Liturgical Music *for the* Revised Common Lectionary

Year **C**

Carl P. Daw, Jr. • Thomas Pavlechko

Church Publishing
NEW YORK

© 2009 by Carl P. Daw, Jr. and Thomas Pavlechko
All rights reserved.

Church Publishing, Incorporated.
445 Fifth Avenue
New York, New York 10016

www.churchpublishing.com

5 4 3 2 1

THE REVISED COMMON LECTIONARY

This lectionary (RCL) will replace the lectionary in The Book of Common Prayer beginning Advent 2007 and is required for use in the Episcopal church by Advent 2010. The lectionary impacts the schedule of readings appointed for the eucharist and for certain Holy Days: All Saints, Thanksgiving Day, The Presentation, The Annunciation, The Visitation, The Transfiguration, and Holy Cross Day. All other Holy Days in the Episcopal calendar, as well as readings for the daily offices are unaffected.

A feature of the RCL is the two track option for the appointed first readings during the long season of Pentecost beginning with Proper 4. The semi-continuous track offers an in-course reading of selected Old Testament texts and the gospel-related track offers Old Testament texts that are closely related to the appointed gospel. In this liturgical guide the readings and their subsequent anthems and hymns for the semi-continuous track use are marked "SC Track" and those for the gospel-related track are marked "GR Track". A parish chooses to use one track or the other for the entire season.

AN INTRODUCTION TO THE HYMNS

The hymns listed in this liturgical guide are intended to be a starting place for those who plan Eucharistic worship following the Revised Common Lectionary. These suggestions are not a substitute for careful local planning but a survey of the possibilities from which choices can be made. They provide a skeleton that will need to be fleshed out according to the needs and capabilities of each worshiping community. For example, in the "green seasons" between Epiphany and Ash Wednesday and between Trinity Sunday and Advent, it may be appropriate in a given situation to use a general "Praise of God" hymn at the Entrance or a "Holy Communion" hymn at that point in the service rather than one of suggestions given here.

Although this listing has been compiled from the authorized hymnal of the Episcopal Church and its supplements published by Church Publishing, Inc., it has been created with the hope that it will also be useful in a larger ecumenical context. In that connection, it must be acknowledged that the quarter-century since the adoption of *The Hymnal 1982* has been a very fruitful one, both for the creation of new texts and tunes and for the compilation of new hymnals. As CPI's own publication of Michael Hudson's *Songs for the Cycle* (2004) attests, numerous writers have published collections of texts related to lectionary readings since the creation of *H82*. Some of these have been incorporated into the supplements indexed here, but there are many more to be explored. Also beyond what can be included here lies a wealth of settings that numerous composers have created for texts old and new.

One of the best ways to become acquainted with the broader ecumenical context from which the CPI supplements have been created is through The Hymn Society in the United States and Canada. A quick glance at the "Author and Composer Collections" section of their Book Service listings in any printed issue of *The Hymn* (or the online version at www.thehymnsociety.org/books) will show how many possibilities there are. In addition to these texts and tunes that have come out of North American and European contexts, there is an abundance of material coming from Africa, Asia, and the other Americas. Glimpses of this bounty can be seen from time to time in the materials indexed here, but the possibilities are constantly increasing. In a world that is becoming increasingly interdependent because of political and economic concerns, we need more than ever to affirm our connections with Christians around the globe by incorporating their sung prayer into our own.

Because this guide is specifically organized by the Revised Common Lectionary, the primary consideration for including hymns in the lists provided here has been their relationship to the appointed scripture passages. First priority has been given to metrical paraphrases or retellings of a passage, followed by texts that allude to portions of it. These directly-related texts are augmented by hymns that share a thematic emphasis or have some cultural association. Ordinarily a hymn is listed only once on a given day, but there are occasionally texts that allude to more than one appointed scripture and therefore appear more than once. Alternatively, hymns that are related to a specific day or season rather than to a specific scripture passage are listed before the lections and are marked [S]. This initial list also includes hymns related to the collect of the day [C] or the appointed psalm [P].

For each listed hymn, a suggestion is made for the place in the service where it is most likely to work well. In general, the beginning, middle, and end positions (Entrance, Offertory, and Postcommunion) are assigned for the more expansive, better-known, and more corporate hymns, while the more reflective, less-familiar, and more personal hymns are assigned to the positions framed by those positions (Sequence and Communion). A number of the hymns appointed for Communion, for example, have a refrain or some other feature than lends them to singing without reference to the printed page, making them appropriate for use while members of the congregation are moving. Also, because experience has shown that most worshipers make the connections between hymns and scripture better if they have heard the scripture first, it has been a general principle to have hymns follow rather than precede the scripture passages to which they are related. This pattern is not applied, however, to occasions in the church year when the emphasis of the day is already generally known (e.g. Christmas, Trinity Sunday, Thanksgiving Day).

In most cases, hymns are listed by the first line of the first stanza rather than by title or the first line of an opening refrain or antiphon, though there are occasions where exceptions have been made in order to use a well-known title or part of an identifying refrain. On the few occasions where metrical paraphrases of a relevant canticle (e.g. the Second Song of Isaiah) were not available, the canticle itself is suggested and is listed by first line rather than title.

In the two far-right columns following the hymn numbers are cross references to *The Crowning Glory: New Descants for Church Choirs* (CG descant) and *Trumpet Descants for 101 Noteworthy Hymns* (Inst desc) composed and arranged by Lorna Tedesco. Both resources are available from Church Publishing (www.churchpublishing.org) A shaded cell containing a circle o means that the hymn tune is available, but the text is not the same as hymn indicated. *Trumpet Descants* offers two descants in Bb for each hymn it contains. These descants may be played together or separately. In the organ score for the hymns these same descants appear in C and could be played by other instruments if desired.

In many ways, the present guide is a successor to the weekly Eucharistic listings of *A Liturgical Index to The Hymnal 1982* compiled by Marion J. Hatchett (CPI, 1986), which has helpfully informed what is presented here. Equally valuable has been his *Scriptural Index to The Hymnal 1982* (CPI, 1988), to which I am much indebted. Another great help in locating hymns related to passages not previously appointed has been *A Concordance of The Hymnal 1982* by Robert F. Klepper (Metuchen, NJ: Scarecrow Press, 1989). In addition I am grateful for the responses to preliminary versions of this guide from Carolyn Darr, SSM, Kevin R. Hackett, SSJE, Mark G. Meyer, and (by no means least) May B. Daw, as well as the encouragement from Marilyn Haskel and Frank L. Tedeschi of Church Publishing, Inc. Anthems and hymns from the African-American tradition were supplemented by the work of Dr. Carl MaultsBy.

Carl P. Daw, Jr.

Carl P. Daw, Jr. is an Episcopal priest and writer who has served as the Executive Director of The Hymn Society in the United States and Canada since 1996. This ecumenical and international organization has its headquarters at Boston University School of Theology, where Dr. Daw serves as Adjunct Professor of Hymnology in the Master of Sacred Music program. He has been successively Secretary and Chair of the Standing Commission on Church Music of the Episcopal Church and was a consultant member of the Text Committee for *The Hymnal 1982*, to which he contributed a number of translations, metrical paraphrases, and original hymns. Four collections of his hymns have subsequently been published by Hope Publishing Co., and they have appeared in a wide range of denominational and ecumenical hymnals in the United States, Canada, England, Scotland, Australia, Hong Kong, and Japan as well as in several smaller collections and over sixty anthem settings. He was a member of the Editorial Advisory Committee for *The Hymnal 1982 Companion* and wrote the essay on "The Spirituality of Anglican Hymnody" in Volume I and numerous text commentaries in Volume III. Other Church Publishing, Inc. projects in which he has been involved include: *Breaking the Word: Essays on the Liturgical Dimensions of Preaching* (1994), for which he was the editor and a contributor of two essays, and (with Kevin R. Hackett, SSJE) *A HymnTune Psalter*, 2 vols. (1998-1999), now reissued in a Revised Common Lectionary edition (2007).

We acknowledge with gratitude that the anthems and hymns in the African-American tradition were supplemented by Dr. Carl MaultsBy

AN INTRODUCTION TO THE CHORAL ANTHEMS AND VOCAL SOLOS

The principles guiding the selection of hymns are paralleled in this compilation of choral anthems and vocal solos.

The anthems in this list represent over twelve years of hands-on parish worship planning according to the RCL, plus a concentrated six-month compilation specific to this resource. Considering the diversity represented in all of our churches, it is far from exhaustive. Time and space are major factors to which many good intentions have to be relinquished.

Time limits the ability to include much of the current output of living composers, and space limits us from listing all of the multiple settings of the most common scripture texts, Psalms and canticles. For example, the number of settings available for the text of the Magnificat is daunting, let alone the number of anthems and solos with the theme, "O Sing Unto the Lord." And, as lists grew beyond the pages of this volume, we have had to cut in many places, and refer the reader to other parts of the book, or to the volumes for Years A and B.

The list includes many obvious choices, satisfying the needs of a first-year church musician utilizing this resource. It is our hope that it also includes selections that even seasoned musicians may have missed. For example, in some cases, anthems have been chosen based upon verses of scripture just outside the actual appointed verses, providing a contextual, rather than a literal match. The most important principle to keep in mind when perusing these pages is respecting your local tradition. Your own church or cathedral library is going to dictate how you will narrow your choices and apply them to your choirs. It is our intent that the settings listed here will not only serve as suggestions in themselves, but will also stir your creativity in applying similar choices that are already in your own choir's repertory.

As a practical budgetary consideration, many anthems appear multiple times, and, should you invest in a collection or major work included in these lists, you will find that many more than one movement or anthem are applicable throughout the year. Bach Cantatas and major works are included more for the potential of extracting choruses and solos than for their possible performance as a major work with orchestra. Most of the anthems are for adults, from simple unison/two-part to complex mixed/multi-part, and experienced trebles in unison/two-part. Vocal solos are also included, with a special emphasis during summer months.

My goal was to personally peruse all of the music in the lists with my own eyes, but as gaps appear, and time races by, I have to rely on trusted anthem lists with music by composers with a notable reputation. With time, these lists can expand to nearly limitless proportions. I wish to express my thanks to my liturgical musician friends and colleagues who contributed to these lists, Dr. Neal Campbell, Dr. Jonathan Dimmock, Dr. Jane Gamble, Dr. Philip Gehring, Dr. William Bradley Roberts and Dr. David Stevens.

It will be very apparent where the gaps lie in the availability of musical settings of scripture texts that are lesser known, and especially those which have only recently been introduced to the body of the lectionary. There is a plethora of texts in need of new anthem and solo settings, providing all of us with the opportunity to narrow these gaps in the repertory by writing new textual paraphrases and new musical settings.

Choose wisely, and revel in the creative opportunities that lie ahead.

Thomas Pavlechko

Thomas Pavlechko has planned worship through four 3-year cycles of the Revised Common Lectionary. He is currently the Cantor and Composer in Residence at St. Martin's Lutheran Church in Austin, Texas. He served this church from 1994-2000 as Director of Music and Principal Organist, introducing the RCL in 1995. From 2000-2006, Pavlechko was the Organist-Choirmaster at Calvary Episcopal Church in Memphis, Tennessee, where he also introduced the RCL during its trial-use years in the Episcopal Church. Previously, he served as Organist-Choirmaster at St. Paul's Episcopal Church in Petersburg, Virginia, and All Saints Episcopal Church in Cincinnati, Ohio. Baptized a Lutheran and confirmed an Episcopalian, Pavlechko remains committed to both denominations.

A church musician for over thirty years, Pavlechko has also been a member of the adjunct faculty at Richard Bland College of the College of William and Mary in Prince William, Virginia, and served as chapel musician, adjunct faculty, and liturgical consultant to the Lutheran Seminary Program in the Southwest, Austin. He held a seat on the Liturgical Music Editorial Team for the new hymnal of the Evangelical Lutheran Church in America.

Pavlechko is a published composer of choral anthems and service music settings, along with 84 hymns in print, and nearly 1,000 Psalm settings in three editions of St. Martin's Psalter. He was selected in 2002 as the Emerging Hymn Tune Composer by the Hymn Society, and his hymn tunes appear in hymnals in the United States, Canada and Australia. Pavlechko's music is published with Abingdon Press, Augsburg-Fortress, Church Publishing, E-Libris Editions, GIA, Hope, Live Oak House, Selah and St. James Music Press.

THANK YOU

The Rev. Mark Bangert	Richard Erikson	Dr. Philip Gehring	Dr. Carl MaultsBy
Dr. Neal Campbell	Dr. Jane Gamble	Larry Long	Dr. David Stevens

SOURCES

Aland, Kurt, ed., *Synopsis of the Four Gospels*, English Edition, © 1982 United Bible Societies.

Susan Cherwien, "Solos for a C Summer", Resource Center, Grace Notes, the newsletter of the Association of Lutheran Church Musicians.

Dimmock, Jonathan, "The Cantatas of J. S. Bach as Applied to the Revised Common Lectionary", available on the internet.

Fyfe, Peter, *Anthems Especially Appropriate for the Transfiguration*

Jeffers, Ron, *Translations and Annotations of Choral Repertoire, Vol. I: Sacred Latin Texts*, © 2000, Earthsongs, 220 NW 29th St., Corvallis, Oregon 97330.

Jeffers, Ron, and Gordon Paine, *Translations and Annotations of Choral Repertoire, Vol. II: German Texts*, © 2000, Earthsongs, 220 NW 29th St., Corvallis, Oregon 97330.

Klimas, William, *50 Unison and 2-Part Anthems Using Psalm Texts* (suitable for high-school age church choirs), 1981

Laster, James H., *Catalogue of Choral Music Arranged in Biblical Order*, © 2001, Scarecrow Press Inc., www.scarecrowpress.com.

Laster, James H., *Catalogue of Vocal Solos and Duets Arranged in Biblical Order*, © 2001, Scarecrow Press Inc., www.scarecrowpress.com.

Setterlund, John S., *A Bach Lectionary*, 1995, brochure, 1305 Brian Place, Champaign, Illinois (217) 344-4654.

Slonimnsky, Nicolas, *Baker's Biographical Dictionary of Musicians*, © 1992, Schirmer Books.

Stulken, Marilyn Kay, *Indexes for Worship Planning*, © 1996, Augsburg Fortress, www.augsburgfortress.com

Wolff, Christoph, *The New Grove Bach Family*, © 1997, W.W. Norton & Co.

Vail, James H., "Anthems Extractable from Larger Choral Works," *The Journal of the Association of Anglican Musicians*, Vol. 10, No. 10, Dec 2001

OTHER RESOURCES

Psalters

In addition to the Psalm-based anthems and solos listed in this resource, there are notable Psalters to consult for chanting the Psalms:

Daw, Jr., Carl P. and Hackett, Kevin, *A HymnTune Psalter*, Church Publishing, www.churchpublishing.org

Ford, Bruce, ed. *Gradual Psalms with Alleluia Verses and Tracts*, www.churchpublishing.org

Hallock, Peter, *The Ionian Psalter*, Ionian Arts, www.ionianarts.com

Pavlechko, Thomas, *St. Martin's Psalter*, E-Libris Editions, www.sjmp.com

Shafer, Keith, *Psalms Made Singable: the Songs of David Set to Anglican and Plain Chant with Text and Music Aligned.* http://www.psalmsmadesingable.com/

COMPOSERS OF MULTIPLE CHORALE, HYMN-BASED AND CHANT-BASED PRELUDES

Bach, Johann Sebastian
Bender, Jan
Bingham, Seth
Bolcom, William
Brahms, Johannes
Burkhart, Michael
Buxtehude, Dietrich
Cherwien, David
Darke, Harold
David, Johann Nepomuk
Distler, Hugo
Dupré, Marcel
Ferko, Frank
Gehring, Philip
Hancock, Gerre

Held, Wilbur
Hobby, Robert
Johnson, David
Krapf, Gerhard
Lenel, Ludwig
Manz, Paul
Near, Gerald
Ore, Charles
Pachelbel, Johann
Parry, Charles H. H.
Peeters, Flor
Pepping, Ernst
Pinkham, Daniel
Proulx, Richard
Read, Gardner

Reda, Siegfried
Scheidt, Samuel
Schroeder, Hermann
Schulz-Widmar, Russell
Sowerby, Leo
Stanford, Charles Villiers
Telemann, George Phillip
Vaughan Williams, Ralph
Walcha, Helmut
Walther, Johann
Willan, Healey
Wright, Searle
Wyton, Alec

COLLECTIONS OF CHORALE PRELUDES FOR ORGAN

Augsburg Organ Library: Advent, Christmas, Epiphany, Lent, Easter, Pentecost, November, Augsburg Fortress, www.augsburgfortress.org

Now Thank We All Our God, ed. C. H. Trevor, Oxford University Press, www.oup.co.uk/music

80 Chorale Preludes from the 17th and 18th Centuries, ed. Hermann Keller, Edition Peters, www.edition-peters.com/home.php.

TABLES

ANTHEM COLLECTIONS

16th	A Sixteenth-Century Anthem Book, Oxford University Press
100 CFC	100 Carols for Choirs, Oxford University Press
AFC 1	Anthems for Choirs 1, Oxford University Press
AFC 2	Anthems for Choirs 2, Oxford University Press
AFC 4	Anthems for Choirs 4, Oxford University Press
ANTH	Anthology, Oxford University Press
AUG	Augsburg Choirbook, Augsburg Fortress
BFAS	Bach for All Seasons, Augsburg Fortress
CFC 1	Carols for Choirs 1, Oxford University Press
CFC 2	Carols for Choirs 2, Oxford University Press
CHAN	Chantry Choirbook, Augsburg Fortress
CHES	Chester Books of Motets, Chester Music
CHES CHR	Chester, Christmas/Advent Motets, 4 voices
CHES E5	Chester, English, 5 voices
CHES E6	Chester, English, 6 voices
CHES FG5	Chester, Flemish/German, 5 voices
CHES FG6	Chester, Flemish/German, 6 voices
CHES FL	Chester, Flemish, 4 voices
CHES FR	Chester, French, 4 voices
CHES IT	Chester, Italian, 4 voices
CHES IS5	Chester, Italian/Spanish, 5 voices
CHES IS6	Chester, Italian/Spanish, 6 voices
CON 1	The Concord Anthem Book No. 1
CON 2	The Concord Anthem Book No. 2
MCS	Motets for the Christmas Season, E.C. Schirmer
NNOV	New Novello Anthem Book
NOV ENG 3	English Anthems for 3 Voices, Novello
NOVSING	Sing Nowell, Novello
OXADV	Advent for Choirs, Oxford University Press
OXASH	Ash Wednesday to Easter for Choirs, Oxford University Press
OXCAB	Oxford Church Anthem Book

OXNCAB	Oxford New Church Anthem Book
OXEA	The Oxford Easy Anthem Book, Oxford University Press
OXESM	European Sacred Music, Oxford University Press
OXNOV	Cantica Nova, Oxford University Press
PUBDOM	Public Domain
RSCM TR	Anthems for Soprano or Treble Voices, RSCM
SAS	Choirbook for Saints and Singers
SEW	Sewanee Composers Project, St. James Press
TUD	Oxford Book of Tudor Anthems

COLLECTIONS OF VOCAL SOLOS

LIFT	Lift Up Your Voice, Theodore Presser
RNMS	Rejoice Now My Spirit, Augsburg Fortress (Med High, Med Low)
SCY	Solos for the Church Year, Lawson-Gould (High, Low)
SOS	The Story of the Spirituals, compiled and arr. Boatner, McAfee Music
SSJ	Sing a Song of Joy, Augsburg Fortress (Med High, Med Low)
SUNSOLO	The Sunday Solo, G. Schirmer
TCS	The Church Soloist, Lawson-Gould (High, Low)
WB	Wedding Blessings, Concordia (High, Low)

VOICING

SATB — Choir Voicing	str — strings	tr — treble
satb — Solo Voicing	trb — trombone	trp — trumpet
mez — mezzo soprano	vla — viola	gtr — guitar
instr — instruments	vn — violin	s/t — soprano or tenor

First Sunday of Advent | Year C

Anthem	Solo	Handbells	Voicing	Title	Collection	Composer
				Jeremiah 33:14-16		
■			b	A Spotless Rose		Herbert Howells
■				Come Thou Long-Expected Jesus	OXEA	Henry Ley
■				How Bright Appears the Morning Star	BFAS	J S Bach
■				I Will Sing the Story of Your Love		Paul Weber
■				Lo! How A Rose		arr Hugo Distler
■				Waiting for You		Carl MaultsBy
	■		b	A Spotless Rose		Herbert Howells
	■		a	Prepare Thyself Zion, *Christmas Oratorio*		J S Bach
				Psalm 25:1-9 *See also Lent 1B*		
■				Cast Thy Burden upon the Lord, *Elijah*		F Mendelssohn
■				For Thee I Have Waited		Daniel Pinkham
■				Help from the Hills		Vaclav Nelhybel
■				Ihr habt nun Traurigkeit, *A German Requiem*		J Brahms
■				To You O Lord		Marty Haugen
	■		duet	The Sorrows of My Heart		William Boyce
				1 Thessalonians 3:9-13		
■				A New Commandment		Thomas Tallis
				Luke 21:25-36		
■				And There Will Be Signs		Jan Bender
■				Behold the Days Are Coming		Paul Bouman
■				E'en So Lord Jesus, Quickly Come		Paul Manz
■			SSAA	Introit for Advent	AFC 3	arr Philip Ledger
■			SA	Keep Your Lamps		Alan Hommerding
■			perc			André Thomas
■				Lo! He Comes with Clouds Descending		David H Williams
■				My Lord, What a Morning		Larry Farrow, *et al*
■				God Make You Blameless		Thomas Gieschen
■				Lo! He Comes, with Clouds Descending		David H Williams
■				My Lord, What a Morning		arr William Dawson
■				O Savior, Rend the Heav'ns on High		Johannes Brahms
■			str	Prope est Dominus		J M Haydn
■				Rise Up! Rise Up!	CHAN	Johann Walter
■				Sleepers, Wake, a Voice Is Calling, *St. Paul*		F Mendelssohn
■				Soon and Very Soon		Andraé Crouch
■			SSAATTBB, a	Steal Away		arr Dale Adelmann
■				The Coming		Leon Roberts
■				Wachet auf		J S Bach
■				Wake, Awake, for Night Is Flying	BFAS	J S Bach
■				Wohlauf, wohlauf, mit hellem Ton	CHAN	Johann Walter
■				Zion Hears the Watchmen Singing	BFAS	J S Bach
■	■		s	Ja, komm, Herr Jesu! *Cantata 106*		J S Bach
				Add'l Anthems, Cantatas, Major Works		
■			SAB/SATB	Song of the Advents		Russell Schulz-Widmar
			satb	70: Wachet! betet! betet! wachet!		J S Bach

12

Year C | First Sunday of Advent

	Entrance	Sequence	Offertory	Communion	Postcommunion		H82	WLP	LEVAS II	VF	MHSO	CG descant	Inst. descant
				■		Blest be the King whose coming [S]	74						■
	■					Hark! a thrilling voice is sounding [C]	59						
			■			O very God of very God [S]	672						
	■					Once he came in blessing [S]	53						
						Jeremiah 33:14-16							
	■					Blessed be the God of Israel		889					
	■					Come, thou long-expected Jesus	66					o	
	■					Hail to the Lord's Anointed	616						
			■			How bright appears the Morning Star	496,497						
				■		Lead us, O Father, in the paths of peace [Ps 25]	703						
	■					O come, O come, Emmanuel	56						■
	■					O day of God, draw nigh	600,601						
						1 Thessalonians 3:9-13							
				■		O heavenly Word, eternal Light	63,64						
						Luke 21:25-36							
			■			Better be ready			4				
	■					Hark! the glad sound! the Savior comes	71,72					o	
			■			Jesus came, adored by angels	454					■	
	■					Lo! he comes, with clouds descending	57,58					■	
				■		My Lord, what a morning			13				
			■			Signs of endings all around us		721					■
			■			Songs of praise the angels sang	426					■	
	■					Stay awake, be ready (1-2,4)					62		
				■		Steal away		804	103				
	■					The King shall come when morning dawns	73						

■ Same tune, but not text   [S] Seasonal   [C] Collect   [P] Psalm   [GR] Gospel-related   [SC] Semi-continuous

Second Sunday of Advent | Year C

Anthem	Solo	Handbells	Voicing	Title	Collection	Composer
				Baruch 5:1-9		
■				And the Glory of the Lord, *Messiah*		G F Handel
■				Arise, O Jerusalem		Richard Webster
■				Comfort, Comfort		John Ferguson
■				I Rejoiced When I Heard Them Say		Richard Proulx
				I Was Glad *See Advent 1A*		
■				Jerusalem surge	CHES FLEM	Heinrich Isaac
■				Laetatus sum		Marc-Antonio Charpentier
						Michael Haydn
						Claudio Monteverdi
				Look Toward the East		Thomas Pavlechko
■				O Comfort Now My People	SEW	Thomas Pavlechko
				People Look East		Multiple
				Song of Isaiah		Richard Proulx
	■	t		Comfort Ye, *Messiah*		G F Handel
	■	t		Ev'ry Valley, *Messiah*		G F Handel
				Glorious Jerusalem		Horatio Parker
	■	t		Then Shall the Righteous Shine		F Mendelssohn
				Malachi 3:1-4, alt		
■				And He Shall Purify, *Messiah*		G F Handel
				And He Shall Purify (Soulful Messiah)		Handel/M Jackson/S Becton
				He's Coming Back		Sam Scott and David R. Curry
■	■		a or b	Thus Saith the Lord; But Who may..., *Messiah*		G F Handel
■			atb	Cantata 125		J S Bach
				Canticle 4 or 16 Luke 1:68-79		
				Benedictus		Multiple
■				Blessed Be the God of Israel		John Carter
				Philippians 1:3-11		
■				A New Commandment	OXASH	Richard Shephard
						Thomas Tallis
			SSATBB	Huc me sydereo	ANTH	Josquin Desprez
				I Give You a New Commandment	OXNEA	Peter Aston
			SSA/SSAA	If Ye Love Me		Harvey B Gaul
			SSA			Daniel Pinkham
						Thomas Tallis
			SSA			Healey Willan
						Philip Wilby
				Once He Came in Blessing		John R Addenour
						Mark Sedio
						Charles Wood
				Luke 3:1-6		
■				And the Glory of the Lord, *Messiah*		G F Handel
■				Comfort, Comfort	AUG	arr John Ferguson
				On Jordan's Banks the Baptists' Cry		David Cherwien
			SAB, instr	On Jordan's Bank, *Christmas Vespers*		Claudio Monteverdi
						Michael Wise
				Prepare Ye the Way		Carl MaultsBy
			2 pt	There's a Voice in the Wilderness	AUG	arr Anne Krentz Organ
	■	t		Comfort Ye; Ev'ry Valley, *Messiah*		G F Handel
	■	a		Prepare Thyself Zion, *Christmas Oratorio*		J S Bach
				Add'l Music, Cantatas, Major Works		
				Come Now O Prince of Peace (Korean)		Lee Geonyong
				Come Thou Long-Expected Jesus	AUG	Timothy Shaw
				O Jesus Grant Me Hope and Comfort		Johann Franck
				Savior of the Nations Come	BFAS	J S Bach
			satb	167: Ihr Menschen, rühmet Gottes Liebe		J S Bach

Year C | Second Sunday of Advent

	Entrance	Sequence	Offertory	Communion	Postcommunion		H82	WLP	LEVAS II	VF	MHSO	CG descant	Inst descant
	■					Blessed be the God of Israel [Cant 4/16]	444						
						Blessed be the God of Israel [Cant. 4/16]		889					
		■		■		Redeemer of the nations, come [S]	55						
						Savior of the nations, come! [S]	54						
						Baruch 5:1-9							
	■					All you who love Jerusalem					157		
		■				Be not dismayed whate'er betide				183			
		■				Comfort, comfort ye my people	67				32		
					■	People, look East. The time is near		724			34		
						Malachi 3:1-4							
		■			■	Love divine, all loves excelling	657					■	
						Philippians 1:3-11							
	■					O day of God, draw nigh	600,601						
						O heavenly Word, eternal Light	63,64						
						Once he came in blessing	53						
						Luke 3:1-6							
	■					Christ is coming			6		58		
			■			Hark! a thrilling voice is sounding	59						
	■		■			On Jordan's bank the Baptist's cry	76						■
	■					Prepare the way, O Zion	65						
						Prepare the way of the Lord					61		
						Prepare ye the way of the Lord			11		63		
	■					There's a voice in the wilderness crying	75						
						We sing of the saints [John the Baptist]					118		

■ Same tune, but not text　[S] Seasonal　[C] Collect　[P] Psalm　[GR] Gospel-related　[SC] Semi-continuous

Third Sunday of Advent | Year C

Anthem/Solo/Handbells/Voicing	Title	Collection	Composer
	Collect		
	Kyrie		Multiple
	Zephaniah 3:14-20		
	Fear Thou Not		Randall Thompson
	Rejoice in the Lord Always	16th	Anon
			Andrew Carter
atb			Henry Purcell
U tr	Sing Aloud, O Daughter of Zion		John Eggert
U			Judy Hunnicutt
SAB, s	Sing, O Daughters of Zion		Jan Bender
	Song of Isaiah		Richard Proulx
	The First Song of Isaiah		Jack Noble White
	When the Lord Turned Again	16th	Adrian Batten
s	Rejoice Greatly, *Messiah*		G F Handel
	Canticle 9 Isaiah 12:2-6		
	Behold, God Is My Salvation		Jean Berger
SA			Robert J Powell
SA			Leo Sowerby
TTBB	Cry Out and Shout		Knut Nystedt
	Ecce Deus		Ned Rorem
TTBB	God Is My Salvation		Samuel Adler
			Theron Kirk
	O Lord I Will Praise Thee	OXEA	Gordon Jacob
U			Gerhard Krapf
2 pt	Song of Isaiah		Richard Proulx
2 pt, fl	Surely It Is God Who Saves Me		David Ashley White
			Alec Wyton
	The First Song of Isaiah		Jack Noble White
	The Wells of Salvation		Alice Parker
	Why We Sing		Kirk Franklin
	Philippians 4:4-7		
	Be Peace on Earth	OXEA	William Crotch
U	Rejoice in the Lord		Jane Lindner
	Rejoice in the Lord Always(s)	16th	Anon
			Anon; attr Redford
			Andrew Carter
		OXCAB	Henry G Ley
atb			Henry Purcell
t	Rejoice the Lord Is Near		J William Greene
a	But the Lord Is Mindful of His Own, *St. Paul*		F Mendelssohn
s	Rejoice Greatly, *Messiah*		G F Handel
	Luke 3:7-18		
	Comfort, Comfort	AUG	arr John Ferguson
	On Jordan's Banks the Baptist's Cry		David Cherwien
SAB, instr	On Jordan's Bank, *Christmas Vespers*		Claudio Monteverdi
	Prepare Ye the Way		Michael Wise
str	Prope est Dominus		J M Haydn
2 pt	There's A Voice in the Wilderness	AUG	arr Anne Krentz Organ
	Wade in the Water		Mark Butler, et al
a	Prepare Thyself Zion, *Christmas Oratorio*		J S Bach
	Add'l Music, Cantatas, Major Works		
	Come Thou Long-Expected Jesus	AUG	Timothy Shaw
stb	61: Nun komm, der Heiden Heiland		J S Bach
satb	Solo Can. 132: Bereitet die Wege, bereitet die Bahn!		J S Bach
atb	136: Erforsche mich, Gott, und erfahre mein Herz		J S Bach

Year C | Third Sunday of Advent

	Title	H82	WLP	LEVAS II	VF	MHSO	CG descant	Inst descant
	Watchman, tell us of the night [S]	640						
	Zephaniah 3:14-20							
	Surely it is God who saves me [Cant.]	678,679						
	Philippians 4:4-7							
	O come, O come, Emmanuel	56						
	Rejoice in the Lord always				162			
	Rejoice, the Lord is King!	481						
	Luke 3:7-18							
	Hark! a thrilling voice is sounding	59						
	Herald, sound the note of judgment	70						
	On Jordan's bank the Baptist's cry	76						
	Prepare the way, O Zion	65						
	Prepare the way of the Lord					61		
	Prepare ye the way of the Lord			11		63		
	There's a voice in the wilderness crying	75						
	We sing of the saints [John the Baptist]					118		
	What is the crying at Jordan?	69						

Same tune, but not text [S] Seasonal [C] Collect [P] Psalm [GR] Gospel-related [SC] Semi-continuous

17

Fourth Sunday of Advent | Year C

Anthem/Solo/Handbells/Voicing	Title	Collection	Composer
	Collect		
	The Best of Rooms		Randall Thompson
	Micah 5:2-5a		
	Song of Isaiah		Richard Proulx
	Who Has Measured the Waters		Wilbur Held
sa	He Shall Feed His Flock, *Messiah*		G F Handel
	Canticle 3 or 15 Luke 1:46-55		
SA/opt SATB	A New Magnificat	AUG	Carolyn Jennings
SSA	Canticle of Mary		Libby Larsen
	Dixit Maria	CHES CHR	Hans Leo Hassler
	Gaude virgo mater Christi		Josquin Desprez
	Mary's Magnificat	OXNCAB	Andrew Carter
	Magnificat		Multiple
	O virgo prudentissima		Josquin Desprez
	Praeter rerum seriem		Josquin Desprez
	Song of Mary		Harold Friedell
	Psalm 80:1-7, alt		
	Hear, O Thou Shepherd of Israel		William Mathias
	O Adonai, et Dux domus Israel	OXNOV	Roderick Williams
	Lord, How Long Wilt Thou Be Angry?		Henry Purcell
	Ring Out Your Joy		Harrison Oxley
	Hebrews 10:5-10		
	Come Thou Long Expected Jesus	OXEA	Henry Ley
	Once He Came in Blessing		John R Addenour
			Mark Sedio
			Charles Wood
	Luke 1:39-45 (46-55) *See Advent 4A, 4B*		
	Alma Redemptoris	FLEM, ITAL	G P da Palestrina
	Mary Walks Amid the Thorn	CHAN	Hugo Distler
	My Soul Proclaims with Wonder		David Music
	Nova, Nova		Multiple
	Nun Komm der Heiden Heiland		J S Bach
	The Angel Gabriel		Multiple
	The Linden Tree Carol		Multiple
a	Behold, A Virgin, O Thou That Tellest, *Messiah*		G F Handel
	Optional verses in Luke		
	Gospel Magnificat		Robert Ray
	Magnificat		Multiple
	My Soul Proclaims the Greatness of the Lord		Multiple
	The Mary Canticle		Leon Roberts
	Add'l Music, Cantatas, Major Works		
SSAATTBB	Hymn to the Mother of God, *All Night Vigil*		S Rachmaninoff
SSAA	Hymn to the Virgin	AFC 3	Giuseppe Verdi
SATTB	Illibata dei virgo	ANTH	Josquin Desprez
	Savior of the Nations Come	BFAS	J S Bach
satb	36: Schwingt freudig euch empor		J S Bach
stb	62: Nun komm der heiden Heiland		J S Bach
atb	90: Es reisset euch ein schrecklich Ende		J S Bach
satb	147: Herz und Mund und Tat und Leben		J S Bach
ssatb	Magnificat		J S Bach

Year C | Fourth Sunday of Advent

Hymn	H82	WLP	LEVAS II	VF	MHSO	CG descant	Inst descant
Blest be the King whose coming [S]	74						
God himself is with us [C]	475						
My heart sings out with joyful praise [Cant.]					60		
My soul gives glory to my God [Cant.]				117			
Redeemer of the nations, come [S]	55						
Rejoice for women brave				18			
Savior of the nations, come! [S]	54						
Tell out, my soul, the greatness of the Lord! [Cant.]	437, 438						
Micah 5:2-5a							
O come, O come, Emmanuel	56						
Praise we the Lord this day	267						
Hebrews 10:5-10							
Come, thou long-expected Jesus	66					o	
Once he came in blessing	53						
To the Name of our salvation	248, 249						
Luke 1:39-45 (,46-55)							
Creator of the stars of night	60						
Mary heard the angel's message (1-2)				4			
Mary, when the angel's voice (1,3-4)				64			
Salamu Maria / Hail Mary, O Mother			51	11			
The Word whom earth and sea and sky	263, 264						
Virgin-born, we bow before thee	258						
Ye who claim the faith of Jesus	268, 269						

o Same tune, but not text   [S] Seasonal   [C] Collect   [P] Psalm   [GR] Gospel-related   [SC] Semi-continuous

Christmas Day I | Year C

Anthem/Solo/Handbells/Voicing	Title	Collection	Composer
	Isaiah 9:2-7		
	As Dark Awaits the Dawn	AUGXMAS	Carl F Schalk
	Before the Marvel of This Night	AUG	Carl F Schalk
	Ecce virgo concípiet		Christobal Morales
	Welcome All Wonders	AUG	Mark G Sirett
	Psalm 96		
SATB, div	All That Hath Life & Breath Praise Ye the Lord!		René Clausen
	Ascribe unto the Lord		Samuel Wesley
	Cantate Domino Croce; Gabrieli; Hassler		
		AFC 1	Pitoni
	Cantate Domino, *Psalmfest*		John Rutter
	Comfort, O Lord, the Soul		William Crotch
	Declare His Honor, *Chandos Anthem No. 4*		G F Handel
U, fl	Make a Joyful Noise		Maureen I Sindlinger
	O Come Let Us Sing unto the Lord		Emma Lou Diemer
	O Sing unto the Lord		P Aston; Hassler; J Hinde
			William Mathias
satb, str			Henry Purcell
	O Sing unto the Lord A New Song		P Aston; J Bender; Schütz
U			Stanley Smith
s	O Sing unto the Lord, *Chandos Anthem No. 4*		G F Handel
	Sing to the Lord a New Song		John Leavitt; David Hurd
	Sing to the Lord, New Songs Be Raising	CHAN	Jan Pieterszoon Sweelinck
	Sing unto the Lord a New Song		H Schütz
	The Beauty of Holiness		Kenneth Leighton
	The Beauty of Holiness-Rejoice!		Bob Buroughs
	Three Motets		Daniel Pinkham
	Thy Word Is a Lantern		John Bertalot
	Unto the Lord		Samuel Wesley
s or t	Sing a New Song, *Biblical Songs*		Antonin Dvorák
	Titus 2:11-14 *See Christmas Day I, A & B*		
	Luke 2:1-14 (15-20) *See Christmas Day I, A & B*		
	A Christmas Carol	AUG	John Leavitt
	Amen		Jester Hairston
	Dost Thou in a Manger Lie?	AUG	Franklin D Ashdown
	Gloria, Gloria		David Hurd
	Joyous Christmas Song	AUG	arr Paul J Christiansen
	Lute Book Lullaby	AUG	Graeme Morton
	Mary Had a Baby		arr William Dawson
	O, Bwana, U Tombee Sasa/Shout for Joy		Carl MaultsBy
	The Quempas Carol—The Nunc Angelorum		Michael Praetorius
	The Virgin Mary Had a Baby		Jester Hairston
	Add'l Music, Cantatas, Major Works		
	A Child to Us Is Born, *Ein Kind ist uns geboren*		Heinrich Schütz
	Betelehemu		Wendall Whalum
	From Heaven Above to Earth I Come	BFAS	J S Bach
	Hodie Christus natus est		Multiple
	Now to Us a Child Is Born	CHAN	Hugo Distler
	O magnum mysterium		Multiple
	Raise a Song, Let Praise Abound	CHAN	Johann Eccard
	To Us Is Born Emmanuel, *Enatus est Eman*	CHAN	Michael Praetorius
satb	63: Christen, ätzet diesen Tag		J S Bach
satb	91: Gelobet seist du, Jesu Christ		J S Bach
satb	110: Unser Mund sei voll Lachens		J S Bach
satb	121: Christum wir sollen loben schon		J S Bach
atb	248i: Jauchzet, frohlocket, auf, preiset die Tage		J S Bach
satb	*Christmas Oratorio*, Part I		J S Bach
	Gloria		Multiple

Year C | Christmas Day I

						Hymn	H82	WLP	LEVAS II	VF	MHSO	CG descant	Inst descant
						Isaiah 9:2-7							
						Hark! the herald angels sing	87						
						It came upon the midnight clear	89,90						
						Sing, O sing, this blessed morn	88						
						The people who in darkness walked	125,126						
						Unto us a boy is born!	98						
						Titus 2:11-14							
						Joy to the world! the Lord is come	100						
						Luke 2:1-14 (,15-20)							
						A child is born in Bethlehem	103						
						A stable lamp is lighted	104						
						Angels we have heard on high	96						
						Away in a manger	101		27				
						From heaven above to earth I come	80						
						Go tell it on the mountain	99		21				
						God rest you merry, gentlemen	105						
						In the bleak midwinter	112						
						It came upon the midnight clear	89,90						
						Jesus our brother, kind and good					65		
						Lo, how a Rose e'er blooming	81						
						Mary borned a baby			22	37			
						Niño lindo / Child so lovely					69		
						O come, all ye faithful	83						
						O little town of Bethlehem	78,79					0	
						Once in royal David's city	102			38			
						Shengye qing, shengye jing/ Holy night, blessed night		725					
						Silent night, holy night	111		26				
						Star-Child, earth-Child				35			
						That boy-child of Mary was born in a stable			25		70		
						The first Nowell the angel did say	109						
						The snow lay on the ground	110						

Same tune, but not text [S] Seasonal [C] Collect [P] Psalm [GR] Gospel-related [SC] Semi-continuous

Christmas Day II | Year C

Anthem	Solo	Handbells	Voicing	Title	Collection	Composer
				Isaiah 62:6-12		
■				Fanfares		Daniel Pinkham
	■			The First Song of Isaiah		Jack Noble White
				Psalm 97		
■				A Harvest of Light Is Sown		Daniel Pinkham
■				This Lord Is King		Heinrich Schütz
■			str, ob, 2 hn	Viderunt omnes		J M Haydn
				Titus 3:4-7		
■				All Who Believe and Are Baptized	BFAS	J S Bach
■				Salvation Has Come to Us		J Brahms
■				Salvation unto Us Has Come	BFAS	J S Bach
				Luke 2:(1-7) 8-20		
■				A Sound of Angels	AFC 1	Christopher Tye
■				Amen		Jester Hairston
■				Angelus ad pastores ait		Multiple
■				Der Engel sprach zu dem Hirten		Michael Praetorius
■				Et incarnatus est, *Mass in B Minor*		J S Bach
■				Gloria, gloria		David Hurd
■				Gloria in excelsis		Multiple
■				Glory Be To God, *All Night Vigil*		S Rachmaninoff
■				Glory to God, *Messiah*		G F Handel
■				Mary Had a Baby		arr William Dawson
■				O, Bwana, U Tombee Sasa/Shout for Joy		Carl MaultsBy
■				O magnum mysterium		Multiple
■				Omnis mundus jocundétur		Michael Praetorius
■				Psallite		Michael Praetorius
■				Psallite		Samuel Scheidt
■				Quem vidistis, pastores?		Multiple
■				Resonet in laudibus		Multiple
■				Sleep, Holy Child		Thomas Pavlechko
■				Sweet Little Jesu		Harold Friedell
■			SSAATTBB	Starfare: The Night Went Wild With Angels		Thomas Pavlechko
■			SATB/SATB	The Quempas Carol—The Nunc Angelorum		Michael Praetorius
■				The Virgin Mary Had a Baby		Jester Hairston
■			SSATB	'Twas in the Moon of Wintertime		William Bradley Roberts
■			mezz	What Sweeter Musick		William Bradley Roberts
■				When Christ Was Born of Mary Free		Harold Friedell
■				When God's Time Had Ripened		Alfred V Fedak
■	■		st	Cantata 191: Gloria in excelsis Deo		J S Bach
■				And There Were Shepherds		J S Bach
■				And lo, the Angel of the Lord		J S Bach
■				And the Angel Said unto Them		J S Bach
■				And Suddenly There Was with the Angel, *Messiah*		G F Handel
■			sa duet	Et in unum Dominum, *Mass in B Minor*		J S Bach
■				Recitative & Angel's Message, *The Christmas Story*		Heinrich Schütz
				Add'l Music, Cantatas, Major Works		
■				Betelehemu		Wendell Whalum
■			satb	63: Christen, ätzet diesen Tag		J S Bach
■			satb	91: Gelobet seist du, Jesu Christ		J S Bach
■			satb	110: Unser Mund sei voll Lachens		J S Bach
■			satb	151: Süsser Trost, mein Jesus kömmt		J S Bach
■			satb	248i: Jauchzet, frohlocket, auf, preiset die Tage		J S Bach
■			satb	*Christmas Oratorio*, Part II		J S Bach
■				*Gloria*		Multiple

Year C | Christmas Day II

	H82	WLP	LEVAS II	VF	MHSO	CG descant	Inst descant
Isaiah 62:6-12							
All you who love Jerusalem				157			
Awake, thou Spirit of the watchmen	540						
Surely it is God who saves me	678, 679						
Titus 3:4-7							
Good Christian friends, rejoice	107						
Love came down at Christmas	84						
Luke 2:(1-7) 8-20							
Angels we have heard on high	96						
Christians, awake, salute the happy morn	106						
Go tell it on the mountain	99		21				
O come, all ye faithful	83						
Once in royal David's city	102				38		
Hark! the herald angels sing	87						
There's a star in the east on Christmas morn			24				
'Twas in the moon of wintertime	114						
While shepherds watched their flocks by night	94, 95						

Same tune, but not text [S] Seasonal [C] Collect [P] Psalm [GR] Gospel-related [SC] Semi-continuous

Christmas Day III | Year C

Anthem	Solo	Handbells	Voicing	Title	Collection	Composer
				Isaiah 52:7-10		
				Break Forth into Joy, *Messiah*		G F Handel
				From Heaven Above to Earth I Come	BFAS	J S Bach
				How Beauteous Are Their Feet		C V Stanford
				How Beautiful upon the Mountains	NNOV, OX AD	John Stainer
				How Beautiful/Break Forth, *Anthem on the Peace*		G F Handel
				How Lovely on the Mountains		John Bertalot
				How Lovely Are the Messengers, *St. Paul*		F Mendelssohn
				Lovely Appears, *The Redemption*		Charles Gounod
				O Thou That Tellest, *Messiah*		G F Handel
	s or a			How Beautiful Are the Feet, *Messiah*		G F Handel
	a			O Thou That Tellest, *Messiah*		G F Handel
				Psalm 98		
				Cantate Domino		Pitoni; Purcell; Multiple
				Let All the Rivers Clap Their Hands		Mark Schweizer
				O Sing to the Lord a New Song		Healey Willan
			SSAATB	Recordatus est	CHES FG6	Philippe Rogier
				Shout for Joy! (Ps 100)		John Carter
				Sing to the Lord a New Song		Johann Pachelbel
				Singet dem Herrn ein neues Lied		H Schütz
				Hebrews 1:1-4, (5-12)		
				Dies sanctificatus		Multiple
			SAATB	In nomine Jesu	CHES FG5	Jacob Handl
				Let All the Angels of God, *Messiah*		G F Handel
				Mirabile Mysterium		Multiple
				Non nobis, Domine		Multiple *(see Holy Name)*
				Not unto Us, O Lord	AFC 1	T A Walmisley
				Of the Father's Heart Begotten	100 CFC, AFC	arr David Willcocks
	t			Unto Which of the Angels, *Messiah*		G F Handel
				John 1:1-14		
				Dies sanctificatus		Multiple
				Et incarnatus est, *Mass in B Minor*		J S Bach
				Et verbum caro factum est		Sven-Erik Bäck
				Fruit homo missus a Deo	OX ADV	Palestrina
				Holy Is the True Light		William Harris
				Illibata dei virgo		Josquin Desprez
				In dulci jubilo		Multiple
				In the Beginning Was the Word		Kevin Sadowski
			SATTB	Mirabile mysterium	CHES IS5	Pietro Vinci
				O admirabile commercium		Multiple
			SATTB	O nata lux		William Byrd, Thomas Tallis
				O nata lux		William Mathias
	a			O Thou That Tellest, *Messiah*		G F Handel
	fl			The Word Became Flesh	AUG	Paul Roberts
			SA	The Word Was Made Flesh		Healey Willan
				Thou Wilt Keep Him in Perfect Peace		Samuel Wesley
				Verbum caro factum est		Multiple
				When God's Time Had Ripened		Alfred V Fedak
	sa duet			Et in unum Dominum, *Mass in B Minor*		J S Bach
				Add'l Music, Cantatas, Major Works		
				A Holy Child Is Born Today	AUG	Bob Burroughs
				Christmas Day		Gustav Holst
				Hodie Christus natus est		Multiple
				Song 46 (Christmas Day)		Orlando Gibbons
				This Day Christ Was Born	TUD	William Byrd
			satb	63: Christen, ätzet diesen Tag		J S Bach
			satb	133: Ich freue mich in dir		J S Bach
			satb	*Christmas Oratorio*, Part III		J S Bach

Year C | Christmas Day III

							H82	WLP	LEVAS II	VF	MHSO	CG descant	Inst descant
					Isaiah 52:7-10								
					Watchman, tell us of the night	640							
					Hebrews 1:1-4 (,5-12)								
					Angels, from the realms of glory	93							
					Dost thou in a manger lie	97							
					Now yield we thanks and praise	108							
					Once in royal David's city	102			38				
					The first Nowell the angel did say	109							
					Where is this stupendous stranger?	491	726						
					John 1:1-14								
					Eternity touched hands with time				39				
					Father eternal, Ruler of creation	573							
					From the dawning of creation		748						
					Joy to the world! the Lord is come	100							
					Let all mortal flesh keep silence	324							
					Listen, my friends					68			
					Love came down at Christmas	84							
					O Savior of our fallen race	85,86							
					Of the Father's love begotten	82							
					On this day earth shall ring	92							
					Sing, O sing, this blessed morn	88							
					What child is this, who, laid to rest	115							

Same tune, but not text   [S] Seasonal   [C] Collect   [P] Psalm   [GR] Gospel-related   [SC] Semi-continuous

First Sunday after Christmas | Year C

Anthem/Solo/Handbells/Voicing	Title	Collection	Composer
	Isaiah 61:10—62:3		
SSA	Arise, Shine		Charles Callahan
S(A)B, instr			Marty Haugen
	Arise, Shine, For Thy Light Is Come	AUG	Kenneth Jennings
			Healey Willan
	Dies sanctificatus		Multiple
s or t	He Delivered the Poor, *Hear My Words, Ye People*		Charles H H Parry
	I Will Greatly Rejoice		Knut Nystedt
satb	Rejoice in the Lord Always (Phil 4:1-9)		Henry Purcell
	Surge, Illuminare		W Byrd; R Webster; Multiple
	The Spirit of the Lord Is upon Me		Edward Elgar
sa duet	Et in unum Dominum, *Mass in B Minor*		J S Bach
	I Will Greatly Rejoice in the Lord		Philip Young
s	Rejoice Greatly, *Messiah*		G F Handel
	Psalm 147 or 147:13-21		
	From All That Dwell Below the Skies		T Attwood; G Young
	Laudate		Knut Nystedt
	Laudate Dominum		A Gretchaninov; W A Mozart; Tallis; Victoria; Vivaldi
	Laudate Jehovam		Georg Telemann
	Lobet den Herren		J S Bach; Gallus Dressler
	Praise Our Lord, All Ye Gentiles		William Byrd
	O Praise the Lord For It Is a Good Thing		Leo Sowerby
	Praise Ye the Lord, *Twelve Canticles*		Randall Thompson
	Galatians 3:23-25; 4:4-7		
	All Who Believe and Are Baptized	BFAS	J S Bach
	Bring Low Our Ancient Adam	BFAS	J S Bach
	Of the Father's Heart Begotten	100 CFC, AFC 1	arr David Willcocks
	O Morning Star How Fair and Bright	BFAS	J S Bach
	Salvation Has Come to Us		J Brahms
	Salvation unto Us Has Come	BFAS	J S Bach
sa duet	Et in unum Dominum, *Mass in B Minor*		J S Bach
	John 1:1-18 *See Christmas Day III & Chr 1, A & B*		
	Dies sanctificatus		Multiple
	Let All Mortal Flesh		E Bairstow; Gustav Holst
	Mirabile mysterium		Multiple
	O admirabile commercium		Multiple
SATTB	O nata lux		Multiple
	Of the Father's Love Begotten	AUG	arr William Miller
	Verbum caro factum est		Multiple
a	O Thou That Tellest, *Messiah*		G F Handel
	Add'l Music, Cantatas, Major Works		
	Dies sanctificatus		Multiple
	The Blessed Son of God, *Hodie*		Ralph Vaughan Williams
sb	32: Liebster Jesu, mein Verlangen		J S Bach
satb	41: Jesu, nun sei gepreiset		J S Bach
satb	63: Christen, ätzet diesen Tag		J S Bach
satb	122: Das neugeborne Kindelein		J S Bach
satb	133: Ich freue mich in dir		J S Bach
sb	152: Tritt auf die Glaubensbahn		J S Bach
atb	154: Mein Liebster Jesus ist verloren		J S Bach
satb	171: Gott, wie dein Name, so ist auch dein Ruhm		J S Bach
satb	*Christmas Oratorio*, Part III, Cantata 248		J S Bach

Year C | First Sunday after Christmas

Entrance	Sequence	Offertory	Communion	Postcommunion		H82	WLP	LEVAS II	VF	MHSO	CG descant	Instr descant
	■				**Isaiah 61:10-62:3**							
	■				Arise and shine, the prophet sang				156		o	
	■				Arise, shine for your light has come	S 223ff	883					
					Galatians 3:23-25; 4:4-7							
■		■			How bright appears the Morning Star	496,497						
					John 1:1-18							
		■			Father eternal, Ruler of creation	573					■	
		■			From the dawning of creation		748					
		■			Let all mortal flesh keep silence	324						■
■					Listen, my friends					68		
				■	Of the Father's love begotten	82						
■					Word of God, come down on earth	633						

[o] Same tune, but not text [S] Seasonal [C] Collect [P] Psalm [GR] Gospel-related [SC] Semi-continuous

Holy Name, January 1 | Year C

Anthem	Solo	Handbells	Voicing	Title	Collection	Composer
				Collect		
■			SAB	Jesus! Name of Wondrous Love		Everett Titcomb
				Numbers 6:22-27		
■				The Lord Bless You and Keep You		Peter Lutkin
■				The Lord Bless You and Keep You		John Rutter
				Psalm 8 *See Holy Name B*		
				Die Himmel erzählen die Ehre Gottes		H Schütz
				O Lord Our Lord		Robert J Powell
			U	Psalm 8		Eugene Butler
						Richard Smallwood
				The Heavens are Telling		Beethoven
				Galatians 4:4-7		
■			SATB div	Little Lamb		David Cherwien
			U	Little Lamb, Who Made Thee		William Bradley Roberts
				The Lamb		John Tavener
				Philippians 2:5-11, alt		
				Adoramus te, Christe		Multiple
				At the Name of Jesus		Ralph Vaughan Williams
				Christe, adoramus te		Claudio Monteverdi
				Christus factus est		Bruckner, Multiple
■			SAATB	In Nomine Jesu	CHES FG5	Jacob Handl
				Jesu, dulcis memoria		Multiple
■			SAB	Jesus, Name of Wondrous Love		Everitt Titcomb
				Let This Mind Be in You		Lee Hoiby
				Let Thy Hand be..., *Coron. Anth. No. 2*		G F Handel
				Non nobis, Domine		Multiple
				Praise to You Lord Jesus	CHAN	Heinrich Schütz
				The Lord Will Surely Come		Gerre Hancock
				Luke 2:15-21		
				Hail Mary		William Dawson
				Jesu, dulcis memoria		Multiple
■			SAB	Jesus! Name of Wondrous Love		Everett Titcomb
				Laud Ye the Name of the Lord, *All Night Vigil*		S Rachmaninoff
				Non nobis, Domine		Multiple
				Not unto Us, O Lord	AFC 1	T A Walmisley
				O admirabile commercium		Multiple
				Praise the Lord, Ye Servants		John Blow
				Quem vidistis, pastores?		Multiple
				Resonet in laudibus		Multiple
			U or SA	What You Gonna Call Your Baby		Greg Gilpin
				Ye Nations, Offer to the Lord, *Hymn of Praise*		F Mendelssohn
				I Just Came from the Fountain	SOS	Spiritual, arr Boatner
				O Jesu, Name Most Lovely, *3 Short Scrd Concert*		Heinrich Schütz
				O Most Kind and Most Merciful Jesu		Heinrich Schütz
				What You Goin' to Name the Baby?	SOS	Spiritual, arr Boatner
				Add'l Music, Cantatas, Major Works		
			atb	16: Herr Gott, dich loben wir		J S Bach
			satb	28: Gottlob! nun geht das Jahr zu Ende		J S Bach
			satb	41: Jesu, nun sei gepreiset		J S Bach
			satb	171: Gott, wie dein Name, so ist auch dein Ruhm		J S Bach
			atb	190: Singet dem Herrn ein neues Lied!		J S Bach
			stb	248iv: Fallt mit Danken, *Christmas Oratorio*		J S Bach
				Das neugeborne Kindelein, BuxWV 13		D Buxtehude

Year C | Holy Name, January 1

	Entrance	Sequence	Offertory	Communion	Postcommunion	Hymn	H82	WLP	LEVAS II	VF	MHSO	CG descant	Inst descant
						Blessed be the name! [S]			78				
						Glorious is the Name of Jesus [S]			63				
						How sweet the Name of Jesus sounds [S]	644						
						Jesus, name above all names [S]				81			
						Jesus, the very thought of thee [S]	642						
						Now greet the swiftly changing year [S]	250						
						O for a thousand tongues to sing [S]	493						
						The Virgin Mary had a baby boy [S]					67		
						There is a name I love to hear [S]			95				
						There's something about that Name [S]			107				
						To the Name of our salvation [S]	248, 249						
						Numbers 6:22-27							
						God be with you				234			
						God be with you till we meet again		801					
						May the Lord bless us					56		
						The Lord bless you and keep you			231				
						Galatians 4:4-7							
						Sing praise to our Creator	295						
						You're called by name, forever loved		766					
						Philippians 2:5-11							
						A stable lamp is lighted	104						
						All hail the power of Jesus' Name!	450, 451						o
						All praise to thee, for thou, O King divine	477						
						At the Name of Jesus	435			135			
						From east to west, from shore to shore	77						
						Luke 2:15-21							
						Jesus, name above all names				81			
						Jesus! Name of wondrous Love!	252						

o Same tune, but not text [S] Seasonal [C] Collect [P] Psalm [GR] Gospel-related [SC] Semi-continuous

Second Sunday after Christmas | Year C

Anthem/Solo/Handbells/Voicing	Title	Collection	Composer
	Jeremiah 31:7-14		
	For I Went with the Multitude	NNOV	Peter Aston
	Tomorrow Shall Be My Dancing Day		Multiple
s/a	He Shall Feed His Flock, *Messiah*		G F Handel
	Psalm 84:1-8 (9-12)		
	Behold, O God, Our Defender		Herbert Howells
	Gott der Herr ist Sonn und Schild, *Cantata 79*		J S Bach
	How Dear to Me Is Your Dwelling		Bruce Neswick; David Hurd
	How Lovely Are the Temples, *Saul*		G F Handel
	How Lovely Is Your Dwelling Place	AUG	Jane Marshall
	How Lovely Is Thy Dwelling Place, *Ger. Requiem*		J Brahms
	How Lovely Is Thy Dwelling Place		Multiple
	Jubilate Deo (Ps 100)		Multiple
	Locus iste		Anton Bruckner
SSAATTBB	Lord God of Hosts, How Lovely Leland		Sateren
	O How Amiable		John Gardner
U			Maurice Greene
			Thomas Tomkins
			Thomas Weelkes
SS			Healey Willan
			Ralph Vaughan Williams
SSA	Psalm 84		Jan Bender
	Quam Dilecta!		Gerald Bales
			Kenneth Leighton
			Charles-Marie Widor
	The Lord Is My Strength		Daniel Moe
	Wie lieblich sind deine Wohnungen, *Ger. Requiem*		J Brahms
	Wie lieblich sind deine Wohnungen		Heinrich Schütz
a	Gott, der Herr, ist Sonn' und Schild, Contralto, *Cantata 79*		J S Bach
	Ephesians 1:3-6, 15-19a		
	Blessed be the Father		Paul Christiansen
SATBB	Glory and Worship, *Coronation Anthem III, No. 3*		G F Handel
SAATB	The King Shall Rejoice, *Coronation Anthem III*		G F Handel
	Matthew 2:13-15, 19-23 *See Chr 2B*		
	For unto Us a Child is Born, *Messiah*		G F Handel
	Luke 2:41-52, *alt See Chr 2B*		
	Hail Mary		William Dawson
SAB, instr	Mein Sohn, warum hast Du uns das getan?		Heinrich Schütz
U or SA	What You Gonna Call Your Baby		Greg Gilpin
	Matthew 2:1-12, alt *See Chr 2B*		
	For unto Us a Child is Born, *Messiah*		G F Handel
SSA	Lo, the Star Which They Saw		Healey Willan
	Magi véniunt ab oriente	CHES CHR	Clemens non Papa
SSATB	Magi videntes stellam	CHES FG5	Blasius Amon
	Omnes de Saba		Multiple
	Reges terrae	CHES FR	Jean Mouton
	Tribus miráculis	CHES IT	Lucas Marenzio
	Viderunt omnes		Multiple
	We Three Kings	NOVSING	Richard Drakeford
	Add'l Music, Cantatas, Major Works		
	Dies sanctificatus		Multiple
	Jubilate Deo (Ps 100)		Multiple
	O Be Joyful (Ps 100)		Multiple
satb	122: Das neugeborne Kindlein		J S Bach
satb	124: Meinen Jesum lass ich nicht		J S Bach
satb	171: Gott, wie dein Name, so ist auch dein Ruhm	J S Bach	
	Das neugeborne Kindelein, BuxWV 13		D Buxtehude

Year C | Second Sunday after Christmas

	Entrance	Sequence	Offertory	Communion	Postcommunion		H82	WLP	LEVAS II	VF	MHSO	CG descant	Instr descant
						How bright appears the Morning Star [C]	496,497						
						How lovely is thy dwelling-place [P]	517						
						Once in royal David's city [C]	102			38			
						Jeremiah 31:7-14							
						O God of Bethel, by whose hand	709						
						Ephesians 1:3-6, 15-19a							
						In your mercy, Lord, you called me	706						
						Sing praise to our Creator	295						
						Matthew 2:13-15,19-23							
						Duérmete, Niño lindo/Oh, sleep now, holy baby	113						
						In Bethlehem a newborn boy	246						
						Lully, lullay, thou little tiny child	247						
						On this day earth shall ring	92						
						Unto us a boy is born!	98						
						Luke 2:41-52							
						Our Father, by whose Name	587						
						When Jesus left his Father's throne	480						
						Matthew 2:1-12							
						As with gladness men of old	119						
						Brightest and best of the stars of the morning	117,118						
						Duérmete, Niño lindo/Oh, sleep now, holy baby	113						
						Earth has many a noble city	127						
						Father eternal, Ruler of creation	573						
						Los magos que llegaron a Belén / The Magi who to Bethlehem did go					71		
						On this day earth shall ring	92						
						The first Nowell the angel did say	109						
						Unto us a boy is born!	98						
						We three kings of Orient are	128						
						What star is this, with beams so bright	124						o
						Where is this stupendous stranger?	491	726					
						Who are these eastern strangers?					72		

Same tune, but not text [S] Seasonal [C] Collect [P] Psalm [GR] Gospel-related [SC] Semi-continuous

The Epiphany, January 6 | Year C

Voicing	Title	Collection	Composer
	Collect		
	Almighty God, Who by the Leading		John Bull
	O God, Who by the Leading of a Star	AFC 1	Thomas Attwood
	Isaiah 60:1-6 *See also Years A & B*		
SSA	Arise, Shine		Charles Callahan
	As Dark Awaits the Dawn		Carl F Schalk
	Dies sanctificatus		Multiple
SAB	Eternal Light	AUGXMAS	Aaron David Miller
	Kings to Thy Rising		Frank C Butcher
	O Christ Who Art the Light and Day *(evening)*	OXCAB	William Byrd
	O Gladsome Light, O Grace *(evening)*	OXCAB	Bourgeois/Goudimel
SATTB	O nata lux		William Byrd; Thomas Tallis
	O nata lux		William Mathias
	O Thou That Tellest, *Messiah*		G F Handel
	Omnes de Saba		Multiple
	Rise! Up! Arise!, *St. Paul*		F Mendelssohn
	Surge, Illuminare		Richard Webster, et al
SAB	The King Shall Come When Morning Dawns	AUG	arr David N Johnson
	Welcome All Wonders	AUG	Mark G Sirett
sa duet	Et in unum Dominum, *Mass in B Minor*		J S Bach
b	For Behold, Darkness Shall Cover, *Messiah*		G F Handel
fl, cont	Ihr Volkers, Hört, *A Solo Cantata for Epiphany*		G P Telemann
s, 2 vio	Mache dich auf, werde licht		Melchior Franck
	Psalm 72:1-7, 10-14 *See also Years A & B*		
	Omnes de Saba		Multiple
b	The Three Kings	100 CFC	Peter Cornelius
	Viderunt omnes		Multiple
	Ephesians 3:1-12		
b	For This Cause		Harold Friedell
	O magnum mysterium		Multiple
	Matthew 2:1-12 *See also Years A & B*		
	Ballad of the Brown Kings		Margaret Bonds
	Behold the Star		arr William L Dawson
	Betelehemu		Wendell Whalum
	Et incarnatus est, *Mass in B Minor*		J S Bach
	Go Back Another Way		Glenn Burleigh
	Lo! Star-led Chiefs	OXCAB	William Crotch
SSA	Lo, the Star Which They Saw		Healey Willan
	Magi véniunt ab oriente	CHES CHR	Clemens non Papa
SSATB	Magi videntes stellam	CHES FG5	Blasius Amon
	Now to the Earth in Mercy	OXCAB	Percy C Buck
	Omnes de Saba		Multiple
	Out of the Orient Crystal Skies	AUGXMAS	Richard Zgodava
	Reges Terrae	CHES FR	Jean Mouton
	Ring De Christmas Bells		Jester Hairston
SSATB	Surge Illuminare Jerusalem		Francesco Corteccia
	The Three Kings		Healey Willan
	Videntes stellam		Francis Poulenc
	Viderunt omnes		Multiple
	We Have Seen His Star in the East		John Carter
	Where Is the Newborn King?		Andreas Hammerschmidt
tb	Cantata 65: Sie werden aus Saba alle kommen		J S Bach
satb	Cantata 248v: Ehre sei dir, Gott, *Christmas Oratorio*		J S Bach
satb	Cantata 248vi: Herr, wenn die, *Christmas Oratorio*		J S Bach
sa duet	Et in unum Dominum, *Mass in B Minor*		J S Bach
	Add'l Music, Cantatas, Major Works		
	O Morning Star, How Fair and Bright	AUGXMAS	arr David N Johnson
satb	*Christmas Oratorio*, parts v & vi		J S Bach

Year C | The Epiphany, January 6

Hymn	H82	WLP	LEVAS II	VF	MHSO	CG descant	Inst descant
Hail to the Lord's Anointed [P]	616						
How bright appears the Morning Star [S]	496,497						
Now the silence [S]	333						
We stand within the circle [S]				77			
Isaiah 60:1-6							
Arise and shine, the prophet sang				156		o	
Arise, shine for your light has come	S223ff	883					
O very God of very God	672						
O Zion, tune thy voice	543						
Ephesians 3:1-12							
Now, my tongue, the mystery telling	329,331						
Our God, to whom we turn	681						
Matthew 2:1-12							
As with gladness men of old	119						
Brightest and best of the stars of the morning	117,118						
Duérmete, Niño lindo/Oh, sleep now, holy baby	113						
Earth has many a noble city	127						
Father eternal, Ruler of creation	573						
Los magos que llegaron a Belén / The Magi who to Bethlehem did go					71		
On this day earth shall ring	92						
Songs of thankfulness and praise	135						
The first Nowell the angel did say	109						
Unto us a boy is born!	98						
We three kings of Orient are	128						
What star is this, with beams so bright	124						o
When Christ's appearing was made known (1,2,5)	131,132						
Where is this stupendous stranger?	491	726					
Who are these eastern strangers?					72		

o Same tune, but not text   [S] Seasonal   [C] Collect   [P] Psalm   [GR] Gospel-related   [SC] Semi-continuous

First Sunday after Epiphany | Year C

Anthem/Solo/Handbells/Voicing	Title	Collection	Composer
	Isaiah 43:1-7		
SATB/SATB	Be Not Afraid		J S Bach
SATB/SATB	Isaiah 43		Randall Z Stroope
	Motet: Fürchte dich nicht		J S Bach
	Be Not Afraid		Craig Courtney
	Psalm 29		
	Exaltabo te		Orlandus Lassus
SSATB	Exaltabo te, Domine		Palestrina
	Give God the Glory		James Hill
	Give unto the Lord		Edward Elgar
SAB			Samuel Wesley
U	Psalm 29		Jane Marshall
			Heinrich Schütz
SSATB			J P Sweelinck
	Give God, the Father, Praise		Heinrich Schütz
	Acts 8:14-17		
	All Who Believe and Are Baptized	BFAS	J S Bach
	Luke 3:15-17, 21-22		
	Come to the Water		Joseph & Mary Martin
	Inter natos mulierum		W A Mozart
	I Wander as I Wonder		Multiple
	Joys Seven	100 CFC	arr Stephen Cleobury
	Lord of the Dance		arr John Ferguson
		100 CFC	David Willcocks
	O Come Everyone that Thirsteth, *Elijah*		F Mendelssohn
	Of the Father's Heart Begotten	100 CFC, AFC 1	arr David Willcocks
	Of the Father's Love Begotten	AUG	arr William Miller
	On Jordan's Bank the Baptist's Cry, *Christmas Vespers*		Claudio Monteverdi
	The Blessed Son of God, *Hodie*		Ralph Vaughan Williams
	The Only Son from Heaven	AUGXMAS, BFAS	J S Bach
	The Spirit of the Lord Is upon Me, *The Apostles*		Edward Elgar
	This Is My Beloved Son		Knut Nystedt
	Tomorrow Shall Be My Dancing Day		John Gardner
			Gerald Near
		100 CFC	David Willcocks
	Tribus miráculis	CHES	Lucas Marenzio
	Wade in the Water		arr Howard Roberts
	Cantata 7, Christ unser Herr zum Jordan kam		J S Bach
	I Wander as I Wonder		Multiple
satb	O Come Everyone that Thirsteth, *Elijah*		F Mendelssohn
	Add'l Music, Cantatas, Major Works		
	Asperges me, Domine		Multiple
	Confiteor unum Baptisma, *Mass in B Minor*		J S Bach
	Once, as I Remember	100 CFC	arr Charles Wood
	The Waters of Life	AUG	James Biery
st	Domine Deus, Rex coelestis, *Mass in B Minor*		J S Bach
	Search Me, O God		A Dvorak
atb	7: Christ unser Herr zum Jordan kam		J S Bach
satb	37: Wer da gläubet und getauft wird		J S Bach
atb	123: Liebster Immanuel, Herzog der Frommen		J S Bach

Year C | First Sunday after Epiphany

	H82	WLP	LEVAS II	VF	MHSO	CG descant	Inst descant
Songs of thankfulness and praise [S]	135						
Isaiah 43:1-7							
How firm a foundation	636,637						
You shall cross the barren desert		811					
Acts 8:14-17							
Baptized in water	294	767	121				
Luke 3:15-17,21-22							
Christ, when for us you were baptized	121						
Crashing waters at creation				67	95		
From God Christ's deity came forth	443						
"I come," the great Redeemer cries	116						
O love, how deep, how broad, how high (1-3,6)	448,449						
Spirit of God, you moved over the waters					58		
The sinless one to Jordan came	120						
When Christ's appearing was made known (1,3,5)	131,132						
When Jesus went to Jordan's stream	139						

Same tune, but not text   [S] Seasonal   [C] Collect   [P] Psalm   [GR] Gospel-related   [SC] Semi-continuous

Second Sunday after Epiphany | Year C

Anthem	Solo	Handbells	Voicing	Title	Collection	Composer
				Collect		
				Christ Whose Glory Fills the Skies	OXEA	T Frederick H Candlyn
				Christ Is the World's True Light		W K Stanton
				O Morning Star How Fair and Bright	BFAS	J S Bach
				O Almighty God	AFC 1	George Barcrofte
				Isaiah 62:1-5		
				Fanfares		Daniel Pinkham
			2 pt	Go Through the Gates		Eugene Butler
			SAB/SATB	Prepare the Way!		arr George Brandon
	b			For Behold, Darkness Shall Cover, *Messiah*		G F Handel
	a			O Thou That Tellest Good Tidings, *Messiah*		G F Handel
				Psalm 36:5-10		
				Dixit Dominus		Multiple
				How Precious Is Thy Loving Kindness		Samuel Adler
						Daniel Pinkham
				How Precious Is Your Steadfast Love		Robert Buckley Farlee
				I Sat Down under His Shadow	AFC	Edward Bairstow
				Laudate Dominum		Multiple
				They Are Happy	NNOV	John Joubert
			TB	Thy Mercy Jehovah		Benedetto Marcello
				Thy Mercy O Lord Reacheth unto the Heavens		Pazul C Edwards
				Thy Word Is a Lantern		John Bertalot
				Loving Kindness	SUNSOLO	Henry Purcell
				1 Corinthians 12:1-11		
				Draw Us in the Spirit's Tether		Harold Friedell
				I'm Gonna Sing 'Til the Spirit Moves in My Heart		arr. Moses Hogan
				King Jesus Hath a Garden	CFC 1	arr Charles Wood
				Like the Murmur of the Dove's Song		Peter Cutts
				One Bread One Body		John Foley
				John 2:1-11		
				Come, Join in Cana's Feast		Sally Ann Morris
				I Sat Down under His Shadow	AFC	Edward Bairstow
				Jesus Son of Life, My Splendor		G F Handel
				Joys Seven	100 CFC	arr Stephen Cleobury
				Tribus miráculis	CHES ITAL	Luca Marenzio
				Add'l Music, Cantatas, Major Works		
				Laudate Dominum omnes gentes		Multiple
			satb	3: Ach Gott, wie manches Herzeleid		J S Bach
			satb	13: Meine Seufzer, meine Tränen		J S Bach
			satb	155: Mein Gott, wie lang, ach lange		J S Bach
			stb	196: Der Herr denket an uns		J S Bach

Year C | Second Sunday after Epiphany

Hymn	H82	WLP	LEVAS II	VF	MHSO	CG descant	Inst descant
Blessed Jesus, at thy word [C]	440						
Christ, whose glory fills the skies [C]	6,7						
Christ is the world's true light [C]	542						
How bright appears the Morning Star [C]	496,497						
The light of Christ [C]					80		
Thou, whose almighty word [C]	371						
Isaiah 62:1-5							
How wondrous and great thy works, God of praise!	532,533						
1 Corinthians 12:1-11							
Holy Spirit, font of light	228						
O Holy Spirit, by whose breath	501,502						
O Holy Spirit, flowing light				54			
O Spirit of Life, O Spirit of God	505						
Praise the Spirit in creation	506,507						
We all are one in mission		778					
John 2:1-11							
All praise to you, O Lord	138						
From God Christ's deity came forth	443						
Songs of thankfulness and praise	135						
When Christ's appearing was made known	131,132						

Same tune, but not text   [S] Seasonal   [C] Collect   [P] Psalm   [GR] Gospel-related   [SC] Semi-continuous

Third Sunday after Epiphany | Year C

Anthem	Solo	Handbells	Voicing	Title	Collection	Composer
				Collect		
			satb	O Sing Unto the Lord		Henry Purcell
				Nehemiah 8:1-3, 5-6, 8-10		
				Psalm 19		
				Always, Only for My King		Robert Wetzler
			SSATTB	Die Himmel erzählen die Ehre Gottes		Heinrich Schütz
				Heaven and Earth, and Sea and Air, *12 Songs of Praise*		Samuel Adler
			SATTB	Justitiae Domini		Palestrina
				Let the Words of My Mouth		Henry Purcell
						K Lee Scott
				Lord, You Have the Words		Richard Proulx
				O Verbum Patris		Frank Ferko
						K Lee Scott
						Everett Titcomb
				Psalm 19		Benedetto Marcello
						Richard Proulx
				Silver and Gold		Kirk Franklin
				The Heavens Are Telling	CON 1	Beethoven
						Richard McKinney
				The Heavens Are Telling, *The Creation*		F J Haydn
				The Heavens Declare		William Billings
			TTBB			Thomas Tomkins
				The Heavens Declare God's Mighty, *Samson*		G F Handel
			U	The Heavens Declare the Creator's Glory	OXCAB	Beethoven
				The Heavens Tell Out the Glory of God		Daniel Pinkham
				The Law of the Lord		William Mathias
				The Law of the Lord is Perfect		Alec Wyton
				Their Sound Is Gone Out, *Messiah*		G F Handel
			satb	Cantata 76: Die Himmel erzählen die Ehre Gottes		J S Bach
				1 Corinthians 12:12-31a		
				All Who Believe and Are Baptized	BFAS	J S Bach
				One Bread, One Body		John Foley
				The Spirit of the Lord Is upon Me, *The Apostles*		Edward Elgar
				Ubi Caritas		Maurice Duruflé
				The Spirit of the Lord Is upon Me		Arthur Sullivan
				Luke 4:14-21		
				Ain'-a That Good News		arr William Dawson
				Every Time I Feel the Spirit		William Dawson
						Jester Hairston
				How Beautiful Are Their Feet	NNOV	Charles Stanford
				How Beautiful upon the Mountains	NNOV	John Stainer
				How Lovely Are the Messengers, *St. Paul*		F Mendelssohn
				I'm Goin' to Sing When the Spirit Says Sing		Alice Parker
	a			O Thou That Tellest Good Tidings, *Messiah*		G F Handel
				Song of Isaiah		Richard Proulx
				The Spirit of the Lord Is upon Me, *The Apostles*		Edward Elgar
				There Shall a Star from Jacob Shine		arr Joy F Patterson
	s			How Beautiful Are the Feet, *Messiah*		G F Handel
				I Know De Lord's Laid His Hands on Me		arr Harry T Burleigh
				I Know the Lord Laid His Hands on Me	SOS	Edward Boatner
	s			Rejoice Greatly, *Messiah*		G F Handel
	a			O Thou That Tellest Good Tidings, *Messiah*		G F Handel
				The Spirit of the Lord Is upon Me	LIFT	Arthur Sullivan
	a			Then Shall the Eyes of the Blind, *Messiah*		G F Handel
				Add'l Music, Cantatas, Major Works		
				Motet: Lobe den Herrn, meine Seele, BWV 143		J S Bach

Year C | Third Sunday after Epiphany

						Hymn	H82	WLP	LEVAS II	VF	MHSO	CG descant	Inst descant
			■			As we gather at your Table [C]		763				o	
			■			Christ for the world we sing! [C]	537						
			■			How wondrous and great thy works, God of praise! [C]	532,533						
			■			My God, thy table now is spread [C]	321						
■						O Spirit of the living God [C]	531						
■						Spread, O spread, thou mighty word [C]	530						
■						The spacious firmament on high [P]	409						
■						The stars declare his glory [P]	431						
						Nehemiah 8:1-3,5-6,8-10							
■						Help us, O Lord, to learn	628						
■						Open your ears, O faithful people	536						
						Thanks to God whose Word was spoken	630					■	
		■				We all are one in mission		778				■	
						1 Corinthians 12:12-31a							
			■			God is love, and where true love is	576,577						
			■			Like the murmur of the dove's song	513						
			■			Muchos resplandores/Many are the light-beams		794					
			■			O God of gentle strength		770,771				o	
			■			Sing praise to our Creator	295						
			■			Ubi caritas et amor		831					
			■			We are a part of all creation					131		
			■			Where charity and love prevail	581						
			■			Where true charity and love dwell	606						
						Luke 4:14-21							
						Gracious Spirit, give your servants		782					
■						Hail to the Lord's Anointed	616						■
						Hark! the glad sound! the Savior comes	71,72					o	
	■					O Christ, the Word Incarnate	632						
		■				O I know the Lord's laid his hands on me			131				
		■				O Zion, haste, thy mission high fulfilling	539						■
	■					Word of God, come down on earth	633						

b Same tune, but not text [S] Seasonal [C] Collect [P] Psalm [GR] Gospel-related [SC] Semi-continuous

Fourth Sunday after Epiphany | Year C

Anthem/Solo/Handbells/Voicing	Title	Collection	Composer
	Jeremiah 1:4-10		
	Be Not Afraid, *Elijah*		F Mendelssohn
t	Be Thou Faithful unto Death, *St. Paul*		F Mendelssohn
b, vio	Behold I Have Put My Words in Your Mouth		Stephen P Folkemer
	How Lovely Are the Messengers, *St. Paul*		F Mendelssohn
	Thou Knowest Lord the Secrets		Henry Purcell
	Psalm 71:1-6		
	Descendit sicut pluvial	MCS	Orlando Lassus
	Descendit sicut pluvial		Orlando Lassus
	Go Not Far from Me O God		Nicola Zingarelli
SSATB	Herr, auf dich Traus ich		Heinrich Schütz
	I Go to the Rock		Briggs & Rambo/arr L Larson
	I Waited on the Lord, *Lobgesang*, vs 14		F Mendelssohn
	In te, Domine speravi		Josquin; Halsey Stevens
SATTB	In te speravi		Palestrina
	In Thee, O Lord		Jane Marshall
b			Thomas Weelkes
	Jesus, Lover of My Soul (in *Playing Gospel Piano*)		Edwin Hawkins/arr MaultsBy
	My God Is a Rock		Shaw/Parker
	O How Amiable		Ralph Vaughan Williams
	O Lord in Thee Have I Trusted		G F Handel
2 pt	O Lord, My God, (Bist Du bei mir)		J S Bach, arr Hopson
	They That Wait upon the Lord		Jean Berger
st duet	My Song Shall Be Always, *Lobgesang*, vss 22-24		F Mendelssohn
	Nobody Knows the Trouble I've Seen		Spiritual, Various
	1 Corinthians 13:1-13		
	Faith, Hope and Love		Alexander Peloquin
	I Sat Down under His Shadow		Edward Bairstow
instr	Love Never Fails		Jack Noble White
	Not for Tongues		Timothy Dudley-Smith
	Not for Tongues of Heaven's Angels		Roy Hopp
	Now Abideth Faith, Hope, and Charity		Herbert Howells
	The Corinthians		Ned Rorem
U or 2 pt	The Gift of Love		Hal Hopson
3 pt	The Greatest of These is Love		William Zeitler
	Though I Speak with the Tongues of Men	OXNCAB	Edward Bairstow
SATTBB	Ubi caritas		Maurice Duruflé
SSATBB			Petr Eben
U			Jean Langlais
			Flor Peeters
			Richard Proulx
2 pt, cello	With All I Am		Taylor David
	Who Shall Separate Us (Romans 8)		Richard Webster
	Love Never Faileth		Gabriel Fauré
	O God in All Thy Might		Austin Lovelace
t or b	The Call, *Five Mystical Songs*		Ralph Vaughan Williams
	The Greatest of These is Love		Roberta Bitgood
			René Clausen
			Daniel Moe
			Robert Wetzler
	Wenn ich mit Menschen, *Vier ernste Gesang*		J Brahms
	Luke 4:21-30		
	Joys Seven	100 CFC	arr Stephen Cleobury
	Where There Are Prophecies		Thomas Gieschen
s	Jerusalem, Jerusalem, *St. Paul*		F Mendelssohn
	Add'l Music, Cantatas, Major Works		
satb	181: Leichtgesinnte Flattergeister		J S Bach

Year C | Fourth Sunday after Epiphany

	H82	WLP	LEVAS II	VF	MHSO	CG descant	Inst descant
God the omnipotent! King, who ordainest [C]	569						
Jeremiah 1:4-10							
Be not dismayed whate'er betide			183				
From my birth, from my birth					126		
God of the prophets, bless the prophets' heirs!	359						
1 Corinthians 13:1-13							
God is love, and where true love is	576, 577						
Gracious Spirit, Holy Ghost	612						
Love astounding, love confounding				143			
Muchos resplandores/Many are the light-beams		794					
Ubi caritas et amor		831					
Where charity and love prevail	581						
Where true charity and love dwell	606						
Luke 4:21-30							
Blessed Jesus, at thy word	440						
O love, how deep, how broad, how high	448, 449						
Spread, O spread, thou mighty word	530						
Thanks to God whose word was spoken	630						
Word of God, come down on earth	633						

Same tune, but not text [S] Seasonal [C] Collect [P] Psalm [GR] Gospel-related [SC] Semi-continuous

Fifth Sunday after Epiphany | Year C

Anthem	Solo	Handbells	Voicing	Title	Collection	Composer
				Isaiah 6:1-8, (9-13)		
				Above Him Stood the Seraphim	OXEA	Richard Dering
				Duo Seraphim clamabant		Multiple
				Here I Am, Lord		Donald J Reagan
						Michael Ward
				Heilig		F Mendelssohn
						Franz Schubert
				Holy, Holy, Holy, *Hymn to the Trinity*	OXCAB, OXNCAB	P I Tchaikovsky
				In the Year That King Uzziah Died		David McK Williams
				Let All Mortal Flesh Keep Silence		Edward Bairstow
						Gustav Holst
				Sanctus		Multiple
				Te Deum		Multiple
				The Cherubic Hymn (Izhe kheruvimyi)		Mikhail Glinka
				Psalm 138		
	U			A Joyous Psalm		Eugene Butler
				Attend to the Music Divine (Ps. 134)		Richard Webster
				Confitebor tibi, *Solemn Vespers*		W A Mozart
			SATB/STTB			Francesco Cavalli
				Follow Me		Don Harper & Ben Tankard
				He Watching Over Israel, *Elijah*		F Mendelssohn
				I Was Glad		Multiple
				Laetatus sum		Marc-Antonio Charpentier
						Michael Haydn
						Claudio Monteverdi
	U			I Will Worship		George Dyson
				Let Thy Hand, *Coronation Anthem No. 2*		G F Handel
				Locus iste		Anton Bruckner
			SAB	O Give Thanks unto the Lord		John Wood
				Psalm 138		Thomas Hoekstra
						Knut Nystedt
						J P Sweelinck
				Why We Sing		Kirk Franklin
				Bring to Jehovah, *Five Sacred Songs*		Heinrich Schütz
				Bring to the Lord God, *5 Short Sacred Concertos*		Heinrich Schütz
				Give God the Glory		Heinrich Schütz
				1 Corinthians 15:1-11		
				Christ the Lord Is Risen! Alleluia!		Johan Helmich Roman
				Exultate Deo		Multiple
				I Know That My Redeemer Lives	OXCAB	Johann Michael Bach
				Jesus, Son of Life, My Splendor		G F Handel
				Scio enim	CHES FL	Jacob Vaet
				Since by Man Came Death, *Messiah*		G F Handel
				Since by Man	SEW	Thomas Pavlechko
				Te Deum		Multiple
				Awake All Ye People, *Cantata 15*	LIFT	J S Bach
				Exultate Deo		Multiple
	s			I Know That My Redeemer Liveth, *Messiah*		G F Handel
				Luke 5:1-11		
				I Heard Him Once		Taylor Davis
	U			Master, We Toiled All Night		Gerhard Krapf
				The Fisherfolk		Betty Carr Pulkingham
				The Spirit of the Lord Is Upon Me, *The Apostles*		Edward Elgar
				There Is a Balm in Gilead		arr William Dawson
	t			Meister, wir habe die ganze Nacht		H Schütz
				Add'l Music, Cantatas, Major Works		
			satb	88: Siehe, ich will viel Fischer aussenden		J S Bach

42

Year C | Fifth Sunday after Epiphany

	Entrance	Sequence	Offertory	Communion	Postcommunion		H82	WLP	LEVAS II	VF	MHSO	CG descant	Inst descant
The church of Christ in every age [C]								779					
Thy strong word did cleave the darkness [C]							381						

Isaiah 6:1-8(,9-13)

	Entrance	Sequence	Offertory	Communion	Postcommunion		H82	WLP	LEVAS II	VF	MHSO	CG descant	Inst descant
"Holy, holy, holy," angel hosts are singing/ Santo, santo, santo											26		
Holy, holy, holy! Lord God Almighty!							362						
I, the Lord of sea and sky								812			77		
Let all mortal flesh keep silence							324						
Let all that is within me cry, "Holy!"									85				
My God, how wonderful thou art							643						
O day of radiant gladness							48						
O God, we praise thee, and confess							364						
Round the Lord in glory seated							367						
Santo, santo, santo								785					
The God of Abraham praise							401						
Thuma mina / Send me, Lord								808			35		
We see the Lord											114		

1 Corinthians 15:1-11

	Entrance	Sequence	Offertory	Communion	Postcommunion		H82	WLP	LEVAS II	VF	MHSO	CG descant	Inst descant
Amazing grace! how sweet the sound							671		181				
Come, thou fount of every blessing							686		111				
Glorious the day when Christ was born							452						
In your mercy, Lord, you called me							706						
Now the green blade riseth							204						

Luke 5:1-11

	Entrance	Sequence	Offertory	Communion	Postcommunion		H82	WLP	LEVAS II	VF	MHSO	CG descant	Inst descant
As we gather at your table								763				o	
Christ for the world we sing							537						
My God, thy table now is spread							321						
Put down your nets and follow me								807					
There is a balm in Gilead							676		203				
Tú has venido a la orrilla/You have come down to the lakeshore								758					
When Jesus saw the fishermen											76		
Will you come and follow me								757					
Ye servants of God, your Master proclaim							535						

o Same tune, but not text   [S] Seasonal   [C] Collect   [P] Psalm   [GR] Gospel-related   [SC] Semi-continuous

Sixth Sunday after Epiphany | Year C

Anthem	Solo	Handbells	Voicing	Title	Collection	Composer
				Jeremiah 17:5-10		
■				Blessed Are They Who Trust in the Lord		Thomas Keesecker
■			SAB/SSA/SATB	Blessed Is the Man		Stanley L Glarum
■				Blessed Is the Man That Trusteth in the Lord		Alan Hovhaness
■				Immortal, Invisible		Eric Thiman
■				Jesus Christ the Apple Tree	100 CFC	Elizabeth Poston
				Psalm 1		
■			SA	Beatus vir		Orlando Lassus
■						W A Mozart
■						A Vivaldi
■			SA	Blessed Is He Who Walks Not		Heinrich Schütz
■			SAB	Blessed Is the Man		Archangelo Corelli
■						Sven Lekberg
■						Jane Marshall
■				Blessed Is the Man, *All Night Vigil*		S Rachmaninoff
■				Blest Is the Man		Hans Leo Hassler
■			SSA			Orlando Lassus
■			U, ob, fl	Happy Is the Man Who Fears the Lord		Richard Proulx
■				O for a Closer Walk	AFC 1	C V Stanford
■				Psalm 1		S Rachmaninoff
■						Halsey Stevens
	ss duet			Gloria et divitiae, *Beatus vir*		A Vivaldi
	s			Jucundus homo, *Beatus vir*		A Vivaldi
	t			Peccator videbit (Ps 112), *Beatus vir*		A Vivaldi
				1 Corinthians 15:12-20		
■				Alleluia. Christus Surrexit	OXASH	Felice Anerio
■				But Thanks Be to God, *Messiah*		G F Handel
■				Christ Our Passover		Richard Dirksen
■						Will C MacFarlane
■				If We Believe	OXNCAB	John Goss
■				I Know That My Redeemer Lives	OXCAB	Johann Michael Bach
■				Jesus, Son of Life, My Splendor		G F Handel
■				Scio enim	CHES FL	Jacob Vaet
■				Since by Man Came Death, *Messiah*		G F Handel
■				Since by Man	SEW	Thomas Pavlechko
■				This Joyful Eastertide	OXASH	arr Philip Ledger
	s			I Know That My Redeemer Liveth, *Messiah*		G F Handel
	s			Awake All Ye People, *Cantata 15*	LIFT	J S Bach
				Luke 6:17-26		
■				Blessed Are the Pure in Heart	OXCAB	H Walford Davies
■				Blessed Are They		David Haas
■				Blessed Are You		Emma Lou Diemer
■			SSAATTBB	Blessed Is the Man, *All Night Vigil*		S Rachmaninoff
■				Exceeding Glad, *Coronation Anthems III, No. 2*		G F Handel
■				Glory and Worship, *Coron. Anthems III, No 3*		G F Handel
■				Let Nothing Ever Grieve Thee		Johannes Brahms
■				O Give Thanks Unto the Lord	NNOV	Arthur Bliss
■				Sit Down Servant		Linda Twine
■			SSAATTBB	Swing Low, Sweet Chariot		arr Dale Adelmann
■				Soon-ah Will Be Done		arr William Dawson
■				The Beatitudes		Virgil T Ford
■						Micki Grant
■						Russian Chant
	mez			There Is a Balm in Gilead		arr William Dawson
				Add'l Music Cantatas, Major Works		
■			atb	20: O Ewigkeit, du Donnerwort		J S Bach

44

Year C | Sixth Sunday after Epiphany

						H82	WLP	LEVAS II	VF	MHSO	CG descant	Inst. descant
					If thou but trust in God to guide thee [C]	635						
					Jeremiah 17:5-10							
					Immortal, invisible, God only wise	423						
					The tree of life my soul hath seen		749			149		
					1 Corinthians 15:12-20							
					God's Paschal Lamb is sacrificed for us		880				o	
					Jesus lives! thy terrors now	194,195						
					Love's redeeming work is done	188,189						
					We know that Christ is raised and dies no more	296					o	
					Luke 6:17-26							
					Blessed Jesus, at thy word	440						
					Blest are the poor in spirit					74		
					Christ for the world we sing!	537						
					From miles around the sick ones came		774					
					Gracious Spirit, give your servants		782					
					Heal me, hands of Jesus		773					
					Heal me, Lord				91			
					Jesus shall reign where'er the sun	544						
					O Christ, the healer, we have come		772					
					O for a thousand tongues to sing	493						
					Remember your servants, Lord	560						
					You shall cross the barren desert		811					

o Same tune, but not text [S] Seasonal [C] Collect [P] Psalm [GR] Gospel-related [SC] Semi-continuous

Seventh Sunday after Epiphany | Year C

Anthem/Solo/Handbells/Voicing	Title	Collection	Composer
	Collect		
	See Easter 5C, Gospel		
	Genesis 45:3-11, 15		
	Every Eye Waiteth upon Thee		Heinrich Schütz
	O God My King	AFC 1	John Amner
	O Lord I Will Praise Thee	OXEA	Gordon Jacob
	Oculi omnium		Charles Wood
	Praise to the Lord		Hugo Distler
	Prope est Dóminus	CHES ADV CHR	Jacob Regnart
	The Eyes of All Wait upon Thee		Jean Berger
			Orlando Gibbons
			William Harris
U			Richard Proulx
		SEW	Richard Shephard
			Robert Edward Smith
	The Lord Is Good to All		Jean Berger
	Psalm 37:1-12, 41-42		
	Commit Your Life to the Lord		Liebhold
	Habe deine Lust an dem Herrn		Christopher Bernhard
ss duet	I Waited for the Lord, *Lobgesang, Hymn of Praise*		F Mendelssohn
div	Os justi	OXESM	Anton Bruckner
	Proclaim the Lord		Dan Locklair
	Psalm 37		John Leavitt
U			Jane Marshall
	Novit Dominus	CHES FG6	Leonhard Lechner
	The Paper Reeds..., *The Peaceable Kingdom*		Randall Thompson
b	Habe deine Lust am Herrn, *Cantata 4, Alles was*		Dietrich Buxtehude
a	O Rest in the Lord, *Elijah*		F Mendelssohn
	1 Corinthians 15:35-38, 42-50		
	But Thanks Be to God, *Messiah*		G F Handel
	Nolo mortem peccatoris	16th	Thomas Morley
	Since by Man, *Messiah*		G F Handel
	Since by Man	SEW	Thomas Pavlechko
2 pt	Thanks Be to God		Paul Bouman
at	O Death Where Is Thy Sting? *Messiah*		G F Handel
	Luke 6:27-38		
	A Prayer of St. Richard of Chichester	OXEA	L J White
U	Be Merciful, Even as Your Father Is Merciful		Gerhard Krapf
	Beatitudes		Russian Chant
	Blessed Are the Pure in Heart		Walford Davies
	Blessed Are They That Mourn	OXCAB	J Brahms
	Blessed Is the Man, *All Night Vigil*		S Rachmaninoff
	Give Almes of Thy Goods	AFC 1	Christopher Tye
	Greater Love Hath No Man		John Ireland
t	Grieve Not the Holy Spirit		T Tertius Noble
	Let Nothing Ever Grieve Thee		J Brahms
	On Love of One's Enemies		Virgil T Ford
	Ubi caritas		Maurice Duruflé
	Add'l Music, Cantatas, Major Works		
satb	138, Warum betrübst du dich, mein Herz?		J S Bach
satb	185: Barmherziges Herze der ewigen Liebe		J S Bach

Year C | Seventh Sunday after Epiphany

	H82	WLP	LEVAS II	VF	MHSO	CG descant	Inst descant
Commit thou all that grieves thee [P]	669						
Gracious Spirit, Holy Ghost [C]	612						
Love divine, all loves excelling [C]	657						
Genesis 45:3-11,15							
Before the Lord's eternal throne	391						
God moves in a mysterious way	677						
Praise to the Lord, the Almighty, the King of creation	390						
1 Corinthians 15:35-38,42-50							
Give thanks for life		775				O	
Now the green blade riseth	204						
Praise to the Holiest in the height	445,446						
Luke 6:27-38							
Brother, sister, let me serve you				124	94		
Father all loving, who rulest in majesty	568						
"Forgive our sins as we forgive"	674						
Go forth for God, go to the world in peace	347						
God is love, and where true love is	576,577						
I come with joy to meet my Lord	304						
If I have wounded any soul today			176				
Jesu, Jesu, fill us with your love	602			74			
Lord, make us servants of your peace	593						
Lord, whose love through humble service	610						
Out in the highways and byways of life			158				
We are all children of the Lord					105		
Where charity and love prevail	581						
Where true charity and love dwell	606						

[O] Same tune, but not text [S] Seasonal [C] Collect [P] Psalm [GR] Gospel-related [SC] Semi-continuous

Eighth Sunday after Epiphany | Year C

Anthem/Solo/Handbells	Voicing	Title	Collection	Composer
		Collect		
		Praise to the Lord		Hugo Distler
		Sirach 27:4-7		
		God Be in My Head		John Rutter
		Thou Knowest Lord the Secrets of Our Hearts		Henry Purcell
		Isaiah 55:10-13, alt		
	SATB/SATB, st	But These Are They, *The Peaceable Kingdom*		Randall Thompson
		For as the Rain and Snow Come Down		Hal Hopson
		For Ye Shall Go Out with Joy		Emma Lou Diemer
		Seek the Lord		René Clausen
				Knut Nystedt
		The First Song of Isaiah		Jack Noble White
		This Is Our God		Paul Christiansen
		Ye Shall Go Out with Joy		Jean Berger
		You Shall Go Out with Joy		Carl Schalk
		Psalm 92:1-4, 11-14		
		All That Have Life and Breath		Rene Clausen
	SSAA	Exult		Alison Bauld
		Give Thanks unto the Lord		Richard Dirksen
	U	How Good to Offer Thanks	SAS	Rolf Schweizer
	SATB div	In medio Ecclesiae	OXNOV	John Joubert
		It Is Good to Give Thanks		David Hurd
	U	It Is Good to Sing Thy Praises, *Twelve Songs of Praise*		Samuel Adler
		1 Corinthians 15:51-58		
		But Thanks Be to God, *Messiah*		G F Handel
		Death Where Is Thy Sting		C P E Bach
	b	For We Have on Earth, *A German Requiem*		J Brahms
		O Jesus Christ, My Life, My Light	BFAS	J S Bach
	b	Behold I Tell You a Mystery, *Messiah*		G F Handel
	b	The Trumpet Shall Sound, *Messiah*		G F Handel
	a	Then Shall Be Brought to Pass, *Messiah*		G F Handel
	at duet	O Death, Where Is Thy Sting? *Messiah*		G F Handel
		Luke 6:39-49		
		Christ Is Made the Sure Foundation		Dale Wood
		God Is a Rock		Robert Shaw/Alice Parker
		Jesus Christ the Apple Tree	100 CFC	Elizabeth Poston
		Song of the Mustard Seed		Hal Hopson
		Tu es Petrus		Maurice Duruflé
	b			Gabriel Fauré
				Palestrina
				Charles-Marie Widor
		Add'l Music, Cantatas, Major Works		
	atb	24: Ein ungefärbt Gemüte		J S Bach
	sat	177: Ich ruf zu dir, Herr Jesu Christ		J S Bach
	satb	Solo Cantata 185: Barmherziges Herze der ewigen		J S Bach

Year C | Eighth Sunday after Epiphany

					Title	H82	WLP	LEVAS II	VF	MHSO	CG descant	Instr descant
	■				Praise, my soul, the King of heaven [C]	410						■
	■				Praise to the Lord, the Almighty [C]	390						■
					Sirach 27:4-7							
	■				God be in my head, and in my understanding	694						
					Isaiah 55:10-13							
	■				Surely it is God who saves me	678,679						
					1 Corinthians 15:51-58							
			■		Abide with me: fast falls the eventide	662					■	
			■		Holy God, we praise thy Name (1,5-7)	366						■
		■			Jesus lives! thy terrors now	194,195						
		■			Love's redeeming work is done	188,189						
			■		O God, we praise thee, and confess (1,6-8)	364						
					Luke 6:39-49							
	■				Blessed Jesus, at thy word	440						
	■				Come, we that love the Lord	392		12				
	■				Help us, O Lord, to learn	628						
	■				How firm a foundation, ye saints of the Lord	636,637						■
			■		How sweet the Name if Jesus sounds	644						
			■		If thou but trust in God to guide thee	635						
	■				Lord, be thy word my rule	626						
				■	Lord, dismiss us with thy blessing	344						■
			■		My hope is built on nothing less			99				
			■		O God, unseen yet ever near	332						

Same tune, but not text   [S] Seasonal   [C] Collect   [P] Psalm   [GR] Gospel-related   [SC] Semi-continuous

49

Last Sunday after Epiphany | Year C

Anthem/Solo/Handbells/Voicing	Title	Collection	Composer
	Exodus 34:29-35		
	Psalm 99		
	Cry Out with Joy		Christopher Walker
SATB/SATB	Derr Herr ist König		Johann Pachelbel
	Dominus Regnavit, *Seven Short Anthems*		Peter Hallock
	Let All Mortal Flesh Keep Silence		Edward Bairstow
			Gustav Holst
	Sanctus		Multiple
	The Lord Is King		David Ashley White
	2 Corinthians 3:12—4:2		
	Thee We Adore		T Frederick Candlyn
	Luke 9:28-36, (37-43a)		
	And Then Shall Your Light Break Forth, *Elijah*		F Mendelssohn
	Beautiful Savior		F Melius Christiansen
	Christ upon the Mountain Peak		John Bertalot
			Paul Bouman
	Christ, Whose Glory Fills the Skies	OXCAB	Thomas Armstrong
			T Frederick Candlyn
SAB	Fairest Lord Jesus	AUGXMAS	Walter L Pelz
			Russell Schulz-Widmar
U	Jesus on the Mountain Peak	AUGXMAS	Mark Sedio
	O Christ Who Art the Light and Day *(evening)*	OXCAB	William Byrd
	O Gladsome Light, O Grace *(evening)*	OXCAB	Bourgeois/Goudimel
	O nata lux		William Mathias
SATTB	O nata lux		Thomas Tallis; Wm Byrd
a	O Thou That Tellest, *Messiah*		G F Handel
	Of the Father's Heart Begotten	100 CFC, AFC	arr David Willcocks
	Of the Father's Love Begotten	AUG	arr William Miller
	The Only Son from Heaven	AUGXMAS BFAS	J S Bach
	The Spirit of The Lord Is upon Me		Edward Elgar
	The Transfiguration		Sven-Erik Bäck
	The Transfiguration of Christ		Hampson A Sisler
	The Transfiguration of our Lord		Nancy Maeker
	This Is My Beloved Son		Knut Nystedt
			Dan Uhl
	Transfiguration		Alan Hovhaness
			Alec Wyton
	Add'l Music, Cantatas, Major Works		
	Alleluia		Multiple
SAB/SATB	Alleluia, Song of Gladness		David Ashley-White
	Deo Gracias, O Wondrous Type		arr Robert Scholz
	In Splendenti Nube		Peter Philips
	Jesus, Take Us to the Mountain		Carl Schalk
	O Morning Star How Fair and Bright	BFAS	J S Bach
	O Wondrous Type		Roger Petrich
	Prayer for Transfiguration Day		John Weaver
	Shine, Jesus, Shine		Graham Kendrick
	Te Deum		Multiple
	The Glory of Christ		K Lee Scott
	The Heavens Are Telling		G F Handel
			F J Haydn
	This Glimpse of Glory		David Ashley White
	We Are Marching in the Light of God (Siyahamba)		S African Song, Multiple
	50: Nun ist das Heil und die Kraft		J S Bach
satb	130: Herr Gott, dich loben alle wir		J S Bach

Year C | Last Sunday after Epiphany

	Hymn	H82	WLP	LEVAS II	VF	MHSO	CG descant	Inst descant
Entrance/Postcommunion	Songs of thankfulness and praise [S]	135						
Sequence	Alleluia, song of gladness [S]	122,123						
	Exodus 34:29-35							
Offertory	We sing of God, the mighty source (1-2)	386,387						
	2 Corinthians 3:12-4:2							
Offertory	All my hope on God is founded	665					●	
Communion	Come with us, O blessed Jesus	336						
Postcommunion	From glory to glory advancing, we peaise thee, O Lord	326						
Postcommunion	Go forth for God; go to the world in peace	347						
Communion	Humbly I adore thee, Verity unseen	314						
Communion	O Bread of life, for sinners broken	342						
Communion	Spirit of the Living God			115				
	Luke 9:28-36(,37-43a)							
Entrance	Christ upon the mountain peak	129,130						
Entrance	O Light of Light, Love given birth	133,134						
Entrance	O wondrous type! O vision fair	136,137					●	

○ Same tune, but not text [S] Seasonal [C] Collect [P] Psalm [GR] Gospel-related [SC] Semi-continuous

Ash Wednesday | Year C

Anthem/Solo/Handbells/Voicing	Title	Collection	Composer
	Collect		
Anthem	Create in Me		J Brahms
			Carl F Mueller
	Hide Not Thou Thy Face	TUD	Richard Farrant
	Lord, for Thy Tender Mercy's Sake	TUD	Richard Farrant
	Joel 2:1-2, 12-17		
SSSAATTTBB	Blow Up the Trumpet in Sion		Henry Purcell
	Blow Ye the Trumpet in Zion		Francis Jackson
	Fear Not, O Lord		William Harris
	Return to the Lord, Your God Carl Schalk		
SAB	Sound Forth the Trumpet in Zion		Thomas Morley, ed Proulx
	Isaiah 58:1-12, alt		
U	A Lenten Carol		Glen Darst
	Psalm 103:(1-7), 8-14, (15-22)		
SA	Bless the Lord My Soul, *Cantata 196*		J S Bach, arr Hopson
	Bless the Lord, O My Soul		Austin Lovelace
			Sam Batt Owens
	Lord for Thy Tender Mercy's Sake	TUD	Richard Farrant
	Not Only unto Him, *St. Paul*		F Mendelssohn
	The Lord Has Established His Throne		Daniel Pinkham
	The Paper Reeds..., *The Peaceable Kingdom*		Randall Thompson
	2 Corinthians 5:20b-6:10		
	The Beatitudes		Russian Chant
	Matthew 6:1-6, 16-21		
	Ah, Thou Poor World	AFC 1	J Brahms
TTBB	Lay Not Up for Yourselves		John Heath
	Lay Up for Yourselves		Ned Rorem
	Lord, Teach Us How to Pray Aright		Thomas Tallis
	Steal Away		arr Dale Adelmann
			arr William Dawson
	Treasures in Heaven		Joseph W Clokey
	Recit & Chorale: O Mortal World, *Cantata 95*	LIFT	J S Bach
	Steal Away		Spiritual, Multiple
	Psalm 51:1-17 *See Proper 13B*		
	I'm Glad Salvation Is Free		Shelton Becton
	Open Our Eyes		Leon Lumpkins
	Add'l Music, Cantatas, Major Works		
SATTB	Emendemus in melius		William Byrd
	Give Rest O Christ *Permission granted by the composer to replace the Alleluias with Laudamus Domino*		Russell Schulz-Widmar
	Jesu, meine Freude	BFAS	J S Bach
	My Spirit Longs for Thee	OXEA	John Dowland
	Peccantem me quotidie		Cristobal Morales
	The Blood of Jesus Christ	CHAN	Heinrich Schütz
	Denn es gehet dem Menschen, *4 Script. Songs*		J Brahms
sb	32: Liebster Jesu, mein Verlangen		J S Bach
atb	135: Ach Herr, mich armen Sünder		J S Bach
s	Solo Cantata 199: Mein Herze schwimmt im Blut		J S Bach
	Motet: Jesu, meine Freude, BWV 227		J S Bach

Year C | Ash Wednesday

	H82	WLP	LEVAS II	VF	MHSO	CG descant	Inst descant
Note: There is no Entrance Hymn on this day (see BCP, p. 264).							
Almighty Lord Most High draw near [S]		888					
Bless the Lord, my soul [P]		825					
Bless the Lord, O my soul [P]			65				
Come, ye disconsolate [S]			147				
Eternal Lord of love, behold your Church [S]	149						
O bless the Lord, my soul! [P]	411						
The glory of these forty days [S]	143						
Joel 2:1-2, 12-17							
Before thy throne, O God, we kneel	574,575						
Kind Maker of the world, O hear	152						
Lord Jesus, Sun of Righteousness	144						
Isaiah 58:1-12							
Creator of the earth and skies	148						
Gracious Spirit, give your servants		782				o	
Lord, whose love through humble service	610						
Now quit your care	145						
O day of God, draw nigh	600,601						
2 Corinthians 5:20b-6:10							
Lead us, heavenly Father, lead us	559						
Thou my everlasting portion			122				
Matthew 6:1-6, 16-21							
God himself is with us	475						
Jesus, all my gladness	701						

o Same tune, but not text   [S] Seasonal   [C] Collect   [P] Psalm   [GR] Gospel-related   [SC] Semi-continuous

First Sunday in Lent | Year C

Anthem/Solo/Handbells/Voicing	Title	Collection	Composer
	Deuteronomy 26: 1-11		
	Come See the Wonders		William Billings
sa	Go Down Moses		Robert Harris; Norman Luboff
	Give Almes of Thy Goods	AFC 1	Christopher Tye
	Psalm 91:1-2, 9-16		
	For He Has Commanded His Angels, *Elijah*		F Mendelssohn
SSAATTB	For He Shall Give His Angels Charge, *Elijah*		F Mendelssohn
	Lord, Thou Hast Been Our Refuge		Bairstow; Joubert; V Williams
	On Eagle's Wings		Michael Joncas
	Swing Low, Sweet Chariot		arr Dale Adelmann; Multiple
	I've Got Peace Like a River		Spiritual, Multiple
a	Lobe den Herren, Cantata 137		J S Bach
sb	Lobe den Herren, Cantata 137		J S Bach
	Romans 10:8b-13		
	All Who Believe and Are Baptized	BFAS	J S Bach
	Bring Low Our Ancient Adam	BFAS	J S Bach
	How Lovely Are the Messengers, *St Paul*		F Mendelssohn
	If Thou Shalt Confess with Thy Mouth		C V Stanford
	Lovely Appear, *The Redemption*		Charles Gounod
	Oh, for a Closer Walk with God	AFC 1	Charles Stanford
	Salvation unto Us Has Come	BFAS	J S Bach
	Swing Low, Sweet Chariot		Spiritual, Multiple
	Their Sound Is Gone Out, *Messiah*, (Rom 10:18)		G F Handel
s	How Beautiful Are the Feet, *Messiah*		G F Handel
	Luke 4:1-13		
2 pt	A Lenten Walk	AUG	arr Hal Hopson
	A Mighty Fortress Is Our God	CHAN	Hans Leo Hassler
	As Panting Deer		David Ashley White
	As Pants the Hart		Orlando Lassus
	As Pants the Hart, *Chandos Anthem No. 6*		G F Handel
	As the Deer, for Water Yearning	CHAN	Claude Goudimel
	As the Deer Pants for Streams of Water		Jim Taylor
	As the Deer Longs for the Waterbrooks		Peter Pindar Stearns
U, 2 pt	Begone, Satan		Jan Bender
	Behold the Lamb of God, *Messiah*		G F Handel
	Ein feste Burg	BFAS	J S Bach
	He That Shall Endure to the End, *Elijah*		F Mendelssohn
	Jesus, So Lowly		Harold Friedell
	Jesus Walked That Lonesome Valley		arr John Ferguson
			arr William Dawson
	Like As the Hart		H Howells; M Williamson
	On Eagle's Wings		Michael Joncas
fl	My Soul Is Thirsting for You, O Lord, My God		Charles Callahan
ob	Psalm 42		Daniel Kean
	Put Thy Trust in God, *Chandos Anthem No. 6*		G F Handel
	Sicut cervus	FLEM, ITAL	G P da Palestrina
			Reginald Unterseher
	The Serpent	SEW	Thomas Pavlechko
	The Temptation of Christ		Lloyd Pfautsch
	Cantata 80, Ein feste Burg ist unser Gott		J S Bach
	I Ain't Got Weary Yet	SOS	Spiritual, arr Boatner
	Jesus Walked That Lonesome Valley		Multiple
	Add'l Music, Cantatas, Major Works		
str	Sweet Spirit, Comfort Me		Russell Schulz-Widmar
atb	40, Dazu ist erschienen der Sohn Gottes		J S Bach
a	Solo Cantata 54: Widerstehe doch der Sünde		J S Bach

54

Year C | First Sunday in Lent

			Hymn	H82	WLP	LEVAS II	VF	MHSO	CG descant	Inst descant
			Eternal Lord of love, behold your Church [S]	149						
			Lead us, heavenly Father, lead us [C]	559						
			O God of Bethel, by whose hand [P]	709						
			You who dwell in the shelter of the Lord [P]		810					
			Deuteronomy 26:1-11							
			As those of old their first fruits brought	705						
			Wisdom freed a holy people		905		155			
			Romans 10:8b-13							
			In Christ there is no East or West	529		62				
			Lord, speak to me, that I may speak				98			
			Luke 4:1-13							
			Christ, when for us you were baptized	121						
			Forty days and forty nights (1)					84		
			Forty days and forty nights	150						
			From God Christ's deity came forth	443						
			Lord, who throughout these forty days	142						
			Now let us all with one accord	146,147						
			O love, how deep, how broad, how high	448,449						
			Spirit of God, you moved over the waters				58			
			The glory of these forty days	143						
			The sinless one to Jordan came	120						

Same tune, but not text [S] Seasonal [C] Collect [P] Psalm [GR] Gospel-related [SC] Semi-continuous

Second Sunday in Lent | Year C

Anthem/Solo/Handbells	Voicing	Title	Collection	Composer
		Collect		
		All We Like Sheep, *Messiah*		G F Handel
		Lord, Thee I Love	BFAS	J S Bach
		Genesis 15:1-12, 17-18		
	SSA	God's Promise		Samuel Adler
		Laudate pueri		Multiple
		Magnificat		Multiple
		Offertory, *Requiem Mass*		Multiple
		Psalm 27		
		Arise, Shine, for Thy Light Is Come		Joel Martinson
				William Mathias
				Healey Willan
	SAB	God Is My Strong Salvation		Robert J. Powell
		Hearken to My Voice, O Lord	AUG	Bruce Neswick
		Hide Not Thou Thy Face		Richard Farrant
		Nobody Knows the Trouble I've Seen		Spiritual, Multiple
		One Thing Have I Desired		Herbert Howells
		One Thing I Seek		Robert Hobby
		Psalm 27 Multiple		
		The Lord Is My Light		Clara Edwards
				Peter Hallock
		The Lord Is My Light, *Psalmfest*		John Rutter
		The Lord is My Strength		Daniel Moe
		Thou Knowest, Lord, the Secrets		Henry Purcell
		Nobody Knows the Trouble I've Seen		Spiritual, Multiple
		Psalm 27		Multiple
		Philippians 3:17—4:1		
		Lord, Thee I Love	BFAS	J S Bach
		Children of the Heavenly Father		arr Robert Scholz
				arr Paul Sjolund
		Stand		Donny McClurkin
		Luke 13:31-35		
		Benedictus qui venit		Multiple
	SSATB	Gloria laus	CHES IS5	Juan Ginés Perez
		He Is Blessed That Cometh, *Requiem*	OXCAB	W A Mozart
		Hosanna! Blessed Is He	AUG	Knut Nystedt
		Hosanna to the Son of David	OXASH	Arthur Hutchings
			TUD	Orlando Gibbons
			TUD	Thomas Weelkes
		Hosanno filio David		Tomas Luis de Victoria
		Hosianna dem Sohne Davids	OXAS	Bartholomäus Gesius
	s	O Pray for the Peace of Jerusalem		John Blow
				Leo Nester
				Herbert Howells
			16th	Thomas Tomkins
		Sing Hosanna to the Son of David		Bartholomäus Gesius
	2 pt	When Twilight Comes		arr Robert Buckley Farlee
	s	Jerusalem, Thou That Killest..., *St. Paul*		F Mendelssohn
		Add'l Music, Cantatas, Major Works		
		Lord, Thee I Love with All My Heart	BFAS	J S Bach
	atb	46: Schauet doch und sehet		J S Bach

Year C | Second Sunday in Lent

	Entrance	Sequence	Offertory	Communion	Postcommunion		H82	WLP	LEVAS II	VF	MHSO	CG descant	Inst descant
Genesis 15:1-12,17-18													
God it was who said to Abraham (1,5)											85		
Now let us all with one accord							146,147						
The God of Abraham praise							401						
We are on our way to the promised land											96(1-2)		
You shall cross the barren desert								811					
Philippians 3:17-4:1													
Hail, thou once despised Jesus!							495						
My Jesus, I love thee									89				
O love, how deep, how broad, how high							448,449						
O Love of God, how strong and true							455,456						
Luke 13:31-35													
All who love and serve your city							570,571						
And now, O Father, mindful of the love							337						
Day by day							654				33		
Draw nigh and take the Body of the Lord							327,328						
Mother hen, mother hen											141		
New every morning is the love							10						
O Jesus Christ, may grateful hymns be rising							590						
Praise the Lord through every nation							484,485						
Take up your cross, the Savior said							675						
Weary of all trumpeting							572						

Same tune, but not text [S] Seasonal [C] Collect [P] Psalm [GR] Gospel-related [SC] Semi-continuous

Third Sunday in Lent | Year C

Anthem/Solo/Handbells/Voicing	Title	Collection	Composer
	Exodus 3:1-15		
A	De profundis		Multiple
A	Go Down, Moses		Spiritual, Multiple
A	Out of the Depths		Jacques Charpentier
A	Out of the Deep, *Requiem*		John Rutter
A	Psalm 130		Multiple
A	When Israel Was in Egypt's Land		Spiritual, Multiple
S	Go Down Moses		Spiritual, Multiple
A	When Israel Was in Egypt's Land		Spiritual, Multiple
	Psalm 63:1-8		
A	As Panting Deer		David Ashley White
A	As Pants the Hart		Orlando Lassus
A	As Pants the Hart, *Chandos Anthem No. 6*		G F Handel
A	As the Deer, for Water Yearning	CHAN	Claude Goudimel
A	As the Deer Pants for Streams of Water		Jim Taylor
A	As the Deer Longs for the Waterbrooks		Peter Pindar Stearns
A	Behold the Tabernacle of God		William Harris
A	Like as the Hart		Herbert Howells
		OXASH	Noel Rawsthorne
			Malcolm Williamson
ob	Psalm 42		Daniel Kean
A	Sicut cervus	FLEM, ITAL	G P da Palestrina
			Reginald Unterseher
fl	My Soul Is Thirsting for You, O Lord, My God		Charles Callahan
A	Sicut cervus	FLEM, ITAL	G P da Palestrina
			Reginald Unterseher
	The Lord Is My Light		Peter Hallock
A / s or t	Lord, O Harken Unto My Crying, *Biblical Songs*		Antonin Dvorák
	Hear My Prayer, *Biblical Songs*		Antonin Dvorák
	1 Corinthians 10:1-13		
A	He That Is Down Need Fear No Fall		Philip Moore
A	We Fall Down		Kyle Matthews
A	He That Is Down Need Fear No Fall		Ralph Vaughan Williams
A	Hear My Prayer		Antonin Dvorák
	Luke 13:1-9		
A	Come Ye, Sinners		Carl MaultsBy
A	Kyrie		Multiple
A	O, Sinner		Davis Sisters
A	Save Me, O God		William Boyce
ssatb			Alan Hovhaness
			Henry Purcell
	Add'l Music, Cantatas, Major Works		
satb	124: Meinen Jesum lass ich nicht		J S Bach

58

Year C | Third Sunday in Lent

	Entrance	Sequence	Offertory	Communion	Postcommunion		H82	WLP	LEVAS II	VF	MHSO	CG descant	Inst descant
					■	Kind Maker of the world, O hear [S]	152						
						Exodus 3:1-15							
	■					Praise to the living God!	372					o	
						The God of Abraham praise	401						■
			■			We sing of God, the mighty source	386,387						
			■			What wondrous love is this	439					■	
						When from bondage we are summoned		753,754				■	
			■			When Israel was in Egypt's land	648		228				
						1 Corinthians 10:1-13							
			■			Come, ye disconsolate			147				
	■					Creator of the earth and skies	148						
	■					Eternal Lord of love, behold your Church	149						
	■					Forty days and forty nights	150						
				■		If thou but trust in God to guide thee	635						
	■					Lord, who throughout these forty days	142						■
			■			O God, unseen yet ever near	332						
			■			Rock of ages, cleft for me	685						
			■			Shepherd of souls, refresh and bless	343					■	
	■					The glory of these forty days	143						
						Luke 13:1-9							
	■					Before thy throne, O God, we kneel	574,575						■
					■	Kind Maker of the world, O hear	152						
					■	Lord, dismiss us with thy blessing	344						
				■		Now let us all with one accord	146,147						

o Same tune, but not text   [S] Seasonal   [C] Collect   [P] Psalm   [GR] Gospel-related   [SC] Semi-continuous

59

Fourth Sunday in Lent | Year C

Anthem/Solo/Handbells/Voicing	Title	Collection	Composer
	Collect		
	Bread of Heaven		Roy Hopp
	Ego sum panis vitae		Sven-Erik Bäck
	Ego sum panis vivus	CHES IT	Palestrina
			William Byrd
	Lauda Sion		Multiple
2 pt	O Bread of Life from Heaven	AUG	David Ashley White
ATB	O Sacred Communion		Larry Long
	O Sacred Feast		Healey Willan
	O Sacrum Convivium		Multiple
	O Bread of Life from Heaven	BFAS	J S Bach
s or t	Panis Angelicus		César Franck
SATB div			Pierre Villette
		SEW	Thomas Pavlechko
	Verbum caro		Multiple
	Verily, Verily, I Say unto You		Thomas Tallis
	Bread of Life, *Lauda Sion*	LIFT	F Mendelssohn
	Thine O Father, Thine..., *Fall of Jerusalem*	LIFT	Martin Blumner
	Joshua 5:9-12		
	Deep River		Spiritual, Multiple
	On Jordan's Stormy Banks		Southern Harmony, Multiple
	Deep River		Spiritual, Multiple
	On Jordan's Stormy Banks		Southern Harmony, Multiple
	Psalm 32		
	A Choral Flourish		Ralph Vaughan Williams
SAB	Be Glad You Righteous		Robert J Powell
	Beati quorum via (Ps. 119)		C V Stanford
ATB	Blessed Is He Whose Unrighteousness Is Forgiven		Thomas Tomkins
	Exultate Deo		Multiple
	Exultate justi		Multiple
SST or SAB	Psalm 32		Paul Weber
	Thou Knowest, Lord, the Secrets of Our Hearts		Henry Purcell
TTBB	Whom the Lord Hath Forgiven		Alan MacMillan
	2 Corinthians 5:16-21		
	How Lovely Are the Messengers, *St. Paul*		F Mendelssohn
	If We Believe		John Goss
	Sing, My Soul, His Wondrous Love		Ned Rorem
	Thou Knowest, Lord, the Secrets of Our Hearts		Henry Purcell
tb	Now We Are Ambassadors, *St. Paul*		F Mendelssohn
	Luke 15:1-3, 11b-32		
	Amazing Grace		Multiple
	Come Ye, Sinners		Carl MaultsBy
	He Knows Just How My Much You Can Bear		Phyllis Hall
	He That Is Down Need Fear No Fall		Philip Moore
	How Much We Can Bear		David Frazier
U or 2 pt	Rejoice! I Found the Lost		Rusty Edwards, arr Wold
	Satisfied		M McGhee & R Martin
	See What Love, *St. Paul*		F Mendelssohn
	Thou Knowest, Lord, the Secrets of Our Hearts		Henry Purcell
a, fl	Our Father We Have Wandered		arr Larry Harris
	Our Loving Father, *Nine Sacred Songs*	LIFT	Peter Cornelius
	Add'l Music, Cantatas, Major Works		
t	O Lord Most Holy		César Franck
	O Lord I Will Praise Thee	OXEA	Gordon Jacob
satb	5: Wo soll ich fliehen hin		J S Bach

Year C | Fourth Sunday in Lent

	Entrance	Sequence	Offertory	Communion	Postcommunion		H82	WLP	LEVAS II	VF	MHSO	CG descant	Inst descant
					■	Shepherd of souls, refresh and bless [C]	343					■	
						Joshua 5:9-12							
			■			Deep river, my home is over Jordan			8				
	■					Guide me, O thou great Jehovah	690					■	
	■					On Jordan's stormy banks I stand			9				
	■					Praise our great and gracious Lord	393						
						2 Corinthians 5:16-21							
			■			All who believe and are baptized	298						
						Come now, O Prince of peace		795			82		
	■			■		O love, how deep, how broad, how high	448,449					■	
	■					O Love of God, how strong and true	455,456						
	■					O Spirit of the living God	531						
	■					Sing, my soul, his wondrous love	467						
	■					The great Creator of the worlds	489						
	■					When Christ was lifted from the earth	603,604						
						Luke 15:1-3,11b-32							
						A long lost lamb				95			
				■		Bread of the world, in mercy broken	301						
				■		Come, thou fount of every blessing	686		111			■	
						From my birth, from my birth					126		
						God of the sparrow					129		
			■			Just as I am, without one plea	693		137	82,83,84			■
	■					Lead us, heavenly Father, lead us	559						
				■		Lord Jesus, think on me	641	798					
			■			Now the silence	333						
	■					O bless the Lord, my soul!	411						
						Softly and tenderly Jesus is calling			101				
				■		There's a wideness in God's mercy	469,470						■
				■		Wilt thou forgive that sin where I begun	140,141						

Same tune, but not text [S] Seasonal [C] Collect [P] Psalm [GR] Gospel-related [SC] Semi-continuous

61

Fifth Sunday in Lent | Year C

Anthem	Solo	Handbells	Voicing	Title	Collection	Composer
				Isaiah 43:16-21		
				As Panting Deer		David Ashley White
				As Pants the Hart		Orlando Lassus
				As Pants the Hart, *Chandos Anthem No. 6*		G F Handel
				As the Deer, for Water Yearning	CHAN	Claude Goudimel
				As the Deer Pants for Streams of Water		Jim Taylor
				As the Deer Longs for the Waterbrooks		Peter Pindar Stearns
				Bless the Lord O My Soul	OXEA	C Armstrong Gibbs
				Like As the Hart		Herbert Howells
						Malcolm Williamson
				O Comfort Now My People	SEW	Thomas Pavlechko
	fl			My Soul Is Thirsting for You, O Lord, My God		Charles Callahan
	ob			Psalm 42		Daniel Kean
				Ride the Chariot		Noah Ryder
				Sicut cervus	FLEM, ITAL	G P da Palestrina
						Reginald Unterseher
				The First Song of Isaiah		Jack Noble White
				Psalm 126		
				Blessed Are They, *A German Requiem*	CAB	J Brahms
				Die mit Tränen säen		Johann Schein
						Heinrich Schütz
				He Has Done Great Things *(Lead Me, Guide Me)*		Jesse Dixon
				I Will Greatly Rejoice		Harold Darke
				Selig sind, die da Leid tragen, *A German Requiem*		J Brahms
				The 126th Psalm		Ernst Krenek
				Weeping (Joy, Joy)		Edwin Hawkins
				When the Lord Turned Again	16th	Adrian Batten
				Jesus Take Me by the Hand		Stephen Foster
				Philippians 3:4b-14		
				Fight the Good Fight		John Gardner
				I Am Pressing On		James Cleveland
				Since by Man Came Death, *Messiah*		G F Handel
				Since by Man Came Death *(Lent version)*	SEW	Thomas Pavlechko
				When I Survey the Wondrous Cross		Gilbert Martin
				John 12:1-8		
				A Litany/ Drop, Drop Slow Tears	AFC 4	William Walton
				Drop, Drop, Slow Tears	OXNEA	Gibbons/arr Blackwell
		SSA		Introit for Lent or Passiontide	AFC 3	Orlando Gibbons
				Jesu, meine Freude	BFAS	J S Bach
		SATB, instr		The Anointing, *Sacred Symphonies*		Alice Parker
				The Feet O' Jesus		William Averitt
				Wondrous Love		Multiple
				How Beautiful Are the Feet, *Messiah*		G F Handel
				Add'l Music, Cantatas, Major Works		
				Grief and Pain, *St. Matthew Passion*		J S Bach
				Motet: Jesu, meine Freude		J S Bach

Year C | Fifth Sunday in Lent

	H82	WLP	LEVAS II	VF	MHSO	CG descant	Inst descant
Eternal Lord of love, behold your Church [S]	149						
I sing the almighty power of God [C]	398					o	
Isaiah 43:16-21							
Come, thou fount of every blessing	686		111				
Crashing waters at creation				67	95		
Lord, dismiss us with thy blessing	344						
O God, unseen yet ever near	332						
Sing now with joy unto the Lord	425						
Surely it is God who saves me	678,679						
When from bondage we are summoned		753,754					
Wisdom freed a holy people		905		155			
Philippians 3:4b-14							
Awake, my soul, stretch every nerve	546						
Fight the good fight with all thy might (1-2)	552,553						
If the world from you withhold			197				
I'm pressing on the upward way			165				
Jesus, all my gladness	701						
Lo! what a cloud of witnesses	545						
Not far beyond the sea, nor high	422						
We sing the praise of him who died	471						
When from bondage we are summoned		753,754					
When I survey the wondrous cross	474						
John 12:1-8							
Delivered from shame, the woman came				14			
Holy woman, graceful giver				1			
In boldness, look to God for help				94			
Let thy Blood in mercy poured	313						
Lord, whose love through humble service	610						
Not here for high and holy things (4-6)	9						

o Same tune, but not text   [S] Seasonal   [C] Collect   [P] Psalm   [GR] Gospel-related   [SC] Semi-continuous

Palm Sunday | Year C

Anthem/Solo/Handbells/Voicing	Title	Collection	Composer
	Luke 19:28-40 *See Palm Sunday A & B*		
	Hosanno filio David		Tomas Luis de Victoria
	Ride On	OXASH	Grayston Ives
	Ride on King Jesus *(Not the spiritual)*		Dorothy Norwood
	Ride on King Jesus		arr Hairston; Hall Johnson
	Ride on, King Jesus		Robert Shaw/Alice Parker
	Ride On! Ride on in Majesty!		T Frederick Candlyn
	Sing Hosanna to the Son of David		Bartholomäus Gesius
	Psalm 118:1-2, 19-29 *See Palm Sunday A & B*		
	Isaiah 50:4-9a		
	God Be in My Head	OXNCAB	H Walford Davies; J Rutter
	Os justi		Anton Bruckner
	Strengthen for Service	AUG	Richard Proulx
	He Was Despised, *Messiah*		G F Handel
s or t	How Hast Thou Offended		Heinrich Schütz
	Psalm 31:9-16 *See Palm Sunday A & B*		
	Philippians 2:5-11 *See Palm Sunday A & B*		
SAATB	In Nomine Jesu	CHES FG5	Jacob Handl
	The Lord Will Surely Come		Gerre Hancock
	Luke 22:14—23:56 or Luke 23:1-49		
	Ah, Holy Jesus		Roger T. Petrich
	Daughters of Zion	OXCAB	F Mendelssohn
SATTB	In manus tuas		Multiple
	In monte Olivéti	SEW	Thomas Pavlechko
	The Way to Jerusalem		Harold Friedell
	Stabat Mater		Multiple
	Words of Institution	SEW	Thomas Pavlechko
	Vexilla Regis		John Ireland
b	Heute, wirst du mi mir im Paradies, *Cantata 106*		J S Bach
s or t	How Hast Thou Offended		Heinrich Schütz
a	Mit Fried und Freud ich fahr..., *Cantata 106*		J S Bach
	Add'l Music, Cantatas, Major Works		
	Agnus Dei		Multiple
	A Lamb Goes Uncomplaining Forth	CHAN	Hugo Distler
	Crux fidelis		Multiple
	Ecce quomodo moritur justus		Jacob Handl
SSATBB	Huc me sydereo	ANTH	Josquin Desprez
	Lamb of God		Multiple
	SAA O crux benedicta	AFC 3	Claudio Monteverdi
SAA	O Domine Jesu Christe		Claudio Monteverdi
	O vos omnes		Multiple
SSAA		AFC 3	Tomás Luis de Victoria
	Pange Lingua		Multiple
	Praise to Thee, Lord Jesus, *St. Mt. Passion*	OXNCAB	Heinrich Schütz
	Salvator mundi		Thomas Tallis
	Sing, O Tongue/ Sing, My Tongue		Multiple
	Solus ad Victimam (Alone to Sacrifice...)	AFC 1	Kenneth Leighton
	The Feast of Palms	OXASH	Alan Bullard
	Were You There		arr Harold Friedell
		AUG	arr Richard Proulx
	Bleed and break Thou, *St. Matthew Passion*		J S Bach
	My Heart Breaks in Anguish, *St. John Passion*		J S Bach
	Quis non posset, *Stabat Mater*		F J Haydn
satb	106: Gottes Zeit ist die allerbeste Zeit		J S Bach
atb	182: Himmelskönig, sei willkommen		J S Bach
	The Passion According to St. Matthew		J S Bach
	St. Matthew Passion		Heinrich Schütz
	Stabat Mater		Multiple

Year C | Palm Sunday

	H82	WLP	LEVAS II	VF	MHSO	CG descant	Inst descant
At the Liturgy of the Palms: Luke 19:28-40							
Palm Sunday Anthems	153						
All glory, laud, and honor	154, 155						
Mantos y palmas esparciendo / Filled with excitement		728					
Ride on, King Jesus			97				
Ride on! ride on in majesty!	156						
Sanna, sannanina					91		
Isaiah 50:4-9a							
Alone thou goest forth, O Lord	164						
Hail, thou once despised Jesus! (1-2)	495						
To mock your reign, O dearest Lord	170						
Philippians 2:5-11							
At the Name of Jesus, every knee shall bow	435			135			
Cross of Jesus, cross of sorrow	160						
Jesus, living word incarnate				75			
Morning glory, starlit sky (4-6)	585						
The flaming banners of our king	161						
The royal banners forward go	162						
What wondrous love is this	439						
Luke 22:14-23:56 or 23:1-49							
Ah, holy Jesus, how hast thou offended	158						
And now, O Father, mindful of the love (1-2)	337						
Holy woman, graceful giver				1			
Let thy Blood in mercy poured	313						
My song is love unknown	458						
Nature with open volume stands	434						
O Lord, how the fallen woman wept				41			
O sacred head, sore wounded	168, 169	735	36				
She poured the perfume lavishly				137			
There is a green hill far away	167			49			
When I survey the wondrous cross	474						
Would you share Christ's passion?				42			

Same tune, but not text [S] Seasonal [C] Collect [P] Psalm [GR] Gospel-related [SC] Semi-continuous

65

Monday in Holy Week | Year C

Anthem	Solo	Handbells	Voicing		Title	Collection	Composer
				Isaiah 42:1-9			
	■			Behold My Servant		Bruce Bengston
				Ein jeder Lauft, der In den Schranken kauft		G P Telemann
				Psalm 36:5-11		
■				How Precious Is Thy Loving Kindness		Samuel Adler
■						Daniel Pinkham
			TB	Thy Mercy Jehovah		Benedetto Marcello
				Thy Mercy O Lord Reacheth unto the Heavens		Paul C Edwards
				Thy Word is a Lantern		John Bertalot
	■			Loving Kindness	SUNSOLO	Henry Purcell
				Hebrews 9:11-15		
■			Unison	The Promise of Eternal Inheritance		Rudolf Moser
				John 12:1-11		
				A Litany/Drop, Drop, Slow Tears	AFC 4	William Walton
				Jesu, meine Freude	BFAS	J S Bach
			SATB, inst	The Anointing, *Sacred Symphonies*		Alice Parker
				Wondrous Love		Multiple
	■			How Beautiful Are the Feet, *Messiah*		G F Handel

Year C | Monday in Holy Week

	Hymn	H82	WLP	LEVAS II	VF	MHSO	CG descant	Inst descant
Postcommunion	We sing the praise of him who died [S]	471						
	Isaiah 42:1-9							
	Ancient of Days, who sittest throned in glory	363						
	Jesus shall reign where'er the sun	544						
	Thy strong word did cleave the darkness	381						
	Weary of all trumpeting	572						
	Hebrews 9:11-15							
	Come, thou fount of every blessing	686	111					
	Cross of Jesus, cross of sorrow	160						
	Draw nigh and take the Body of the Lord	327, 328						
	Glory be to Jesus	479						
	Holy Father, great Creator	368						
	Let thy Blood in mercy poured	313						
	John 12:1-11							
	God himself is with us	475						
	Holy woman, graceful giver				1			
	Jesus, all my gladness	701						
	Jesus, the very thought of thee	642						
	Just as I am, without one plea	693		137	82, 83, 84			
	She poured the perfume lavishly				137			
	There's a wideness in God's mercy	469, 470						

[o] Same tune, but not text [S] Seasonal [C] Collect [P] Psalm [GR] Gospel-related [SC] Semi-continuous

Tuesday in Holy Week | Year C

Anthem	Solo	Handbells	Voicing	Title	Collection	Composer
				Isaiah 49:1-7		
	■			Hear Ye, Israel, *Elijah*		F Mendelssohn
				I Will Give You as a Light to the Nations		Carl Schalk
				Sing O Heavens		Emma Lou Diemer
				Psalm 71:1-14		
■				Descendit sicut pluvial		Orlando Gibbons
				Go Not Far from Me O God		Nicolo Zingarelli
			SSATB	Herr, auf dich Traus ich		Heinrich Schütz
				I Waited on the Lord, *Hymn of Praise*		F Mendelssohn
				In te, Domine speravi		Josquin des Prés
						Halsey Stevens
				In te, speravi		Palestrina
				In Thee, O Lord		Jane Marshall
						Thomas Weelkes
				My God Is a Rock		Shaw/Parker
				O Lord, in Thee Have I Trusted		G F Handel
			2 pt	O Lord, My God, You Are… (Bist Du bei mir)		J S Bach, arr Hopson
				They That Wait upon the Lord		Jean Berger
	■		st duet	My Song Shall Be Always, *Hymn of Praise*		F Mendelssohn
				Nobody Knows the Trouble I've Seen		Spiritual, Various
				1 Corinthians 1:18-31		
■				Crux fidelis		Multiple
				The Foolishness Carol		Austin Lovelace
				The Wisdom of God		Austin Lovelace
				John 12:20-36		
■				As Moses Lifted Up the Serpent		Edward Bairstow
				Jesus, So Lowly		Harold Friedell
				Lift Up Your Heads	16th	John Amner
				Lift Up Your Heads, *Messiah*		G F Handel
				Sicut Moses serpentem		Heinrich Schütz
				The Way to Jerusalem		Harold Friedell
			SATB, vla	Who Is This?		John Ferguson
■			SSATB	Yet a Little While		Knut Nystedt

Year C | Tuesday in Holy Week

	Hymn	H82	WLP	LEVAS II	VF	MHSO	CG descant	Inst descant
	My song is love unknown (1-2,7) [S]	458						
	Isaiah 49:1-7							
	Christ, whose glory fills the skies	6,7						
	God of mercy, God of grace	538						
	How wondrous and great thy works, God of praise!	532,533						
	1 Corinthians 1:18-31							
	Beneath the cross of Jesus	498						
	Cross of Jesus, cross of sorrow	160						
	In the cross of Christ I glory	441,442						
	Jesus, keep me near the cross			29				
	Nature with open volume stands	434						
	On a hill far away stood an old rugged cross			38				
	We sing the praise of him who died	471						
	When I survey the wondrous cross	474						
	John 12:20-36							
	I heard the voice of Jesus say	692						
	I want to walk as a child of the light	490						
	O Jesus, I have promised	655						
	The great Creator of the worlds	489						
	When Christ was lifted from the earth	603,604					o	

[o] Same tune, but not text   [S] Seasonal   [C] Collect   [P] Psalm   [GR] Gospel-related   [SC] Semi-continuous

Wednesday in Holy Week | Year C

Anthem/Solo/Handbells/Voicing	Title	Collection	Composer
	Isaiah 50:4-9a		
	God Be In My Head	OXNCAB	H Walford Davies
		OXNCAB	John Rutter
	Os justi		Anton Bruckner
	Strengthen for Service	AUG	Richard Proulx
Solo a	He Was Despised, *Messiah*		G F Handel
Solo s or t	How Hast Thou Offended		Heinrich Schütz
	Psalm 70		
	Auxilium meum	CHES FR	Pierre Passereau
	Deus in adjutorium		J Pachelbel
	Domine, ad adjuvandum me festina		Giovanni Gastoldi
			Padre Martini
	Eile, mich, Gott, zu erretten		Heinrich Schütz
	Haste Thee, O God	AFC 1	Adrian Batten
	Make Haste		Alan Hovhaness
TTBB	Psalm 70		Leo Sowerby
			David Ashley White
Solo	Hasten, O Lord, To…, *Five Sht Scrd Concertos*		Heinrich Schütz
	Hebrews 12:1-3		
	Adoramus te		Multiple
	Christus factus est		Multiple
	He Endured the Cross		Carl H Graun
	Seeing We Also		Leo Sowerby
	John 13:21-32		
	Adoramus te		Multiple
	Ah, Holy Jesus	AFC 4	arr Roger T Petrich
	Christus factus est		Multiple

Year C | Wednesday in Holy Week

							H82	WLP	LEVAS II	VF	MHSO	CG descant	Inst descant
					Isaiah 50:4-9a								
					Alone thou goest forth, O Lord	164							
					Bread of heaven, on thee we feed	323							
					Let thy Blood in mercy poured	313							
					To mock your reign, O dearest Lord	170							
					Hebrews 12:1-3								
					Hail, thou once despised Jesus!	495							
					Lo! what a cloud of witnesses	545							
					The head that once was crowned with thorns	483							
					John 13:21-32								
					Ah, holy Jesus, how hast thou offended	158							
					Bread of the world, in mercy broken	301							
					O love, how deep, how broad, how high	448,449							

Same tune, but not text   [S] Seasonal   [C] Collect   [P] Psalm   [GR] Gospel-related   [SC] Semi-continuous

71

Maundy Thursday | Year C

Anthem	Solo	Handbells	Voicing	Title	Collection	Composer
				Exodus 12:1-4 [5-10] 11-14		
				Psalm 116:1, 10-17		
■				I Love the Lord		Richard Smallwood
■				What Shall I Render to My God		Austin Lovelace
				1 Corinthians 11:23-26		
■				Ave Verum		Multiple
■				Of the Glorious Body Telling		Multiple
■				Pange lingua		Multiple
■				Tantum ergo (Genitori, Genitoque)		Multiple
■				Verily, Verily I Say unto You	AFC 1	Thomas Tallis
■				Words of Institution	SEW vol 11	Thomas Pavlechko
				John 13:1-17, 31b-35		
■				A New Commandment	OXASH	Richard Shephard
■				A Litany/Drop, Drop, Slow Tears	AFC 4	William Walton
■				Asperges me, Domine		Multiple
■				Christus factus est		Multiple
■				In the Heart Where Love Is Abiding	OXASH	arr John Barnard
■				Non nobis, Domine		Multiple
			SATTBB	Ubi caritas		Maurice Duruflé
			SATTBB			Petr Eben
						Jean Langlais
		U				Flor Peeters
■						Richard Proulx
■				Behold the Son of God	LIFT	W A Mozart
				Add'l Music, Cantatas, Major Works		
■				Beautiful Savior		F Melius Christiansen
				In monte Olivéti	SEW	Thomas Pavlechko
						Multiple
				Jesu, dulcis memoria		Multiple
				Nolo Mortem Peccatoris	16th	Thomas Morley
				O sacrum convivium (without Alleluias)		Multiple
				O Salutaris Hostia		Multiple
■				Thee We Adore		T Frederick Candlyn
■			satb	180: Schmücke dich, o liebe Seele		J S Bach
				Christ on the Mount of Olives		Beethoven

Year C | Maundy Thursday

	Entrance	Sequence	Offertory	Communion	Postcommunion		H82	WLP	LEVAS II	VF	MHSO	CG descant	Inst descant
						Go to dark Gethsemane [S]	171						
	■		■			Praise to the Holiest in the height [S]	445,446						
				■		We gather at your table, Lord [S]				89			
						Exodus 12:1-4, (5-10) 11-14							
	■		■			What wondrous love is this	439						■
						1 Corinthians 11:23-26							
				■		As we proclaim your death				80			
				■		In remembrance of me, eat this bread			149				
				■		Lord God, revealed in gifts of bread and wine				78			
				■		Now, my tongue, the mystery telling	329,330,331						
				■		O wheat whose crushing was for bread		760		74			
				■		Pan de Vida, cuerpo del Señor					93		
				■		This is my body given for you			155				
	■			■		When Jesus died to save us	322						
				■		Zion, praise thy Savior singing	320						
						John 13:1-17-31b-35							
				■		A new commandment that I give to you					92		
			■			As in that upper room you left your seat		729,730					
			■			Thou, who at thy first Eucharist didst pray	315						
			■			Three holy days enfold us now		731,732,733					
	■		■			You laid aside your rightful reputation		734					
						At the footwashing:							
						Brother, sister, let me serve you				124	94		
						God is love, and where true love is	576,577						
						Jesu, Jesu, fill us with your love	602			74			
						Ubi caritas et amor		831					
						Where charity and love prevail	581						
						Where true charity and love dwell	606						
						At the stripping of the altar:							
						Stay with me		826					

Same tune, but not text   [S] Seasonal   [C] Collect   [P] Psalm   [GR] Gospel-related   [SC] Semi-continuous

Good Friday | Year C

Anthem/Solo/Handbells/Voicing	Title	Collection	Composer
	Isaiah 52:13—53:12		
	Agnus Dei		Multiple
	And with His Stripes, *Messiah*		G F Handel
	Behold the Lamb of God, *Messiah*		G F Handel
	Furwahr! Er trug unsre Krankheit (Surely)		M Franck; C H Graun
	God So Loved the World		Multiple, *see Trinity Sunday*
	Surely He Hath Borne Our Griefs, *Messiah*		G F Handel
			Multiple
3 pt	Vere languores		André Campra
3 pt or SATB			Antonio Lotti
			Tomás Luis de Victoria
satb	*Messiah*, Part 2		G F Handel
	Psalm 22 *See Good Friday, A & B*		
	Hebrews 10:16-25		
	Agnus Dei		Multiple
	Ave Verum		Multiple
	Christus factus est		Multiple
	Hebrews 4:14-16; 5:7-9, alt		
	Adoramus te		Multiple
	Christus factus est		Multiple
	John 18:1—19:42		
	Crucifixion		Hall Johnson
	Crucifixus, *Mass in B Minor*		J S Bach
	Crucifixus		Multiple
	I Wonder as I Wander		Multiple
SATTB	In manus tuas		Multiple
	In monte Oliveti	SEW	Thomas Pavlechko
			Multiple
SAA	O crux benedicta	AFC 3	Claudio Monteverdi
SAA	O Domine Jesu Christe	AFC 3	Claudio Monteverdi
	O vos omnes		Multiple
SSAA		AFC 3	Tomás Luis de Victoria
	Nolo mortem peccatoris	16th	Thomas Morley
	Stabat Mater		Multiple
	Tenebrae factae sunt		Multiple
	Tristis est anima mea		Multiple
	When We Are Tempted to Deny Your Son		Sally Ann Morris
s or t	How Hast Thou Offended		Heinrich Schütz
	Add'l Music, Cantatas, Major Works		
	Adoramus te Christe		Multiple
	Crux fidelis		Multiple
	Ecce quomodo moritur justus		Jacob Handl
SATB div	Faithful Cross		Thomas Pavlechko
SSATBB	Huc me sydereo	ANTH	Josquin Desprez
	Improperium	CHES FL	Orlando DiLasso
SSA	Is It Nothing to You?	RSCM TR	Sue Fairhurst
	Praise to Thee, Lord Jesus, *St. Matthew Passion*	OXNCAB	Heinrich Schütz
	Salvator mundi		Thomas Tallis
	Sing My Tongue	OXASH	Richard Shephard
SSAATTBB	The Veneration of the Cross, *All Night Vigil*		S Rachmaninoff
	Were You There		arr H Friedell; H Johnson
		AUG	arr Richard Proulx
	Bleed and Break Thou..., *St. Matthew Passion*		J S Bach
	My Heart Breaks in Anguish, *St. John Passion*		J S Bach
	Quis non posset, *Stabat Mater*		F J Haydn
	Stabat Mater		Multiple
satb	*The Passion According to St. John*		J S Bach
	The Passion According to St. John		Multiple

74

Year C | Good Friday

Entrance	Sequence	Offertory	Communion	Postcommunion		H82	WLP	LEVAS II	VF	MHSO	CG descant	Inst descant
					Note: There is no Entrance Hymn on this day (see BCP, p. 276).							
		×			For this day, hymns in this column are for singing after the sermon;							
			×		hymns in this column are for singing before the cross;							
				×	and hymns in this column are for singing to end the service after the Solemn Collects.							
					Isaiah 52:13-53:12							
					Ah, holy Jesus, how hast thou offended	158						
					He never said a mumbalin' word			33				
					O sacred head, sore wounded	168,169	735	36				
					To mock your reign, O dearest Lord	170						
					Hebrews 10:16-25							
					Alone thou goest forth, O Lord	164						
					Cross of Jesus, cross of sorrow	160						
					Hebrews 4:14-16; 5:7-9							
					From God Christ's deity came forth	443						
					There is a green hill far away	167			49			
					John 18:1-19:42							
					At the cross her vigil keeping	159						
					At the foot of the cross (1-3)				43			
					Every time I think about Jesus [Calvary]			32				
					Faithful cross, above all other		737					
					Go to dark Gethsemane	171						
					In the cross of Christ I glory	441,442						
					Jesus, keep me near the cross			29				
					King of my life I crown thee now			31				
					Lord Christ, when first thou cam'st to earth	598						
					Morning glory, starlit sky	585						
					O how he loves you and me			35				
					On a hill far away stood an old rugged cross			38				
					Sing, my tongue the glorious battle	165,166						
					Sunset to sunrise changes now	163						
					There is a fountain filled with blood			39				
					They crucified my Lord			33				
					Were you there when they crucified my Lord?	172		37(1-3)				
					When I survey the wondrous cross	474						
					When Jesus came to Golgotha		736					
					When on the cross of Calvary			34				
					Would you share Christ's passion?				42			

Same tune, but not text [S] Seasonal [C] Collect [P] Psalm [GR] Gospel-related [SC] Semi-continuous

Holy Saturday | Year C

Anthem	Solo	Handbells	Voicing	Title	Collection	Composer
				Job 14:1-14		
●				Man That Is Born of a Woman	OXCAB	Samuel Wesley
				The Lord Is My Shepherd, *Requiem*		John Rutter
				The Paper Reeds..., *The Peaceable Kingdom*		Randall Thompson
				Lamentations 3:1-9, 19-24, alt		
				De profundis		Multiple
				Hear My Cry, Holy One		David Ashley White
				Out of the Depths		Multiple
			SAB			John Horman
			SATB, SAB			W A Mozart
			2 pt			K Lee Scott
						Heinrich Schütz
				Out of the Deep, *Requiem*		John Rutter
			SAB	Out of the Deep		Henry Purcell
			ATB			Thomas Tompkins
				Psalm 130		Multiple
			SAATB	Lord, to Thee I Make My Moan		Thomas Weelkes
			TTB	Si iniquitates observaveris		Samuel Wesley
			satb	Cantata 38: Aus tiefer Not schrei ich zu dir		J S Bach
			satb	Cantata 131: Aus der Tiefen rufe ich, Herr, zu dir		J S Bach
				Psalm 31:1-4, 15-16		
				In te, Domine		Heinrich Schütz
			SAB	In te, Domine speravi		D Buxtehude
			Unison	In Thee, O Lord Do I Put My Trust		Jan Bender
				In Thee, O Lord, Have I Trusted	CON	G F Handel
				1 Peter 4:1-8		
			SSA or SSAA	If Ye Love Me		Harvey B Gaul
			SSA			Daniel Pinkham
						Thomas Tallis
			SSA			Healey Willan
						Philip Wilby
				Matthew 27:57-66		
●				Sepulto Domino		Tomás Luis de Victoria
				John 19:38-42, alt		
●				Sepulto Domino		Tomás Luis de Victoria
				Add'l Music, Cantatas, Major Works		
●				Ave verum		Multiple
			satb	38: Aus tiefer Not schrei ich zu dir		J S Bach

Year C | Holy Saturday

						Reading / Hymn	H82	WLP	LEVAS II	VF	MHSO	CG descant	Inst. descant
						Note: There is no Entrance Hymn on this day (see BCP, p. 283).							
						Job 14:1-14							
						From deepest woe I cry to thee	151						
						Immortal, invisible, God only wise	423						
						Out of the depths I call	666						
						Lamentations 3:1-9,19-24							
						Great is thy faithfulness			189				
						The steadfast love of the Lord never ceases		755					
						1 Peter 4:1-8							
						In deepest night, in darkest days				97			
						O love, how deep, how broad, how high (1-4,6)	448,449						
						O Love of God, how strong and true (1-3)	455,456						
						Matthew 27:57-66							
						My song is love unknown (1-2,6-7)	458						
						O sorrow deep!	173						
						Were you there when they crucified my Lord?	172		37(1-3)				
						John 19:38-42							
						My song is love unknown (1-2,6-7)	458						
						O sorrow deep!	173						
						Were you there when they crucified my Lord?	172		37(1-3)				

Same tune, but not text [S] Seasonal [C] Collect [P] Psalm [GR] Gospel-related [SC] Semi-continuous

The Great Vigil of Easter | Year C

Anthem	Solo	Handbells	Voicing	Title	Collection	Composer
				Genesis 1:1-2:4a		
	s			He's Got the Whole World in His Hands		Margaret Bonds
				Exodus 14:10-31; 15:20-21		
				Go Down Moses		Moses Hogan
				Zephaniah 3:14-20		
			Unison	Sing Aloud, O Daughter of Zion		John Eggert
			SAB, s	Sing, O Daughters of Zion		Jan Bender
	s			Rejoice Greatly, *Messiah*		G F Handel
				Psalm 98		
				Cantate Domino		Multiple
				Let All the Rivers Clap Their Hands		Mark Schweizer
			U, fl	Make a Joyful Noise		Maureen I. Sindlinger
				Psalm 98		Multiple
			SSAATB	Recordatus est	CHES FG6	Philippe Rogier
				Ring Out Your Joy		Harrison Oxley
				Shout for Joy! (Ps 100)		John Carter
				Singet dem Herrn		J S Bach
				Singet dem Herrn ein neues Lied		Heinrich Schütz
				Sing to the Lord a New Song		Multiple
				Sing unto the Lord		Multiple
				Sing unto the Lord a New Song		Healey Willan
				Sing a New Song, *Biblical Songs*		A Dvořák
				Sing unto the Lord	LIFT	Peter Cornelius
				Romans 6:3-11		
			SSAB	Alleluia, Christ Our Passover		Jan Bender
				Canticle for Communion		Jane Marshall
				Christ, Our Passover		Alan Gibbs; John Goss
			SATB, brass			Richard Dirksen
						Will C MacFarlane
			2 pt			Robert J Powell
				Christ Rising Again		William Byrd
				Christ the Lord Is Risen Again		Richard Proulx
				Easter Triumph		Ronald Arnatt
				Since by Man Came Death, *Messiah*		G F Handel
				Since by Man Came Death	SEW, 2006	Thomas Pavlechko
				Psalm 114		
				In exitu Israel		Antonio Vivaldi
				Psalm 114		Zoltan Kodaly
				When Israel Came Out of Egypt (In exita Israel)		W Byrd; H L Hassler; Wesley
				Luke 24:1-12 See also *Easter Day*		
				All Night Vigil		S Rachmaninoff
				Blessed Art Thou, O Lord		
				Today Hath Salvation Come		
				Veneration /We Have Seen Thy Resur…		
				When Thou, O Lord, Hadst Arisen		
				An Easter Dialogue		Andreas Hammerschmidt
			brass	Arise and Shine		Mona Lyn Reese
				Easter Dawning at the Tomb		Robert Wetzler
				Magdalen, Cease from Sobs		Peter Hurford
				Mary Magdalen		J Brahms
				On Easter Morn, Ere Break of Day		Simon Lindley
				The Angel Said to the Women		Harald Rohlig
				Who Rolls Away the Stone		Andreas Hammerschmidt
				Add'l Music, Cantatas, Major Works		
				Et Resurrexit, *Mass in B Minor*		J S Bach
	satb			4: Christ lag in Todes Banden		J S Bach
	stb			31: Der Himmel lacht! die Erde jubilieret		J S Bach
	satb			137: Lobe den Herren, den mächtigen König		J S Bach

Year C | The Great Vigil of Easter

	H82	WLP	LEVAS II	VF	MHSO	CG descant	Inst. descant
It is preferable to sing the appointed Psalm or Canticle after each lesson,							
but the following suitable hymns and songs may be sung instead.							
Genesis 1:1-2:4a							
Creator of all time and space				102			
Give thanks to the Lord [P]		93					
I sing the almighty power of God	398					0	
Let us, with a gladsome mind [P]	389						
Many and great, O God, are thy works	385				128		
Most High, omnipotent, good Lord	406,407						
Most Holy God, the Lord of heaven	31,32						
O blest Creator, source of light (1-4)	27,28						
Genesis 7:1-5, 11-18; 8:6-18; 9:8-13							
A mighty fortress is our God [P]	687,688						
Eternal Father, strong to save	608						
It rained on the earth forty days, forty nights (1,3-4)					97		
Lord Jesus, think on me	641	798					
Genesis 22:1-18							
O sorrow deep!	173						
The God of Abraham praise	401						
Exodus 14:10-31; 15:20-21							
And Miriam was a weaver of unique variety				15			
Come, sing the joy of Miriam				121			
O Mary, don't you weep				122			
Sing now with joy unto the Lord [Canticle]	425						
We give thanks unto you, O God of might					98		
When Israel was in Egypt's land	648		228				
Wisdom freed a holy people		905			155		
With Miriam we will dance (1,4)				16		0	
Isaiah 55:1-11							
God moves in a mysterious way	677						
Surely it is God who saves me [Canticle]	678,679						
Baruch 3:9-15,32-4:4							
Come and seek the ways of Wisdom					60		
Even when young, I prayed for wisdom's grace		906					
The stars declare his glory [P]	431						
Proverbs 8:1-8; 19-21; 9:4b-6							
Come and seek the ways of wisdom					60		
God, you have given us power to sound	584						
The stars declare his glory [P]	431						
Ezekiel 36:24-28							
As longs the deer for cooling streams [P]	658						
As panting deer desire the waterbrooks [P]		727					
Before thy throne, O God, we kneel	574,575						

continued on page 81

0 Same tune, but not text [S] Seasonal [C] Collect [P] Psalm [GR] Gospel-related [SC] Semi-continuous

This page left blank intentionally.

Year C | The Great Vigil of Easter (con't)

						Hymn	H82	WLP	LEVAS II	VF	MHSO	CG descant	Inst descant
						Ezekiel 37:1-14							
						Breath of God, life-bearing wind				59		0	
						Breathe on me, Breath of God	508						
						Go forth for God; go to the world in peace	347						
						Let it breathe on me			116				
						Put forth, O God, thy Spirit's might	521						
						Spirit of the living God			115				
						Zephaniah 3:14-20							
						New songs of celebration render [P]	413						
						Surely it is God who saves me	678,679						
						At the Eucharist							
						At the Lamb's high feast we sing [S]	174						
						Camina, pueblo de Dios/ Walk on, O people of God [S]		739					
						Christ has arisen [S]			41		100		
						Christ is arisen (Christ ist erstanden) [S]	713						
						Christ Jesus lay in death's strong bands [S]	185,186						
						Christ the Lord is risen again! [S]	184						
						Christians, to the Paschal victim [S]	183						
						Come, ye faithful, raise the strain [S]	199,200						
						Day of delight and beauty unbounded [S]		738					
						God sent his Son, they called him Jesus [S]			43				
						Jesus Christ is risen today [S]	207						
						Oh, how good is Christ the Lord/ Oh, qué bueno es Jesús [S]					103		
						The Lamb's high banquet called to share [S]	202						
						The strife is o'er, the battle done [S]	208						
						Romans 6:3-11							
						All who believe and are baptized	298						
						Baptized in water	294	767	121				
						God's Paschal Lamb is sacrificed for us		880				0	
						Through the Red Sea brought at last	187						
						We know that Christ is raised and dies no more	296					0	
						Luke 24:1-12							
						At break of day three women came				50			
						O sons and daughters, let us sing (1-3,5)	203						
						On earth has dawned this day of days	201						
						At Baptism if after the sermon:							
						All who believe and are baptized	298						
						Baptized in water	294	767	121				
						Crashing waters at creation				67	95		
						It rained on the earth forty days, forty nights					97		
						Over the chaos of the empty waters	176,177						
						Take me to the water			134				
						Wade in the water		740	143				
						We know that Christ is raised and dies no more	296					0	
						You have put on Christ					122		

6 Same tune, but not text   [S] Seasonal   [C] Collect   [P] Psalm   [GR] Gospel-related   [SC] Semi-continuous

Easter Day | Year C

Anthem	Solo	Handbells	Voicing	Title	Collection	Composer
				Acts 10:34-43 (and alt 2nd reading)		
■				Christus factus est		Multiple
■				In nomine Jesu	CHES FG5	Jacob Handl
				Isaiah 65:17-25, alt		
■				And I Saw a New Heaven		Edgar L Bainton
■				Blessed City, Heavenly Salem		Edward Bairstow
■				I Heard a Voice from Heaven	OXCAB	John Goss
■				I Saw a New Heaven and a New Earth	AUG	Carl Schalk
■				Lo, God Is Here	AFC 1	Francis Jackson
■				Locus iste		Anton Bruckner
■				Surge illuminare		Multiple
■				City Called Heaven	SOS	Spiritual, arr Boatner
				Psalm 118:1-2, 14-24		
■				Confitemini Domino		Multiple
■				Easter Antiphon		David Hurd
■				Haec Dies *(editions with Alleluias)*		Multiple
■				Haec es Dies *(editions with Alleluias)*		Multiple
■				This Day		Marvin Curtis
	ss			This Day Was Made by the Lord	SOP TR	Evelyn Stell
■				This Is the Day *(editions with Alleluias)*		Multiple
				1 Corinthians 15:19-26		
■				Adam Lay YBounden		Multiple
■				Christ the Lord Is Risen! Alleluia!		Johan Helmich Roman
■				Exultate Deo		Multiple
■				I Know That My Redeemer Lives	OXCAB	Johann Michael Bach
■				Jesus, Son of Life, My Splendor		G F Handel
■				Scio enim	CHES FL	Jacob Vaet
■				Since by Man Came Death, *Messiah*		G F Handel
■				Since by Man	SEW	Thomas Pavlechko
■				Te Deum		Multiple
■				Awake All Ye People, *Cantata 15*	LIFT	J S Bach
	s			I Know That My Redeemer Liveth, *Messiah*		G F Handel
				John 20:1-18		
■				Easter Morning, Peace Be Unto You	AUG	Paul Christiansen
■				Eheu, sustulerunt	OXASH	Thomas Morley
■				Gloria		Marvin Curtis
■				Low in the Grave He Lay		M. Roger Holland
■				Maria Magdalene	CHES FR	François Dulot
■				Mighty Day		Marvin Curtis
■			SSA	O filii et filiae		F A Gevaert
■			SSAATTBB			V Leising
■				Regina caeli		Multiple
■				Three Days Had Passed		Joel Martinson
■				Victimae paschali laudes		Multiple
				Luke 24:1-12, alt *See the Great Vigil of Easter*		
				Add'l Music, Cantatas, Major Works		
			2 pt tr, instr	All Shall Be Well		Libby Larsen
■				Awake, My Heart, with Gladness	CHAN	Johann Crüger
■				Christ Is Now Ris'n Again	RSCM TR	Ian Ord-Hume
■				Christ the Lord Is Risen Again	AFC 4	John Rutter
■			SSA		AFC 3	John Rutter
■				Das Lamm das erwürget ist, *Cantata 21*		J S Bach
■				Easter Chorale		Samuel Barber
■			SSA	Introit for Easter	AFC 3	arr Philip Ledger
■				Jesus Christ, My Sure Defense—Alleluia	CHAN	F Mendelssohn
■				Today in Triumph Christ Arose	CHAN	Johann Crüger
	stb			145: Ich lebe, mein Herze, zu deinem Ergötzen		J S Bach
	satb			Kommt, eilet und laufet, *Easter Oratorio*, BWV 249		J S Bach

Year C | Easter Day

	H82	WLP	LEVAS II	VF	MHSO	CG descant	Inst descant
At the Lamb's high feast we sing [S]	174						
Christ has arisen [S]			41		100		
Christ is arisen / Christ ist erstanden [S]	713						
Christ is risen from the dead [S]		816,817					
Christ Jesus lay in death's strong bands [S]	185,186						
Come, let us with our Lord arise [P]							
Come, ye faithful, raise the strain [S]	199,200						
Day of delight and beauty unbounded [S]		738					
Good Christians all, rejoice and sing [S]	205						
Jesus Christ is risen today [S]	207						
Look there! the Christ our brother comes [S]	196,197						
Sing hallelujah to the Lord [S]				115			
The day of resurrection [S]	210						
The Lamb's high banquet called to share [S]	202						
The strife is o'er, the battle done [S]	208						
This is the day the Lord hath made [P]			219				
Acts 10:34-43							
Hail thee, festival day	175						
In Christ there is no East or West	529		62				
Sing, ye faithful, sing with gladness	492						
"Welcome, happy morning!" age to age shall say	179						
Isaiah 65:17-25							
Surely it is God who saves me	678,679						
This is the feast of victory for our God	417,418						
This is the hour of banquet and of song	316,317						
1 Corinthians 15:19-26							
Alleluia, alleluia! Hearts and voices heavenward raise	191						
God's Paschal Lamb is sacrificed for us		880				O	
Love's redeeming work is done	188,189						
Now the green blade riseth	204						
We know that Christ is raised and dies no more	296					O	
John 20:1-18							
Apostle of the Word				13			
Christ the Lord is risen again	184						
Christians, to the Paschal Victim	183						
I come to the garden alone			69				
Lift your voice rejoicing, Mary	190						
Myrrh-bearing Mary from Magdala came				2			
That Easter morn at break of day				45	99		
The first one ever, oh, ever to know	673						
They crucified my Savior			40				
Luke 24:1-12							
At break of day three women came				50			
O sons and daughters, let us sing (1-3,5)	203						
On earth has dawned this day of days	201						

O Same tune, but not text   [S] Seasonal   [C] Collect   [P] Psalm   [GR] Gospel-related   [SC] Semi-continuous

Easter Evening | Year C

Anthem/Solo/Handbells/Voicing	Title	Collection	Composer
	Isaiah 25:6-9		
	Festival Canticle: This Is the Feast		Peter Hallock
			Richard Hillert
			Mark Mummert
			Russell Schulz-Widmar
	O sacrum convivium (Editions with alleluias)		Multiple
	O Sacred Communion		Larry Long
	O Sacred Feast		Healey Willan
	Psalm 114		
SATB/SATB	In exitu Israel		Samuel Wesley
			A Vivaldi
	Psalm 114	OXASH	Edward Bairstow
			Zoltan Kodaly
	When Israel Came Out of Egypt		William Byrd
SATB/SATB			Samuel Wesley
	When Israel Went Out of Egypt		H L Hassler
	1 Corinthians 5:6b-8		
	Christ Our Passover		Richard Dirksen
			Will C MacFarlane
	Cantata 4: Christ lag in Todes Banden		J S Bach
	Luke 24:13-49		
	Abendlied: Bleib' bei uns		Josef Rheinberger
	Arisen Is Our Blessed Lord	CHAN	Melchior Vulpius
	Come, Risen Lord	AUG	John Bertalot
	Come, Ye Faithful	OXEA, OXNCAB	S Thatcher
	Cognoverunt discipuli		William Byrd
	Easter Morning "Peace Be unto You"	AUG	Paul Christiansen
	I Believe This Is Jesus	AUG	arr Undine Smith Moore
	If We Believe That Jesus Died	OXCAB, OXNC	John Goss
	O Pascal Lamp of Radiant Light	AUG	Sam Batt Owens
	O Sacred Communion		Larry Long
	O Sacred Feast		Healey Willan
	O sacrum convivium (editions with Alleluias)		Multiple
	O Sons and Daughters	OXASH	H Walford Davies
	O That I Knew Where I Might Find Him	OXNCAB	W Sterndale Bennett
	Stetit Jesus (Then Stood Jesus)		Jacob Handl
SSATB		CHES FG5	Jacob Regnart
SAA	Surgens Jesus	AFC 3	Claudio Monteverdi
		OXNCAB	Peter Phillips
	Surrexit Christus Hodie	OXASH	Samuel Scheidt
va	Who Is This?		John Ferguson
satb	Cantata 6: Bleib bei uns, denn es will Abend ...		J S Bach
atb	Cantata 66: Erfreut euch, ihr Herzen		J S Bach
	Add'l Music, Cantatas, Major Works		
U, 2 pt	O Gracious Light		Russell Schulz-Widmar
	Phos hilaron		Multiple
	Stay with Us, Lord	CHAN	Michael Praetorius
	The Day Draws on with Golden Light	OXCAB	Edward Bairstow
satb	4: Christ lag in Todes Banden		J S Bach
satb	6: Bleib bei uns, denn es will Abend werden		J S Bach
atb	66: Erfreut euch, ihr Herzen		J S Bach
b	158: Der Friede sei mit dir		J S Bach

Year C | Easter Evening

	Entrance	Sequence	Offertory	Communion	Postcommunion		H82	WLP	LEVAS II	VF	MHSO	CG descant	Inst descant
						Christ has arisen [S]			41		100		
						Christ is arisen / Christ ist erstanden [S]	713						
						Christ is risen from the dead [S]		816, 817					
						Day of delight and beauty unbounded [S]		738					
						Good Christians all, rejoice and sing! [S]	205						
						Jesus Christ is risen today [S]	207						
						Look there! the Christ, our Brother, comes [S]	196, 197						
						The strife is o'er, the battle done [S]	208						
						Isaiah 25:6-9							
						This is the feast of victory for our God	417, 418						
						This is the hour of banquet and of song	316, 317						
						1 Corinthians 5:6b-8							
						At the Lamb's high feast we sing	174						
						Christ Jesus lay in death's strong bands	185, 186						
						Christ the Lord is risen again!	184						
						God's Paschal Lamb is sacrificed for us		880				o	
						The Lamb's high banquet called to share	202						
						Luke 24:13-49							
						As we gather at your Table		763				o	
						Come, risen Lord, and deign to be our guest	305, 306						
						Come, ye faithful, raise the strain	199, 200						
						O sons and daughters, let us sing	203						
						Shepherd of souls, refresh and bless	343						
						That Easter day with joy was bright	193						

o Same tune, but not text [S] Seasonal [C] Collect [P] Psalm [GR] Gospel-related [SC] Semi-continuous

This page left blank intentionally.

Year C | Easter Week, Mon-Wed

		H82	WLP	LEVAS II	VF	MHSO	CG descant	Inst descant
MONDAY IN EASTER WEEK								
	Alleluia, alleluia! Hearts and voices heavenward raise [S]	191						
	Christ is arisen / Christ ist erstanden [S]	713						
	Jesus is Lord of all the earth [S]	178						
	O Love of God, how strong and true [S]	455,456						
	Acts 2:14,22b-32							
	Christ the Lord is risen again!	184						
	Good Christians all, rejoice and sing	205						
	Jesus lives! thy terrors now	194,195						
	Sing, ye faithful, sing with gladness	492						
	Matthew 28:9-15							
	Awake, arise, lift up your voice	212						
	Come, ye faithful, raise the strain	199,200						
	The day of resurrection!	210						
TUESDAY IN EASTER WEEK								
	The whole bright world rejoices now [S]	211						
	Acts 2:36-41							
	All who believe and are baptized	298						
	Baptized in water	294	767	121				
	Over the chaos of the empty waters	176,177						
	The head that once was crowned with thorns	483						
	We know that Christ is raised and dies no more	296					O	
	John 20:11-18							
	Christ the Lord is risen again!	184						
	Christians, to the Paschal Victim	183						
	Lift your voice rejoicing, Mary	190						
	Myrrh-bearing Mary from Magdala came				2			
	That Easter morn at break of day				45	99		
	The first one ever, oh, ever to know	673						
	They crucified my Savior			40				
WEDNESDAY IN EASTER WEEK								
	Christ has arisen [S]				41	100		
	Christ is arisen / Christ ist erstanden [S]	713						
	Day of delight and beauty unbounded [S]		738					
	Good Christians all, rejoice and sing! [S]	205						
	Jesus is Lord of all the earth [S]	178						
	Acts 3:1-10							
	From thee all skill and science flow	566						
	The fleeting day is nearly gone (1-2,4)	23						
	Luke 24:13-35							
	As we gather at your Table		763				O	
	Bless now, O God the journey that all your people make					142		
	Come, risen Lord, and deign to be our guest	305,306						
	He is risen, he is risen!	180						
	Let us talents and tongues employ				79	50		
	Lord God, revealed in gifts of bread and wine					78		
	Shepherd of souls, refresh and bless	343						

O Same tune, but not text [S] Seasonal [C] Collect [P] Psalm [GR] Gospel-related [SC] Semi-continuous

This page left blank intentionally.

Year C | Easter Week, Thur-Sat

	H82	WLP	LEVAS II	VF	MHSO	CG descant	Inst descant
THURSDAY IN EASTER WEEK							
Christ is arisen / Christ ist erstanden [S]	713						
O Love of God, how strong and true [S]	455,456						
The strife is o'er, the battle done [S]	208						
Acts 3:11-26							
Awake and sing the song	181						
Glorious the day when Christ was born	452						
Sing, ye faithful, sing with gladness	492						
Luke 24:36b-48							
Awake, arise, lift up your voice	212						
Come, ye faithful, raise the strain	199,200						
Look there! the Christ, our Brother, comes	196,197						
O sons and daughters, let us sing	203						
That Easter day with joy was bright	193						
FRIDAY IN EASTER WEEK							
Christ Jesus lay in death's strong bands [S]	185,186						
Christ the Lord is risen again [S]	184						
He is risen, he is risen! [S]	180						
Jesus lives! thy terrors now [S]	194,195						
Acts 4:1-12							
Christ is made the sure foundation	518						
O love, how deep, how broad, how high	448,449						
To the Name of our salvation	248,249						
John 21:1-14							
Come, risen Lord, and deign to be our guest	305,306						
I come with joy to meet my Lord	304						
O Food to pilgrims given	308,309						
SATURDAY IN EASTER WEEK							
Christ is alive! Let Christians sing [S]	182						
Jesus lives! thy terrors now [S]	194,195						
The Lamb's high banquet called to share [S]	202						
The whole bright world rejoices now [S]	211						
This joyful Eastertide [S]	192						
Acts 4:13-21							
Lord, speak to me that I may speak				98			
Mark 16:9-15,20							
Christians, to the Paschal Victim	183						
Lift your voice rejoicing, Mary	190						
Sing, ye faithful, sing with gladness	492						
The first one ever, oh, ever to know	673						
Ye servants of God, your Master proclaim	535						

Same tune, but not text   [S] Seasonal   [C] Collect   [P] Psalm   [GR] Gospel-related   [SC] Semi-continuous

Second Sunday of Easter | Year C

Anthem	Solo	Handbells	Voicing	Title	Collection	Composer
				Acts 5:27-32		
				Christ the Lord Is Risen Again		John Rutter
				Let Thy Hand, *Coronation Anthem No. 2*		G F Handel
				Now This Man Ceaseth Not, *St. Paul*		F Mendelssohn
				Psalm 118:14-29		
				Benedictus qui venit		Multiple
				Christ Is Our Cornerstone	OXNEA	David Thorne
				Confitemini Domino		Multiple
				Easter Antiphon		David Hurd
				Haec Dies (editions with Alleluias)		Multiple
				Haec es Dies (editions with Alleluias)		Multiple
				Lift Up Your Heads	16th	John Amner
						William Mathias
				Lift Up Your Heads, *Messiah*		G F Handel
	ss			This Day Was Made by the Lord	SOP TR	Evelyn Stell
				This Is the Day (editions with Alleluias)		Multiple
				Psalm 150, alt		
				Anthem of Praise		Richard Smallwood
				Hallelujah! Sing to the Lord a New Song		Bruce Neswick
				Laudate Dominum		Multiple
				Laudate Dominum in Sanctis ejus		Multiple
			SATB/SATB	Lobet den Herrn, Motet: Singet dem Herrn		J S Bach
			2 pt	O Praise God in His Holiness	OXEA	C Armstrong Gibbs
			U/2 pt	Praise God in His Sanctuary		John Harper
			U	Praise the Lord, Twelve Songs of Praise		Samuel Adler
			U/4-pt	Praise the Lord		Richard Stark
				Praise the Lord Who Reigns Above		David Ashley White
			b	Praise Ye the Lord	AFC 1	John Rutter
				Psalm 150		Multiple
			U	Song of Exultation		John Horman
				Revelations 1:4-8 *See Proper 29B*		
				John 20:19-31 *See also Easter Even, Luke; and Years A & B*		
				Arisen Is Our Blessed Lord	CHAN	Melchior Vulpius
				Come, Risen Lord	AUG	John Bertalot
				Come Ye Faithful, Raise the Strain	OXEA, OXNCAB	S Thatcher
				Follow Me		Don Harper & Ben Tankard
				I Believe This Is Jesus	AUG	Spiritual, arr Undine Smith Moore
				If We Believe That Jesus Died	OXCAB, OXNC	John Goss
				O Pascal Lamp of Radiant Light	AUG	Sam Batt Owens
				O Sacred Communion		Larry Long
				O Sacred Feast		Healey Willan
				O sacrum convivium (editions with Alleluias)		Multiple
			SAB	O Sons and Daughters		Luigi Cherubini
					OXASH	H Walford Davies
				O That I Knew Where I Might Find Him	OXNCAB	W Sterndale Bennett
				Real, Jesus Is Real to Me		Beatrice Brown
				Stetit Jesus (Then Stood Jesus)		Jacob Handl
			SSATB		CHES FG5	Jacob Regnart
			SAA	Surgens Jesus	AFC 3	Claudio Monteverdi
					OXNCAB	Peter Phillips
				These Things Did Thomas Count as Real		Richard Webster
			va	Who Is This?		John Ferguson
				Add'l Music, Cantatas, Major Works *See also Yrs A & B*		
				Stay with Us, Lord	CHAN	Michael Praetorius
				Jesus Christ, My Sure Defense—Alleluia	CHAN	F Mendelssohn
			SATB/TTBB	Ye Sons and Daughters of the King	CON	Volckmar Leisring
			satb	149: Man singet mit Freuden vom Sieg		J S Bach

Year C | Second Sunday of Easter

	Entrance	Sequence	Offertory	Communion	Postcommunion		H82	WLP	LEVAS II	VF	MHSO	CG descant	Inst descant
		■				O praise ye the Lord! Praise him in the height [P 150]	432						
						Acts 5:27-32							
	■					Christ the Lord is risen again!	184						
	■					Good Christians all, rejoice and sing!	205						■
	■					Jesus is Lord of all the earth	178						■
	■					Jesus lives! thy terrors now	194,195						
				■		Sing, ye faithful, sing with gladness	492					■	
				■		This joyful Eastertide	192						
						Revelation 1:4-8							
	■					At the Name of Jesus	435			135			■
	■					Crown him with many crowns	494						
				■		Draw nigh and take the Body of the Lord	327,328						
	■					He is King of kings, he is Lord of lords			96				
	■					Jesus came, adored by angels	454						
				■		Let all mortal flesh keep silence	324						
	■					Lo! he comes with clouds descending	57,58					■	
			■			Lord, enthroned in heavenly splendor	307						
			■			Rejoice, the Lord is King!	481						
						John 20:19-31							
	■					Awake, arise, lift up your voice	212					■	
			■			By all your saints still striving [2: Dec. 21]	231,232						
			■			How oft, O Lord, thy face hath shone	242						
						In the bulb there is a flower					86		
	■					O sons and daughters, let us sing	206						
						We stand within the circle				77			
				■		We walk by faith and not by sight	209		206			■	

● Same tune, but not text   [S] Seasonal   [C] Collect   [P] Psalm   [GR] Gospel-related   [SC] Semi-continuous

91

Third Sunday of Easter | Year C

Anthem	Solo	Handbells	Voicing	Title	Collection	Composer
				Collect		
■			vla	Who Is This?		John Ferguson
				Acts 9:1-6, (7-20)		
				Excerpts: St. Paul Oratorio - see below		
■				Here's One *(Oxford Book of Spirituals)*		William Grant Still
	narr			Saul		Egil Hovland
				Psalm 30 *See Proper 5C*		
				Revelations 5:11-14		
■				A Song to the Lamb		David Ashley White
■				Alleluia, I Heard a Voice	TUD	Thomas Weelkes
■				Canticle of Praise		Charles Callahan
■				Das Lamm das erwürget ist, *Cantata 21*		J S Bach
■				Factum est silentium	CHES FG 6	Philippe de Monte
■				Glory and Worship, *All Night Vigil*		Sergei Rachmaninoff
■				Holy Lord God Almighty		Robert Parsons
■				Lo, A Voice to Heaven Sounding	CON	Bortniansky/Tchaikovsky
■				Lo, Round the Throne, a Glorious Band		Henry Ley
■				O Quam Gloriosum	FLEM	Jacob Vaet
■				Salvation unto Us Has Come	CHAN	Hugo Distler
■				These Are They Which Follow the Lamb	AFC 1	John Goss
■				Triumph! Thanksgiving	CON	S Rachmaninoff
■				Way Over in Beulah Lan'		Hall Johnson; Stacey Gibbs
■				Worthy Is the Lamb, Blessing..., Amen, *Messiah*		G F Handel
■				Worthy Is the Lord		Wm Murphy Jr & S Davis
■				Worthy the Lamb		Shaw/Parker
				John 21:1-19 *See also Easter 4, Gospel*		
■				Be Known to Us		Carl Schalk
■				Follow Me		Don Harper & Ben Tankard
■				Hymn to St. Peter		Benjamin Britten
■			SSA or SSAA	If Ye Love Me		Harvey B Gaul
■			SSA			Dan Pinkham; Healey Willan
■						Thomas Tallis; Philip Wilby
■			SSATBB	Huc me sydereo	ANTH	Josquin Desprez
■				Listen to the Lambs		R. Nathaniel Dett
■				Pasce agnos meos	OXNOV	Michael Berkeley
■				Thy Perfect Love	OXNEA	John Rutter
■				True Anointed One		David Ashley White
■			SAB	Tu es pastor		C Monteverdi
■				Tu es Petrus		M Duruflé; Palestrina; Widor
■						Gabriel Fauré
■					CHES	H L Hassler
■			SAB			Cristobal Morales
	sa			He Shall Feed His Flock, *Messiah*		G F Handel
■				Jesus, Redeemer		Anton Bruckner
				Add'l Music, Cantatas, Major Works		
■			satb	93: Wer nur den lieben Gott lässt walten		J S Bach
■			satb	*St. Paul*		F Mendelssohn
■				Lord, Thou Alone Art God		
■			SSAA/tb	The Conversion		
■				I Praise Thee, O Lord		
■				O Great Is the Depth		
	t			And Saul Made Havock of the Church		
	b			Consume Them All		
	a			But the Lord is Mindful of His Own		
	t			And His Companions		
	b			O God, Have Mercy		
	t			And There Was a Disciple		
	s			And Ananias Went His Way		

Year C | Third Sunday of Easter

	H82	WLP	LEVAS II	VF	MHSO	CG descant	Inst descant
Christ has arisen [S]			41		100		
Christ is alive! Let Christians sing [S]	182						
Come, let us with our Lord arise [S]	49						
Day of delight and beauty unbounded [S]		738					
Good Christians all, rejoice and sing! (1,3-5) [S]	205						
Sing hallelujah to the Lord [S]				115			
Acts 9:1-6 (,7-20)							
A Light from heaven shone around	256						
By all your saints still striving [2: Jan. 25]	231,232						
We sing the glorious conquest	255						
Revelation 5:11-14							
Alleluia! sing to Jesus! (1,3-5)	460,461						
Come, let us join our cheerful songs	374						
Hail, thou once despised Jesus!	495						
Lord, enthroned in heavenly splendor	307						
Splendor and honor, majesty and power		892					
This is the feast of victory for our God	417,418						
Ye servants of God, your Master proclaim	535						
John 21:1-19							
Be a shepherd for my flock				100			
By all your saints still striving [2: Jan. 18]	231,232						
Come, risen Lord, and deign to be our guest	305,306						
Gentle Jesus, risen Lord					51		
If you love me, truly love me					83		
Shepherd of souls, refresh and bless	343						
Sing, ye faithful, sing with gladness	492						

Same tune, but not text [S] Seasonal [C] Collect [P] Psalm [GR] Gospel-related [SC] Semi-continuous

Fourth Sunday of Easter | Year C

Anthem/Solo/Handbells/Voicing	Title	Collection	Composer
	Collect		
	You Satisfy the Hungry Heart		Robert E Kreutz
	Acts 9:36-43		
	Agnus Dei, *Requiem*		John Rutter
	I Am the Resurrection		Jan Bender; John Carter
			Gallus Dressler; T Morley
	I Am the Resurrection and the Life	CHAN	Gallus Dressler
SATB/SATB			Heinrich Schütz
SA			Healey Willan
			David H. Williams
	Psalm 23 *See Easter 4A, Proper 11B*		
	Adonai ro-i lo ehsar, *Chichester Psalms*		Leonard Bernstein
	Listen to the Lambs		R. Nathaniel Dett
	Follow Me		Don Harper & Ben Tankard
	O Lord, I Trust Your Shepherd Care	CHAN	Heinrich Schütz
	Psalm 23	AUG	Heinz Werner Zimmermann
			Bobby McFerrin
	The King of Love		Malcolm Williamson
U	The Lord Is My Shepherd		Malcolm Archer
			Thomas Matthews
	Revelation 7:9-17 *See also All Saints' A*		
	Alleluia, I Heard a Voice	TUD	Thomas Weelkes
	Beautiful Savior		arr F Melius Christiansen
	Canticle of Praise		Charles Callahan
	Christ the Lord Is Risen! Alleluia!		Johan Helmich Roman
	Holy Lord God Almighty		Robert Parsons
	Jesus Christ the Apple Tree	100 CFC	Elizabeth Poston
	Lo, A Voice to Heaven Sounding	CON	Bortniansky/Tchaikovsky
	Lo, Round the Throne, A Glorious Band		Henry Ley
	O Quam Gloriosum		Multiple
	Salvation unto Us Has Come	CHAN	Hugo Distler
	The Secret of Christ	OXNCAB	Richard Shephard
	The Song of the Tree of Life		Ralph Vaughan Williams
	Triumph! Thanksgiving	CON	S Rachmaninoff
	Wade in the Water		Spiritual, Multiple
	Worthy Is the Lamb, Blessing..., Amen, *Messiah*		G F Handel
	Worthy the Lamb		Shaw/Parker
	Wondrous Love		arr Alice Parker
	John 10:22-30 *See "resurrection" anthems in Acts reading above*		
	Agnus Dei, *Requiem*		John Rutter
	All We Like Sheep, *Messiah*		G F Handel
2 pt	I Am the Good Shepherd		Jan Bender
			Austin Lovelace; A Parker
	Lauda Sion		Multiple
	Little Lamb		David Cherwien
U	Little Lamb, Who Made Thee?		William Bradley Roberts
	Savior, Like a Shepherd Lead Us William		Bradley Roberts
	Surrexit a mortuis		Charles-Marie Widor
	Surrexit pastor bonus		Multiple
2 pt	The Good Shepherd Anna		Laura Page
	The Lamb		John Tavener
	You Satisfy the Hungry Heart		Robert E Kreutz
vla	Who Is This?		John Ferguson
	Addit. Music, Cantatas, Major Works		
satb	85: Ich bin ein gutter Hirt		J S Bach
satb	112: Der Herr ist mein getreuer Hirt		J S Bach
atb	175: Er rufet seinen Schafen mit Namen		J S Bach
sat	184: Erwünschtes Freudenlicht		J S Bach

Year C | Fourth Sunday of Easter

	H82	WLP	LEVAS II	VF	MHSO	CG descant	Inst descant
Christ the Lord is risen again [S]	184						
Good Christians all, rejoice and sing! (1,3-5) [S]	205						
My shepherd will supply my need [P]	664						
Sing, ye faithful, sing with gladness [S]	492						
The King of love my shepherd is [P]	645,646						
The Lord is my Shepherd [P]			104				
The Lord my God my Shepherd is [P]	663						
The Lord, the Lord, the Lord is my shepherd [P]					102		
The strife is o'er, the battle done [S]	208						
You are my shepherd [P]					104		
You hear the lambs a-cryin' [S]			110				
Acts 9:36-43							
Eternal light, shine in my heart	465,466						
Give thanks for life		775				o	
No saint on earth lives life to self alone		776					
Revelation 7:9-17							
All glory be to God on high	421						
Awake and sing the song	181						
By all your saints still striving [2: Nov. 1]	231,232						
Glorious things of thee are spoken	522,523						
Hark! the sound of holy voices	275						
Hearken to the anthem glorious	240,241						
Holy God, we praise thy name	366						
Jerusalem, my happy home	620						
Jerusalem the golden	624						
My faith looks up to thee	691		88				
O God, we praise thee and confess	364						
Sing alleluia forth in endless praise	619	777					
What wondrous love is this	439						
Who are these like stars appearing	286						
Ye holy angels bright	625						
Ye servants of God, your Master proclaim	535						
John 10:22-30							
Jesus, our mighty Lord	478						
Praise the Lord, rise up rejoicing	334						
Savior, like a shepherd lead us	708						
Shepherd of souls, refresh and bless	343						

o Same tune, but not text [S] Seasonal [C] Collect [P] Psalm [GR] Gospel-related [SC] Semi-continuous

Fifth Sunday of Easter | Year C

Anthem/Solo/Handbells/Voicing	Title	Collection	Composer
	Acts 11:1-18		
	Every Eye Waiteth upon Thee		H Schütz
	Oculi Omnium		Charles Wood
	Prope est Dominus	CHES CHR	Jacob Regnart
	The Eyes of All Wait upon Thee, *See Pentecost C*		Multiple
	Psalm 148		
t, perc	Canticle		William Bradley Roberts
	Canticle of Praise		John Ness Beck
	Hallelujah Is the Highest Praise		Anthony Patton
	Laudate		Knut Nystedt; Kirk Mechem
	Laudate Dominum		Multiple
	Let the Praise Begin		Fred Hammond
	Lobet den Herren		J S Bach; Gallus Dressler
	O Praise the Lord of Heaven	ANTH	John Blow
U			Malcolm Williamson
	O Praise the Lord of Heaven, *Psalmfest*		John Rutter
SATB/SATB			Ralph Vaughan Williams
	O Praise Ye the Lord		Charles Callahan; G Near
SSATBB	Praise Our Lord, All Ye Gentiles		William Byrd
U/4 pt	Praise the Lord		Richard Stark
	Praise Ye the Lord	OXNEA	Alan Bullard
		NNOV	Michael Hurd
	Psalm 148		Gustav Holst; Ned Rorem
	Total Praise		Richard Smallwood
	Revelations 21:1-6 *See also Proper 7, Psalm 42*		
	And I Saw a New Heaven	OXNEA	Malcolm Archer
			Edgar Bainton; Leo Nestor
	Behold I Make All Things New		Robert J Powell
	Blessed Are the Dead, Herr, SWV 281		Heinrich Schütz
	Blessed City, Heavenly Salem		Edward Bairstow
	Faire Is the Heaven	AFC 4	William H Harris
	I Heard a Voice from Heaven	OXCAB	John Goss
	I Saw a New Heaven and a New Earth		Carl Schalk
	I Was Glad and Laetatus sum (Ps 122) *See Advent 1A*		Multiple
	Let All Mortal Flesh Keep Silence		Edward Bairstow; G Holst
	Lo, God Is Here	AFC 1	Francis Jackson
	Locus iste		Anton Bruckner
	My Soul, There Is a Country	OXCAB	Charles H H Parry
	O God, Thou Are My God	ANTH	Henry Purcell
	Rockin' Jerusalem		John W. Work
	Surge illuminare		Multiple
	The Eyes of All Wait upon Thee, *See Pentecost C*		Multiple
	Ye Choirs of New Jerusalem	AFC	Charles V Stanford
	City Called Heaven	SOS	Spiritual, arr Boatner
	John 13:31-35		
	A New Commandment	OXASH	Richard Shephard
			Thomas Tallis
SSATBB	Huc me sydereo	ANTH	Josquin Desprez
	I Give You a New Commandment	OXNEA	Peter Aston
SSA or SSAA	If Ye Love Me, *See Easter 6B*		Multiple
	In the Heart Where Love Is Abiding	OXASH	arr John Barnard
	Thy Perfect Love	OXNEA	John Rutter
	Ubi Caritas, *see Maundy Thursday C*		Multiple
U tr	We Have a King Who Came to Earth	SOP TR	Ian Ord-Hum
	Who Shall Separate Us		Richard Webster
	Behold the Son of God	LIFT	W A Mozart
	Add'l Music, Cantatas, Major Works		
stb	95: Christus, der ist mein Leben		J S Bach

Year C | Fifth Sunday of Easter

	Entrance	Sequence	Offertory	Communion	Postcommunion		H82	WLP	LEVAS II	VF	MHSO	CG descant	Instr descant
						Christ is alive! Let Christians sing [S]	182						
						Come away to the skies [S]	213						
						Come, my Way, my Truth, my Life [C]	487						
						Good Christians all, rejoice and sing! (1,3-5) [S]	205						
						He is the Way [C]	463,464						
						Here, O Lord, your servants gather [C]		793					
						Sing, ye faithful, sing with gladness [S]	492						
						Thou art the Way, to thee alone [C]	457						
						Acts 11:1-18							
						Descend, O Spirit, purging flame	297						
						In Christ there is no East or West	529		62				
						Pan de Vida					93		
						We know that Christ is raised and dies no more	296					o	
						When Christ was lifted from the earth	603,604						
						Revelation 21:1-6							
						Behold, behold, I make all things new					47		
						Blessed city, heavenly Salem	519,520						
						Camina, pueblo de Dios/Walk on, O people of God		739					
						Christ the Victorious, give to your servants	358						
						Draw nigh and take the Body of the Lord	327,328						
						Jerusalem the golden	624						
						Let all mortal flesh keep silence	324						
						Light's abode, celestial Salem	621,622						
						O holy city, seen of John	582,583						
						O what their joy and their glory must be	623						
						Of the Father's love begotten (1,3-4)	82						
						Oh! what a beautiful city			10				
						Soon and very soon			14				
						John 13:31-35							
						A new commandment that I give to you					92		
						God is love, and where true love is	576,577						
						I come with joy to meet my Lord	304						
						Thou, who at thy first Eucharist didst pray	315						
						Ubi caritas et amor		831					
						Where charity and love prevail	581						
						Where true charity and love dwell	606						

[o] Same tune, but not text   [S] Seasonal   [C] Collect   [P] Psalm   [GR] Gospel-related   [SC] Semi-continuous

Sixth Sunday of Easter | Year C

Anthem/Solo/Handbells/Voicing	Title	Collection	Composer
	Acts 16:9-15		
	A Voice from Macedonia Cries		Christopher Tye, ed. Schalk
U	Lydia's Song, *Five Children's Anthems*		Daniel Burton
	The Best of Rooms		Randall Thompson
	Psalm 67		
	Deus, misereatur nostri		H Schütz
2 pt tr	God be Merciful		Paul Bouman
			A Hovhaness; H Schütz; Tye
SSA			Healey Willan
U, 2 pt	God Be Merciful unto Us		Regina Holman Fryxell
U, 2 vln	Let the People Praise Thee O God		Andreas Hammerschmidt
			Martin Shaw
	Let All the Peoples Praise Thee O God		William Mathias
	Let the Peoples Praise You, O God		Bruce Neswick
	Let All the People Sing Praise		Lena McLin
	O God Be Merciful	16th	Christopher Tye
	O Let the Nations Be Glad		Randall Thompson
	Psalm 67		Jane Marshall; David A White
	Thou, O God, Art Praised in Sion		Malcolm Boyle
	Revelation 21:10, 22—22:5 *See Easter 5C, Revelations*		
	A Song to the Lamb		Donald Pearson
	Behold I Make All Things New		Robert J Powell
	Dona Nobis Pacem, *Mass in B Minor*	BFAS	J S Bach
	Jesus Christ the Apple Tree	100 CFC	Elizabeth Poston
	My Soul, There Is A Country	OXCAB	Charles H H Parry
	O Blessed Spring		Robert Buckley Farlee
	O God, Thou Art My God (*Westminster Abby*)	ANTH	Henry Purcell
	O Paschal Lamp of Radiant Light	AUG	Sam Batt Owens
	Shall We Gather at the River		Spiritual, Multiple
	The Secret of Christ	OXNCAB	Richard Shephard
	The Song of the Tree of Life		Ralph Vaughan Williams
	Visions of St John		John Ness Beck
	Glorious Jerusalem, *Hora Novissima*	LIFT	Horatio Parker
	Pilgrim on Earth	LIFT	Hugo Wolf
	John 14:23-29 *See also Easter 6A & 6B Gospels*		
	Dona Nobis Pacem, *Mass in B Minor*	BFAS	J S Bach
	Going Up Yonder		Walter Hawkins
	In the Heart Where Love is Abiding	OXASH	arr John Barnard
SSATBB	Huc me sydereo	ANTH	Josquin Desprez
	Lord Thou Knowest		Andreas Hammerschmidt
	See What Love, *St. Paul*		F Mendelssohn
	The Peace of God	OXNEA	John Rutter
	Thy Perfect Love	OXNEA	John Rutter
	Peace Be unto You	LIFT	Franz Schubert
	John 5:1-9, alt		
	O For a Closer Walk with God	AFC 1	Charles V Stanford
	O Saviour of the World	OXCAB	John Goss; Palestrina
	Teach me Thy Way, O Lord		John Blow
	There's a Wideness in God's Mercy		Calvin Hampton
	Tu solus qui facis mirabilia	CHES FL	Josquin des Prés
	I Know De Lord's Laid His Hands on Me		arr Harry T Burleigh
	I Know the Lord Laid His Hands on Me	SOS	arr Boatner
	Add'l Music, Cantatas, Major Works		
U	We Have A King Who Came to Earth	SOP TR	Ian Ord-Hum
	Pilgrim on Earth	LIFT	Hugo Wolf
sb	59: Wer mich liebet, der wird...(Neumeister)		J S Bach
satb	74: Wer mich liebet, der wird...(Ziegler)		J S Bach
satb	172: Erschallet, ihr Lieder		J S Bach

Year C | Sixth Sunday of Easter

	Entrance	Sequence	Offertory	Communion	Postcommunion	Hymn	H82	WLP	LEVAS II	VF	MHSO	CG descant	Inst descant
						Alleluia, alleluia! Hearts and voices heavenward raise [S]	191						
						As those of old their first fruits brought [Rogation]	705						
						God of mercy, God of grace [P]	538						
						Now the green blade riseth [S]	204						
						O Jesus, crowned with all renown [Rogation]	292						
						Sing, ye faithful, sing with gladness [S]	492						
						Acts 16:9-15							
						Christ for the world we sing!	537						
						How wondrous and great thy works, God of praise!	532,533						
						Spread, O spread thou mighty word	530						
						Ye servants of God, your Master proclaim	535						
						Revelation 21:10,22-22:5							
						All you who love Jerusalem				157			
						Christ is made the sure foundation	518						
						Come, let us join our cheerful songs	374						
						Come, ye disconsolate			147				
						I want to walk as a child of the light	490						
						O blessed spring, where Word and sign		765					
						Shall we gather at the river			141				
						Sing the wondrous love of Jesus			20				
						The tree of life my soul hath seen		749			149		
						This is the feast of victory for our God	417,418						
						John 14:23-29							
						Come, Holy Spirit, heavenly Dove	510						
						Come, thou Holy Spirit bright	226,227						
						Creator Spirit, by whose aid	500						
						Holy Spirit, font of light	228						
						Like the murmur of the dove's song	513						
						O Spirit of Life, O Spirit of God	505						
						Peace before us, peace behind us		791			152		
						Savior, again to thy dear Name we raise	345						
						There's a sweet, sweet Spirit in this place			120				
						To thee, O Comforter divine	514						
						Word of God, come down on earth	633						

Same tune, but not text   [S] Seasonal   [C] Collect   [P] Psalm   [GR] Gospel-related   [SC] Semi-continuous

Ascension Day | Year C

Anthem/Solo/Handbells	Voicing	Title	Collection	Composer
		Collect		
	SSATB	I Will Not Leave You Comfortless		William Byrd
	2 pt			Ron Nelson
				Everett Titcomb
		Acts 1:1-11		
		Can I Ride		Jewel T. Thompson
		King of All Ages, Throned on High	OXNEA	Paul Isom
	SSATB	Men of Galilee		J P Sweelinck
		See God to Heaven Ascending	CHAN	Friedrich Samuel Riegel
		The Parting Word the Savior Spoke		Christopher Tye, ed. Schalk
		Viri Galilaei		William Byrd
			CHES FR	Couillart
		Psalm 47 *See Ascension A, B*		
		Ascendit Deus		Multiple
		Clap Hands All People, *Bay Psalm Book*		Jean Berger
	U	Clap Your Hands, All Ye Children		Judy Hunnicutt
	SSAATB	God Is Gone Up with a Merry Noise		William Croft
				Herbert Howells
		Laudate Dominum in sanctis ejus		Multiple
		O Clap Your Hands, *Psalmfest*		John Rutter
	SSATB	Omnes Gentes Plaudite	CHES E5	Christopher Tye
	SSATB	Psallite Deo	CHES E5	Christopher Tye
		Psalm 93, alt		
		Dominus regnat		Knut Nystedt
		God Omnipotent Reigneth		Pierre Dacques
		Psalm 93		Heinrich Schütz
		The Lord Is King		Leo Sowerby
	2 pt	The Lord Shall Reign		David Hurd
		Ephesians 1:15-23		
		At the Name of Jesus		Ralph Vaughan Williams
		Beautiful Savior		F Melius Christiansen
	SAB	Spring Carol (Fairest Lord Jesus)		Russell Schulz-Widmar
	a	Thou Art Gone Up on High, *Messiah*		G F Handel
		Luke 24:44-53		
	SAB	Christ Sends the Spirit	AUG	Richard Proulx
		Et Resurrexit, *Mass in B Minor*		J S Bach
		Glory and Worship, *Coronation Anthem No. III*		G F Handel
		King of All Ages, Throned on High	OXNEA	Paul Isom
		Lift Up Your Heads	16th	John Amner
	two SATB, 3 tr			Jean Berger
				J Blow; J Carter; Wm Croft
	SSAATB			Orlando Gibbons
	SSATBB			Andreas Hammerschmidt
	SSAA	Introit for Ascension	AFC 3	arr Philip Ledger
	SSATB	Lift Up Your Heads, *Messiah*		G F Handel
	SSA or SATB			Wm Mathias; H Schütz
				Healey Willan
		O God the King of Glory	AFC 1	Henry Purcell
		O Rex Gloriae	CHES IT	Luca Marenzio
		See God to Heaven Ascending	CHAN	Friedrich Samuel Riegel
		The Ascension		Philip Moore
		Add'l Music, Cantatas, Major Works		
	satb	37: Wer da gläubet und getauft wird		J S Bach
	satb	43: Gott fähret auf mit Jauchzen		J S Bach
	atb	128: Auf Christi Himmelfahrt allein		J S Bach
	satb	Lobet Gott in seinen, *Ascens. Oratorio* BWV 11		J S Bach

Year C | Ascension Day

	Entrance	Sequence	Offertory	Communion	Postcommunion		H82	WLP	LEVAS II	VF	MHSO	CG descant	Inst. descant
					■	And have the bright immensities [S]	459						
		■				Clap your hands, all you people [P]					113		
				■		"Go preach my gospel," saith the Lord [S]			161				
	■					Hail thee, festival day! [S]	216					■	
						Acts 1:1-11							
	■					A hymn of glory let us sing	217,218						
			■			Alleluia, sing to Jesus	460,461					■	
			■			Hail the day that sees him rise	214						
			■			See the Conqueror mounts in triumph	215						
			■			The Lord ascendeth up on high	219						
						Ephesians 1:15-23							
	■					Crown him with many crowns	494					■	
				■		Emmanuel! The angels' ancient chorus				46			
				■		Hail, thou once despised Jesus!	495					■	
				■		He is King of kings, he is Lord of lords			96				
				■		It was poor little Jesus, yes, yes	468						
			■			Lord, enthroned in heavenly splendor	307						
	■					O Lord Most High, eternal King	220,221						
				■		Rejoice, the Lord is King!	481						
	■					Rejoice, the Lord of life ascends	222						
				■		We see the Lord					114		
						Luke 24:44-53							
	■					A hymn of glory let us sing	217,218						
	■		■			Alleluia, sing to Jesus	460,461					■	
			■			Hail the day that sees him rise	214						
			■			See the Conqueror mounts in triumph	215						
			■			The Lord ascendeth up on high	219						

■ Same tune, but not text   [S] Seasonal   [C] Collect   [P] Psalm   [GR] Gospel-related   [SC] Semi-continuous

Seventh Sunday of Easter | Year C

	Solo	Handbells	Voicing	Title	Collection	Composer
				Collect		
■				O God the King of Glory		Orlando Gibbons
						Henry Purcell
				Acts 16:16-34		
				All Who Believe and Are Baptized	BFAS	J S Bach
				Salvation unto Us Has Come	BFAS	J S Bach
				Psalm 97		
				A Harvest of Light Is Sown		Daniel Pinkham
				This Lord Is King		Heinrich Schütz
			str, ob, 2 hrn	Viderunt omnes		J M Haydn
■				Clouds and Darkness, *Biblical Songs*		Antonin Dvořák
				Revelation 22:12-14, 16-17, 20-21		
				And I John Saw the Holy City		Thomas Matthews
				Behold I Make All Things New		Robert J Powell
				Christ Is the World's True Light	OXEA	W K Stanton
				Christ Whose Glory Fills the Skies		T Frederick Candlyn
				E'en So, Lord Jesus, Quickly Come		Paul Manz
				I Am the Light		Ralph Johnson
				I Saw a New Heaven and a New Earth		Carl Schalk
				King of All Ages, Throned on High	OXNEA	Paul Isom
				O Come Everyone That Thirsteth, *Elijah*		F Mendelssohn
				The Lord in His Goodness, *St. Paul*		F Mendelssohn
■	s			Ja, komm, Herr Jesu! *Cantata 106*		J S Bach
				John 17:20-26 *See also Easter 6A & 6B Gospels*		
				Christ the Lord Is Risen Again	AFC 4	John Rutter
			SSA		AFC 3	John Rutter
				Church Cantata		Lena McLin
				I Have Known You		Thomas Keesecker
				Look, Oh Look, the Sight Is Glorious		S Drummond Wolff
				Lord Enthroned in Heavenly Splendor		S Drummond Wolff
				Rejoice the Lord Is King	NNOV	Bryan Kelly
				See What Love, *St. Paul*		F Mendelssohn
				Add'l Music, Cantatas, Major Works		
■				Awake, Arise, Lift Up Your Voice		Richard Webster
				O Word, that Goest Forth on High		David Ashley White
			atb	125: Mit Fried und Freud ich fahr dahin		J S Bach

102

Year C | Seventh Sunday of Easter

						H82	WLP	LEVAS II	VF	MHSO	CG descant	Inst. descant
					All hail the power of Jesus name [S]	450,451					●	●
					Alleluia, sing to Jesus [S]	460,461					●	
				●	Hail, thou once despised Jesus! [S]	495					●	
	●				Lord, enthroned in heavenly splendor [S]	307						
			●		Rejoice, the Lord is King! [S]	481						
					The head that once was crowned with thorns [S]	483						
					Acts 16:16-34							
	●				All who believe and are baptized	298						
			●		If you believe and I believe		806					
					Revelation 22:12-14,16-17,20-21							
					Better be ready			4				
			●		Christ is the world's true Light	542						●
●					Christ, whose glory fills the skies	6,7						
			●		Draw nigh and take the Body of the Lord	327,328						
●					How bright appears the Morning Star	496,497						
					I heard the voice of Jesus say	692						
					Lord, my soul is thirsting			166		148		
					O love that casts out fear	700						
					Oh! What a beautiful city			10				
					Thy kingdom come, O God!	613						
					John 17:20-26							
	●				Come now, O Prince of peace		795			82		
					Come, risen Lord, and deign to be our guest	305,306						
					For the bread which you have broken	340,341						
					Thou, who at thy first Eucharist didst pray	315						
					Unidos, unidos / Together, together		796					
				●	We all are one in mission		778				●	

◯ Same tune, but not text [S] Seasonal [C] Collect [P] Psalm [GR] Gospel-related [SC] Semi-continuous

Day of Pentecost: Early/Vigil Service | Year C

Anthem	Solo	Handbells	Voicing	Title	Collection	Composer
				Genesis 11:1-9		
				Psalm 33:12-22		
				Exultate justi		Multiple
				O How Amiable		Ralph Vaughan Williams
				Our Soul Waits for the Lord		Jane Marshall
				We Wait for Thy Loving-kindness		William McKee
				Exodus 19:1-9A; 16-20A; 20:18-20, alt		
				Ev'ry Time I Feel the Spirit		arr William Dawson
				On Eagle's Wings		Michael Joncas
				Tuba mirum		Multiple
				Canticle 2 or 13		
				Benedicamus Domino		Multiple
				Te Deum		Multiple
				Ezekiel 37:1-14, alt		
				Dry Bones		Spiritual, Multiple
				Psalm 130 see Proper 5B		
				De profundis		Multiple
				Out of the Depths		Multiple
			satb	Cantata 38: Aus tiefer Not schrei ich zu dir		J S Bach
			satb	Cantata 131: Aus der Tiefen rufe ich, Herr, zu dir		J S Bach
				Joel 2:28-32, alt		
				Lo! He Comes, with Clouds Descending		David H Williams
			SATTB	My Lord, What a Morning		William Dawson
				Canticle 9		
				Surely It Is God Who Saves Me		Jack Noble White
				Acts 2:1-11		
			SAB	Christ Sends the Spirit	AUG	Richard Proulx
			SAATTB	Dum complerentur dies pentecostes		Palestrina
			SSATB	Dum complerentur dies pentecostes		Tomas Luis Victoria
				Hail, Glorious Spirits, Heirs of Light		Christopher Tye
				Holy Spirit		Richard Smallwood
			SSATBB, va	Hymn to the Spirit		John Ferguson
				In Divers Tongues		Palestrina
				Let Every Tongue		Carl MaultsBy
				O Day Full of Grace		F Melius Christiansen
			U	Pentecost Fire		Jayne Southwick Cool
			SSATB	Replenti sunt omnes	CHES IS5	Juan Esquivel
			SATB/SATB			Jacob Handl
				The Presence of the Lord Is Here		Kurt Carr
				Romans 8:14-17, 22-27, alt		
				As Many As Are Led by the Spirit		David McK Williams
				If Any Man Hath Not the Spirit		H Walford Davies
				Like the Murmur of the Dove's Song		Peter Cutts
				The Spirit Also Helpeth Us		J S Bach
				Motet: Der Geist hilft unsrer ..., BWV 226		J S Bach
				Psalm 104:25-32		
			U	I Will Sing to the Lord As Long As I Live		Carl Schalk
				O Taste and See		Ralph Vaughan Williams
				Panis angelicus		P Villette, T Pavlechko
		t		Panis angelicus		César Franck
				John 7:37-39a		
				As Panting Deer Desire the Waterbrooks		David Ashley White
				Sicut cervus		Multiple
				Add'l Music, Cantatas, Major Works		
				Credo		Multiple
			b	Et in Spiritum Sanctum..., Mass in B Minor		J S Bach
				The Victory of Spirit	LIFT	Franz Schubert
			satb	165: O heilges Geist- und Wasserbad		J S Bach

Year C | Day of Pentecost: Early/Vigil Service

	H82	WLP	LEVAS II	VF	MHSO	CG descant	Inst descant
A Vigil has no entrance hymn (see BCP, pp. 175 and 227); the entrance hymns suggested below are for an Early Service.							
See Day of Pentecost: Early/Vigil Service Year A or B for seasonal selections							
Genesis 11:1-9							
All my hope on God is founded	665						
Creator of the earth and skies	148						
Father eternal, Ruler of creation	573						
Exodus 19:1-9a; 16-20a; 20:18-20							
Every time I feel the Spirit		751	114				
God the Omnipotent! King, who ordainest	569						
Holy Ghost, dispel our sadness	515						
O worship the King, all glorious above	388						
Ezekiel 37:1-14							
Breath of God, life-bearing wind				59		o	
Breathe on me, Breath of God	508						
Go forth for God; go to the world in peace	347						
Let it breathe on me			116				
Put forth, O God, thy Spirit's might	521						
Spirit of the living God			115				
Joel 2:28-32							
O day of God, draw nigh	600,601						
Praise the Spirit in creation	506,507						
"Thy kingdom come!" on bended knee	615						
Acts 2:1-11							
A mighty sound from heaven	230						
Filled with the Spirit's power, with one accord		741					
Hail thee, festival day!	225						
Hail this joyful day's return	223,224						
Spirit divine, attend our prayers	509						
Romans 8:14-17,22-27							
Come, Holy Spirit, heavenly Dove	510						
Eternal Spirit of the living Christ	698						
Holy Spirit, ever living	511					o	
Like the murmur of the dove's song	513						
O Spirit of Life, O Spirit of God	505						
Spirit of God, unseen as the wind				53			
John 7:37-39a							
Draw nigh and take the Body of the Lord	327,328						
I heard the voice of Jesus say	692						
O love that casts out fear	700						

o Same tune, but not text [S] Seasonal [C] Collect [P] Psalm [GR] Gospel-related [SC] Semi-continuous

Day of Pentecost: Principal Service | Year C

Anthem/Solo/Handbells/Voicing	Title	Collection	Composer
	Acts 2:1-21		
	Come Holy Ghost the Maker		Cedric Thorpe Davis
	Every Time I Feel the Spirit		arr. William Dawson
	Holy Spirit		Richard Smallwood
SSATBB, vla	Hymn to the Spirit		John Ferguson
	Let Every Tongue		Carl MaultsBy
	O Spirit of the Living God		Austin Lovelace
	Rushing Wind, Dancing Flame		Matthew H Corl
	The Presence of the Lord Is Here		Kurt Carr
	When Fully Came the Day of Pentecost		Palestrina
	Genesis 11:1-9, alt		
	Psalm 104:25-35, 37		
	Every Eye Waiteth upon Thee		H Schütz
	Oculi Omnium		Charles Wood
	Panis angelicus		Franck, Pavlechko, Villette
	The Eyes of All Wait upon Thee		Jean Berger
			Orlando Gibbons
			William Harris
U			Richard Proulx
		SEW	Richard Shephard
			Robert Edward Smith
	Romans 8:14-17		
	The Spirit Also Helpeth Us		J S Bach
	Acts 2:1-21, alt *See First Reading*		
	John 14:8-17, (25-27)		
	All Who Believe and Are Baptized	BFAS	J S Bach
	Credo		Multiple
	God Is A Spirit	CON	Alexander Kopylov
	Greater Love Hath No Man		John Ireland
SSA or SSAA	If Ye Love Me *See Easter 6A*		Multiple
SSATB	I Will Not Leave You Comfortless *See Easter 6A*		William Byrd
	I Will Not Leave You Desolate, *Three Motets...*		Kevin Sadowski
	My Peace I Give		Antonio Lotti
SSATB or TTBB	Non Vos Relinquam Orphanos		William Byrd
	O rex glóriae	CHES	Luca Marenzio
	Peace I Leave with You		Knut Nystedt
			Walter Pelz
	Salvation unto Us Has Come	BFAS	J S Bach
	Shout for Joy!		John Carter
	Scio enim	CHES	Orlando Lassus
	Transcendent, Holy God	BFAS	J S Bach
	We All Believe in One True God	BFAS	J S Bach
	Wondrous Love		arr Paul J Christiansen
			Multiple
s	I Know That My Redeemer Liveth, *Messiah*		G F Handel
	Peace Be unto You		Franz Schubert
	Add'l Music, Cantatas, Major Works		*See also Pentecost A & B*
	Come Holy Ghost, God and Lord	CHAN	Hugo Distler
	Creator Spirit By Whose Aid		Gerhard Krapf
	Creator Spirit, Heav'nly Dove	CHAN	Hugo Distler
SSA	Introit for Whitsun	AFC 3	arr Philip Ledger
U	Litany to the Holy Spirit	AFC 2	Peter Hurford
	O Lord, Give Thy Holy Spirit	16th	Thomas Tallis
	O Spirit of God, Eternal Source	CHAN	Melchior Vulpius
SSA	Veni Creator	AFC 3	Hector Berlioz
			Leo Sowerby
satb	74: Wer mich liebet, der wird..., (Ziegler)		J S Bach

106

Year C | Day of Pentecost: Principal Service

Hymn	H82	WLP	LEVAS II	VF	MHSO	CG descant	Inst descant
Come down, O Love divine [S]	516					●	
Come, Holy Ghost, Creator blest [S]			112				
Come, Holy Ghost, our souls inspire [S]	503, 504						
Come, Holy Spirit, descend on us [S]					108		
Come, thou Holy Spirit bright [trad. Sequence]	226, 227						
Creator Spirit, by whose breath [S]	500						
From deepest woe I cry to thee [P 130]	151						
Holy Spirit, font of light [trad. Sequence]	228						
If you believe and I believe [S]		806					
I'm goin'-a sing when the Spirit says sing [S]			117				
Loving Spirit, loving Spirit [S]		742		51	111		
May your loving spirit [S]					112		
Now Holy Spirit, ever One [S]	20					○	
O day of radiant gladness [S]	48						
O fiery Spirit [S]				62			
O Holy Spirit by whose breath [S]	501, 502						
O Holy Spirit, flowing light [S]				54			
O Holy Spirit, root of life [S]				55			
O Spirit of the living God [S]	531						
Out of the depths I call [P 130]	666						
She sits like a bird, brooding on the waters [S]					110		
Soplo de Dios viviente/Breath of the living God [S]					107		
Spirit of God, you moved over the waters [S]				58			
Surely it is God who saves me [Canticle 9]	678, 679						
There's a sweet, sweet Spirit in this place [S]			120				
This day at thy creating word [S]	52						
Veni Sancte Spiritus [S]		832					
We the Lord's people, heart and voice uniting [S]	51					●	
Acts 2:1-21							
A mighty sound from heaven	230						
Filled with the Spirit's power, with one accord		741					
Hail thee, festival day!	225					●	
Hail this joyful day's return	223, 224						
Spirit divine, attend our prayers	509						
Genesis 11:1-9							
All my hope on God is founded	665						
Creator of the earth and skies	148						
Father eternal, Ruler of creation	573					●	
Romans 8:14-17							
Come, Holy Spirit, heavenly Dove	510						
Holy Spirit, ever living	511					○	
Like the murmur of the dove's song	513						
O Spirit of Life, O Spirit of God	505						
Sing praise to our Creator	295						
Spirit of God, unseen as the wind				53			
John 14:8-17(,25-27)							
Come, Gracious Spirit, heavenly Dove	512						
Holy Spirit, ever living	511					○	
Sople de Dios viviente / Breath of the living God					107		
Spirit of mercy, truth, and love	229						
To thee, O Comforter divine	514						
At Baptism:							
All who believe and are baptized	298						
Baptized in water	294	767	121				
Crashing waters at creation				67	95		●
Descend, O Spirit, purging flame	297						
Over the chaos of the empty waters	176, 177						
Spirit of God, unleashed on earth	299						

○ Same tune, but not text [S] Seasonal [C] Collect [P] Psalm [GR] Gospel-related [SC] Semi-continuous

Trinity Sunday | Year C

Voicing	Title	Collection	Composer
	Proverbs 8:1-4, 22-31		
	Achieved Is the Glorious Work, *The Creation*		F J Haydn
SAB	Great and Marvelous Are Thy Works		Richard Webster
SSSA	Song of the Sun	AFC 3	Carl Orff
	On Mighty Pens Uplifted Soars, *The Creation*		F J Haydn
	O How Pleasing, *The Seasons*		F J Haydn
	With Verdue Clad the Fields..., *The Creation*		F J Haydn
	Psalm 8		
	Die Himmel erzählen die Ehre Gottes		H Schütz
SSAA	Good-Nature to Animals	AFC 3	Phyllis Tate
U	How Majestic Is Thy Name		Emma Lou Diemer
			G F Handel
U	Lord, How Majestic Is Your Name		Austin Lovelace
	Lord, Our Creator, How Excellent		F Mendelssohn
	O How Excellent Thy Name	CON 2	G F Handel
U	O Lord God, How Excellent Is Thy Name		Don McAfee
SSA	O Lord, How Excellent Is Thy Name		Benedetto Marcello
	O Lord, Our God		Robert Powell
	O Lord, Our God, How Great Is Your Name	NNOV	Anthony Milner
	O Lord Our Governor		Gerre Hancock; Barry Rose
			Healey Willan
SSAB or SSTB			Henry Purcell
	O Lord Our Lord		Robert J Powell
2 pt	O Lord Our Master, How Glorious Is Thy Name		G P Telemann
	Psalm 8		Eugene Butler
U			Richard Hillert
			Heinrich Schütz; R Smallwood
	The Heavens Are Telling		Beethoven; F J Haydn
	Canticle 2 or 13, alt		
	Benedicamus Domino		Multiple
	Te Deum		Multiple
	The Heavens are Telling		Beethoven; F J Haydn
	Romans 5:1-5		
	God So Loved the World		Jan Bender; B Chilcott
			K K Davis; Hugo Distler
			Orlando Gibbons; John Goss
U or 2 pt			John Horman
SA			Joel Martinson
SSATBB			M Praetorius
			Heinrich Schütz; J Stainer
SAB, instr			G P Telemann
			David Ashley White
	Salvation unto Us Has Come	BFAS	J S Bach
	Wondrous Love	AUG	arr Paul J Christiansen
			Multiple
	John 16:12-15		
	All I Have Is Yours		Richard Smallwood
t	Grieve Not the Holy Spirit		T Tertius Noble
SSATB	I Will Not Leave You Comfortless		William Byrd
2 pt			Ron Nelson
			Everett Titcomb
	I Will Not Leave You Desolate, *Three Motets...*		Kevin Sadowski
	O Thou Sweetest Source		Charles Wood
t	Grieve Not the Holy Spirit		T Tertius Noble
	Add'l Music, Cantatas, Major Works		*See also Trinity A & B*
SSA	Anthem for the Trinity	AFC 3	Robert Sherlaw Johnson
	O Trinity, O Trinity		David Hurd
ssatb	*Mass in B Minor*		J S Bach

108

Year C | Trinity Sunday

	H82	WLP	LEVAS II	VF	MHSO	CG descant	Inst descant
All glory be to God on high [S]	421						
Ancient of Days, who sittest throned in glory [S]	363						
Come, thou almighty King [S]	365						
Glory to God [S]					117		
God, beyond all human praises [S]		745					
God the sculptor of the mountains [S]		746,747			130		
Holy Father, great Creator [S]	368						
Holy God we praise thy Name [S]	366						
Holy, holy, holy! Lord God Almighty! [S]	362						
How wondrous great, how glorious bright [S]	369						
I bind unto myself today [S]	370						
In the night, in the day [S]					116		
Laus Trinitati / O praise be to you Holy Trinity [S]				105			
Loving Creator, grant to your children [S]					115		
Mothering God, you gave me birth [S]				71,72	142		
O threefold God of tender unity [S]		743					
O Trinity of blessed light [S]	29,30	744					
Oh Lord, how perfect is your name [P]				57			
Sing praise to our Creator [S]	295						
Proverbs 8:1-4,22-31							
Come and seek the ways of Wisdom					60		
Even when young, I prayed for wisdom's grace		906					
God is Love, let heaven adore him	379						
I sing the almighty power of God	398					o	
Open your ears, O faithful people	536						
People of God, gather together					109	o	
Wisdom freed a holy people		905			155		
Romans 5:1-5							
Come down, O Love divine	516						
Come, thou fount of every blessing	686		111				
Creator Spirit, by whose aid	500						
Veni Sancte Spiritus		832					
John 16:12-15							
Come, gracious Spirit, heavenly Dove	512						
Come, Holy Ghost, Creator blest			112				
Thou, whose almighty word	371						

o Same tune, but not text [S] Seasonal [C] Collect [P] Psalm [GR] Gospel-related [SC] Semi-continuous

Proper 4 | Year C

PROPER 1 = SIXTH SUNDAY AFTER THE EPIPHANY
PROPER 2 = SEVENTH SUNDAY AFTER THE EPIPHANY
PROPER 3 = EIGHTH SUNDAY AFTER THE EPIPHANY

Anthem	Solo	Handbells	Voicing	Title	Collection	Composer
				1 Kings 18:20-21, (22-29) 30-39 SC Track		
			U tr or SATB	Elijah!		Dale Wood
			SATB/b	Lord God of Abraham		F Mendelssohn, arr Willhoite
				O Lord my God	OXNCAB	Samuel Wesley
				Psalm 96 SC Track Psalm 96:1-9 GR Track		
			SATB, div	All That Hath Life & Breath Praise Ye the Lord!		René Clausen
				Ascribe unto the Lord		Samuel Wesley
				Cantate Domino		Multiple
				Comfort, O Lord, the Soul		William Crotch
				Declare His Honor, *Chandos Anthem No. 4*		G F Handel
			SAAATB	Laetentur caeli	CHES FG6	Jacob Handl
			U, fl	Make a Joyful Noise		Maureen I. Sindlinger
				O Come Let Us Sing unto the Lord		Emma Lou Diemer
				O Sing unto the Lord (A New Song)		William Mathias
			satb, str			Henry Purcell
	s			O Sing unto the Lord, *Chandos Anthem No. 4*		G F Handel
				Oh, Sing to the Lord a New Song		John Leavitt
				Sing to the Lord, New Songs Be Raising	CHAN	J P Sweelinck
				Sing unto the Lord a New Song		H Schütz
				The Beauty of Holiness		K Leighton; Bob Buroughs
				Three Motets		Daniel Pinkham
				Thy Word Is a Lantern		John Bertalot
	s or t			Sing a New Song, *Biblical Songs*		A Dvořák
				I Kings 8:22-23, 41-43 GR Track		
			SATB/SSAA/AATB	Hear the [thy] Voice and Prayer		Thomas Tallis
				O Lord My God		Samuel Wesley, ed. Shaw
			SAB	O Lord My God		Samuel Wesley, ed. Knight
				The First Song of Isaiah		Jack Noble White
			brass	The Temple of the Living God		Theron Kirk
				Will God Indeed Dwell on the Earth		Leo Sowerby
			SSAATBB	Zadok the Priest, *Coronation Anthem I*		G F Handel
				Zion's Walls		Aaron Copland
				Galatians 1:1-12		
				Grace Be to You and Peace		Carl F Mueller
				Witness		Spiritual, Multiple
				Luke 7:1-10		
				Agnus Dei, *Requiem*		John Rutter
				I Am the Resurrection		Jan Bender; J Carter
						Gallus Dressler; T Morley
				I Am the Resurrection and the Life	CHAN	Gallus Dressler
			SATB/SATB			Heinrich Schütz
			SA			Healey Willan
						David H Williams
				O Jesus Christ, My Life, My Light	BFAS	J S Bach
				O Lord Increase My Faith		Henry Loosemore
				There Is a Balm in Gilead		arr William Dawson
				Wen es meines Gottes Wille, *Cantata 161*		J S Bach
				What God Ordains Is Good Indeed	BFAS	J S Bach
	ss duet			I Waited for the Lord		F Mendelssohn
	t			Rejoice, O My Spirit, *Cantata 21*		J S Bach
	s			Sighing, Weeping, Trouble, Need, *Cantata 21*		J S Bach
				Add'l Music, Cantatas, Major Works		
	a or b			O Rest in the Lord, *Elijah*		F Mendelssohn
	s			I Know That My Redeemer Liveth, *Messiah*		G F Handel
	sab			72: Alles nur nach Gottes Willen		J S Bach

Year C | Proper 4

PROPER 1 = SIXTH SUNDAY AFTER THE EPIPHANY
PROPER 2 = SEVENTH SUNDAY AFTER THE EPIPHANY
PROPER 3 = EIGHTH SUNDAY AFTER THE EPIPHANY

Hymn	H82	WLP	LEVAS II	VF	MHSO	CG descant	Inst descant
Cantad al Señor [P]		786					
Earth and all stars [P]	412						
Heaven and earth [P]					133		
Our God to whom we turn [C]	681						
1 Kings 18:20-21(,22-29),30-39 SC Track							
Before the Lord's eternal throne	391						
Praise to the living God!	372					o	
Sing praise to God who reigns above	408					o	
1 Kings 8:22-23,41-43 GR Track							
Awake, thou Spirit of the watchmen	540						
Holy Father, great Creator	368						
How wondrous and great thy works, God of praise!	532,533						
My God, thy table now is spread	321						
O God of every nation	607						
Spread, O spread, thou mighty word	530						
Surely it is God who saves me	678,679						
The Lord will come and not be slow	462						
Galatians 1:1-12							
Hope of the world, thou Christ of great compassion	472						
In your mercy, Lord, you called me	706						
O Spirit of the living God	531						
Ye servants of God, your Master proclaim	535						
Luke 7:1-10							
God, creator, source of healing					93	o	
God of mercy, God of grace	538						
Heal me, hands of Jesus		773					
Heal me, Lord					91		
I call on thee, Lord Jesus Christ	634						
O Christ the healer, we have come		772					
There is a balm in Gilead	676		203				
Thine arm, O Lord, in days of old	567						

o Same tune, but not text   [S] Seasonal   [C] Collect   [P] Psalm   [GR] Gospel-related   [SC] Semi-continuous

Proper 5 | Year C

Anthem	Solo	Handbells	Voicing	Title	Collection	Composer
				Collect		
■				God Be in My Head		H W Davies; Rutter, et al
				1 King 17:8-16, (17-24) SC Track		
			U	God's Loving Call		Wayne Wold
■				Praise to the Lord		Hugo Distler
	■		t	Rejoice, O My Spirit, *Cantata 21*		J S Bach
	■		s	Sighing, Weeping, Trouble, Need, *Cantata 21*		J S Bach
	■		sb duet	What Have I to Do/Give Me Thy Son, *Elijah*		F Mendelssohn
				Psalm 146 SC Track		
■				Bless the Lord O My Soul	OXEA	C Armstrong Gibbs
■				Lauda Anima Mea Dominum		Orlando DiLasso
■				My Soul, Sing the Praise, *Seven Short Anthems*		Peter Hallock
■				Praise the Lord		Emma Lou Diemer
■			SSAATTBB	Praise the Lord, O My Soul	ANTH	John Blow
■						Thomas Tomkins
■				Praise the Lord, O My Soul, *Psalmfest*		John Rutter
■				Praise to the Lord		Hugo Distler
■				Praise Ye the Lord		Emma Lou Diemer
	■		b			John Rutter
■				Psalm 146		Samuel Adler; Jean Berger
■						Peter Hallock; Robt J Powell
■				To Thee, O Lord	AFC 1	S Rachmaninoff
■				Sing to the Lord	LIFT	Peter Cornelius
	■		a	Then Shall the Eyes of the Blind, *Messiah*		G F Handel
				1 Kings 17:17-24 GR Track *See above*		
				Psalm 30 GR Track		
■				Blest Are They, *A German Requiem*, 1st mvmt		J Brahms
■			SATTB	Exaltabo te		Palestrina
■				Exaltabo te, Domine		Ned Rorem, *et al*
■				Hide Not Thou Thy Face		Richard Farrant
■			2 pt	I Will Exalt You, O Lord		Raymond H Chenault
■				Kyrie		Multiple
■				Sing Praises, Sing Praises		Kent Newbury
■				Sing unto the Lord	16th	Christopher Tye
■				Thou Hast Turned My Laments Into Dancing		Daniel Pinkham
■				Sing unto the Lord	LIFT	Peter Cornelius
				Galatians 1:11-24 *See also St. Paul below*		
■			Narr/SATB	Saul		Egil Hovland
				Luke 7:11-17		
■				Agnus Dei, *Requiem*		John Rutter
■				Here's One *(Oxford Book of Spirituals)*		William Grant Still
■				I Am the Resurrection		Jan Bender; John Carter
■						Gallus Dressler; T Morley
■				I Am the Resurrection and the Life	CHAN	Gallus Dressler
■			SATB/SATB			Heinrich Schütz
■			SA			Healey Willan
■						David H. Williams
■				O Jesus Christ, My Life, My Light	BFAS	J S Bach
■				What God Ordains Is Good Indeed	BFAS	J S Bach
	■		t	Rejoice, O My Spirit, *Cantata 21*		J S Bach
	■		s	Sighing, Weeping, Trouble, Need, *Cantata 21*		J S Bach
	■		b	The Call		Ralph Vaughan Williams
				Add'l Music, Cantatas, Major Works		
■				*St. Paul*		F Mendelssohn
			satb	8: Liebster Gott, wann [wenn] werd ich sterben?		J S Bach
			satb	27: Wer weiss, wie nahe mir mein Ende?		J S Bach
			stb	95: Christus, der ist mein Leben		J S Bach
			at	161: Komm, du süsse Todesstunde		J S Bach

112

Year C | Proper 5

	Entrance	Sequence	Offertory	Communion	Postcommunion		H82	WLP	LEVAS II	VF	MHSO	CG descant	Inst descant
					■	God be in my head, and in my understanding [C]	694						
					■	Lead us, O Father, in the paths of peace [C]	703						
						1 Kings 17:8-16(,17-24) SC Track							
		■				Be not dismayed whate'er betide			183				
						Commit thou all that grieves thee	669						■
	■					God moves in a mysterious way	677						
	■					I'll praise my Maker while I've breath [P 146]	429						
	■					Lead me, guide me			194				
	■				■	O bless the Lord, my soul	411						
	■					Praise to the Lord, the Almighty, the King of creation	390						■
						1 Kings 17:17-24 GR Track							
		■				Be not dismayed whate'er betide			183				
						Commit thou all that grieves thee	669						■
	■					God moves in a mysterious way	677						
	■					Lead me, guide me			194				
	■				■	O bless the Lord, my soul!	411						
	■					Praise to the Lord, the Almighty, the King of creation	390						■
						Galatians 1:11-24							
	■					A light from heaven shone around	256						
	■					We sing the glorious conquest	255						
						Luke 7:11-17							
		■				Awake, O sleeper, rise from death	547						
				■		Come, my Way, my Truth, my Life	487						
				■		Eternal Light, shine in my heart	465,466						
	■					O for a thousand tongues to sing	493					■	
	■					Thine arm, O Lord, in days of old	567						

○ Same tune, but not text   [S] Seasonal   [C] Collect   [P] Psalm   [GR] Gospel-related   [SC] Semi-continuous

113

Proper 6 | Year C

Anthem	Solo	Handbells	Voicing	Title	Collection	Composer
				1 Kings 21:1-10, (11-14), 15-21a SC Track		
	s			Balm in Gilead		William Dawson
				Surely He's Able (Songs of Zion)		C. Herbert Brewster
				Why Art Thou Cast Down My Soul?		F Mendelssohn
				Psalm 5:1-8 SC Track		
				Give Ear O Lord		Eugene Butler
				Harken unto My Cry		H Schütz
			2 pt	Hear My Words		Stephen Paulus
			U	Hear My Words, *Twelve Songs of Praise*		Samuel Adler
				Lead Me, Lord	AFC 1, OXCAB	Samuel Wesley
			2 pt	Listen to My Words, Lord		Samuel Adler
				Lord, Hear My Words		Georg Schumann
			2 pt	Lord, to You I Pray		Ruth Elaine Schram
			U tr	My Voice Shalt Thou Hear		Joseph Corfe
			TTBB			Thomas Tomkins
				O Hearken Thou		Edward Elgar
			SSAA	Ponder My Words		Thomas Attwood Walmisley
				Praise the Lord My Soul		Samuel Wesley
			SSA	Verba mea auribus		Orlandus Lassus
				2 Samuel 11:26—12:10, 13-15 GR Track		
				Hide Not Thou Thy Face	TUD	Richard Farrant
				Kyrie		Multiple
				Lent Prose	OXASH	Mode V
				Lord, for Thy Tender Mercy's Sake	TUD OXASH	Richard Farrant
					OXCAB	attr. School of Dr. Tye
				Miserere mei, Deus		Multiple
				The Litany (BCP)	OXASH	Henry Loosemore
				Jesus, Redeemer, Our Loving…		Anton Bruckner
				King of Glory	RNMS	K Lee Scott
	s or t			Lord Jesus Christ!		Samuel Barber
	s or t			O Divine Redeemer		Charles Gounod
				O God Have Mercy	TCS	F Mendelssohn
				Redeeming Grace	SSJ	K Lee Scott
				Song of Penitence	SCY	Beethoven
				Psalm 32 GR Track See Lent 4C		
				Galatians 2:15-21		
				But Thanks be to God, *Messiah*		G F Handel
				O Lord, Increase My Faith		Henry Loosemore
				Salvation unto Us Has Come	BFAS	J S Bach
				Luke 7:36—8:3		
				A Litany: Drop Slow Tears		William Walton
				How Beautiful Are the Feet, *Messiah*		G F Handel
				How Lovely Are the Messengers, *St. Paul*		F Mendelssohn
				Jesu dulcis memoria		Tomás Luis de Victoria
				Jesu the Very Thought of Thee		Edward Bairstow
						Eric Thiman
				The Feet O' Jesus		William Averitt
				Jesus, Redeemer, Our Loving…		Anton Bruckner
	s or a			How Beautiful Are the Feet, *Messiah*		G F Handel
				King of Glory	RNMS	K Lee Scott
	s or t			Lord Jesus Christ!		Samuel Barber
	s or t			O Divine Redeemer		Charles Gounod
				O God Have Mercy	TCS	F Mendelssohn
				Redeeming Grace	SSJ	K Lee Scott
				Song of Penitence	SCY	Beethoven
				Add'l Music, Cantatas, Major works		
			satb	150: Nach dir, Herr, verlanget mich		J S Bach

Year C | Proper 6

	H82	WLP	LEVAS II	VF	MHSO	CG descant	Inst descant
Lord, whose love through humble service [C]	610						
1 Kings 21:1-10(,11-14),15-21a SC Track							
Before thy throne, O God, we kneel	574,575						
Father eternal, ruler of creation	573						
O God of earth and altar	591						
What does the Lord require for praise and offering?	605						
2 Samuel 11:26-12:10,13-15 GR Track							
Before thy throne, O God, we kneel	574,575						
Father eternal, Ruler of creation	573						
O God of earth and altar	591						
What does the Lord require for praise and offering?	605						
Galatians 2:15-21							
Alleluia, alleluia! Give thanks to the risen Lord	178						
Hail, thou once despised Jesus	495						
My faith looks up to thee	691		88				
My God, accept my heart this day	697						
Luke 7:36-8:3							
Bread of the world, in mercy broken	301						
Come, ye disconsolate			147				
Delivered from shame				14			
Holy woman, graceful giver				1			
In boldness, look to God for help				94			
King of glory, King of peace	382						
O bless the Lord, my soul!	411						
O Lord, how the fallen woman wept				41			
Praise, my soul, the King of heaven	410						
She poured the perfume lavishly				137			
There's a wideness in God's mercy	469,470						
You laid aside your rightful reputation		734					

Same tune, but not text   [S] Seasonal   [C] Collect   [P] Psalm   [GR] Gospel-related   [SC] Semi-continuous

Proper 7 | Year C

Anthem	Solo	Handbells	Voicing	Title	Collection	Composer
				Collect		
				At the Name of Jesus		Ralph Vaughan Williams
			SAATB	In Nomine Jesu	CHES FG5	Jacob Handl
			SAB	Jesus! Name of Wondrous Love		Everett Titcomb
				Non nobis, Domine		Multiple
				O Lord, Our God, How Great Is Your Name	NNOV	Anthony Milner
				1 Kings 19:1-4, (5-7), 8-15a SC Track *See also Proper 14A*		
				As Panting Deer		David Ashley White
				As Pants the Hart, *Chandos Anthem No. 6*		G F Handel
				As the Deer, for Water Yearning	CHAN	Claude Goudimel
				Elijah Rock		Jester Hairston
				Like As the Hart		Herbert Howells
						Malcolm Williamson
				Sicut cervus	FLEM, ITAL	G P da Palestrina
				Why Are Thou Cast Down My Soul?		F Mendelssohn
				Psalm 42 and 43 SC Track		
				As Panting Deer		David Ashley White
				As Pants the Hart		Orlando Lassus
				As Pants the Hart, *Chandos Anthem No. 6*		G F Handel
				As the Deer, for Water Yearning	CHAN	Claude Goudimel
				As the Deer Pants for Streams of Water		Jim Taylor
				As the Deer Longs for the Waterbrooks		Peter Pindar Stearns
				For I Went with the Multitude		Peter Aston
				Like as the Hart		Herbert Howells
						Malcolm Williamson
				Oh God, Thou Art My God	ANTH	H Purcell
			ob	Psalm 42		Daniel Kean
				Put Thy Trust in God, *Chandos Anthem No. 6*		G F Handel
				Sicut cervus	FLEM, ITAL	G P da Palestrina
						Reginald Unterseher
				Was betrübst du dich, meine Seele, *Cantata 21*		J S Bach
				Why Are Thou Cast Down?		Daniel Pinkham
				With Glad Shouts..., *Chandos Anthem No. 6*		G F Handel
				(Psalm 43) *See Proper 26A*		
				Psalm 43	OXESM	F Mendelssohn
				Isaiah 65:1-9 GR Track		
				I've Been 'Buked		Spiritual, Multiple
				Psalm 22:18-27 GR Track *See also Lent 2B*		
				Go Not Far from Me, O God		N Zingarelli
				Galatians 3:23-29		
				But Thanks Be to God, *Messiah*		G F Handel
				One Bread, One Body		John Foley
				Salvation unto Us Has Come	BFAS	J S Bach
				Luke 8:26-39		
				Follow Me		Don Harper & Ben Tankard
		s		There Is a Balm in Gilead		arr William Dawson
				Ye Servants of God	OXEA	arr Henry Coleman
				I Know De Lord's Laid His Hands on Me		arr Harry T Burleigh
				I Know the Lord Laid His Hands on Me	SOS	Edward Boatner
				Add'l Music, Cantatas, Major Works		
				I Will Sing of Thy Greatness	TCS	F Mendelssohn
				Lord, to Thee Do I Lift Up	SCY	A Vivaldi
			s or t	Out of the Depths		Alan Hovhaness
				Patiently Have I Waited	SSJ	Camille Saint-Saens
			s or t	Psalm 142, *Cycle of Holy Songs*	SMP	Ned Rorem
			stb	127: Herr Jesu Christ, wahr' Mensch und Gott		J S Bach

Year C | Proper 7

	H82	WLP	LEVAS II	VF	MHSO	CG descant	Inst descant
Praise to the living God! [C]	372					0	
1 Kings 19:1-4(,5-7),8-15a SC Track							
As longs the deer for cooling streams [P 42]	658						
As panting deer desire the waterbrooks [P 42]		727					
Dear Lord and Father of mankind	652, 653						
O God of every nation	607						
Praise the Spirit in creation	506, 507						
Isaiah 65:1-9 GR Track							
I've been 'buked and I've been scorned			195				
O worship the King, all glorious above!	388						
Sing praise to God who reigns above	408					0	
Galatians 3:23-29							
Baptized in water	294	767	121				
In Christ there is no East or West	529		62				
One bread, one body			151				
Pan de Vida					93		
Sing praise to our Creator	295						
You have put on Christ					122		
You're called by name, forever loved		766					
Luke 8:26-39							
Heal me, hands of Jesus		773					
Heal me, Lord				91			
How like a gentle spirit deep within			113			0	
I love the Lord, he heard my cry				67			
O bless the Lord, my soul!	411						
O Christ, the healer, we have come		772					
O for a thousand tongues to sing	493						
Thine arm, O Lord, in days of old	567						
Ye servants of God, your Master proclaim	535						

0 Same tune, but not text   [S] Seasonal   [C] Collect   [P] Psalm   [GR] Gospel-related   [SC] Semi-continuous

Proper 8 | Year C

Anthem/Solo/Handbells/Voicing	Title	Collection	Composer
	Collect		
	Christ Is Made the Sure Foundation		Dale Wood
	The Best of Rooms		Randall Thompson
	Tu es Petrus		Maurice Duruflé
b			Gabriel Fauré
			Palestrina
			Charles-Marie Widor
	2 Kings 2:1-2, 6-14 SC Track		
	Elijah Rock		Multiple
	Then did Elijah, *Elijah*, no. 38		F Mendelssohn
	But the Lord from the North, *Elijah*, no. 41		F Mendelssohn
SSAATTBB	Swing Low, Sweet Chariot		arr Dale Adelmann
t	Then Shall the Righteous Shine Forth, *Elijah*, no. 39		F Mendelssohn
s	Behold, God Hath Sent Elijah, *Elijah*, no. 40		F Mendelssohn
	Swing Low, Sweet Chariot		Spiritual, Multiple
	Psalm 77:1-2, 11-20 SC Track		
SATB, a	I Cry Aloud to God		Lois Land
	I Have Considered the Days of Old		Phillip James
SATTB	In die tribulationis, *Ten Venetian Motets*		Giuseppi Guami
U	The Lightnings Lightened the World		Edmund Martens
	1 Kings 19:15-16, 19-21 GR Track		
	Psalm 16 GR Track		
	All the Ways of a Man		Knut Nystedt
	I Have Set the Lord Always before Me		Carl Schalk
	Lord, Thou Hast Been Our Refuge		Edward Bairstow
			John Joubert
			Ralph Vaughan Williams
	My Heart Is Fixed, O God		Leo Sowerby
	O Lord You Are My Portion and My Cup		Jack Noble White
	Preserve Me, O God		B Marcello, ed. Hines
			Jack H Ossewaarde
	Preserve Me, O Lord		Paul Manz
	Psalm 16		Jane Marshall
U, 2 pt, gtr	You Will Show Me the Path of Life		Marty Haugen
t or s	But Thou Didst Not Leave…, *Messiah*		G F Handel
	Galatians 5:1, 13-25		
	Be Ye Followers of God		Leo Sowerby
	King Jesus Hath a Garden	CFC 1	Charles Wood
	Like the Murmur of the Dove's Song		Peter Cutts
	I Love to Dwell in Spirit, *Three Sacred Songs*		David Moritz Michael
	Luke 9:51-62		
	The Summons		John Bell
SATB, b	The Way to Jerusalem		Harold Friedell
	Come, Follow Me		Siegfried Karg-Elert
s	Evangelienmusik		Siegfried Reda
	Add'l Music, Cantatas, Major Works		
atb	12: Weinen, Klagen, Sorgen, Zagen		J S Bach
satb	78: Jesu, der du meine Seele		J S Bach

Year C | Proper 8

	H82	WLP	LEVAS II	VF	MHSO	CG descant	Inst. descant
Christ is made the sure foundation [C]	518					■	
The Church's one foundation [C]	525						
2 Kings 2:1-2,6-14 SC Track							
God of the prophets, bless the prophets' heirs	359						
Swing low, sweet chariot			18				
1 Kings 19:15-16,19-21 GR Track							
God of the prophets, bless the prophets' heirs	359						
Galatians 5:1,13-25							
Brother, sister let me serve you				124	94		
If you believe and I believe		806					
Like the murmur of the dove's song	513						
Lord, whose love through humble service	610						
My God, accept my heart this day	697						
O Holy Spirit, flowing light				54			
When Christ was lifted from the earth	603,604						
Luke 9:51-62							
Day by day	654				33		
He who would valiant be	564,565						
I can hear my Savior calling			144				
I have decided to follow Jesus			136				
In your mercy, Lord, you called me	706						
Jesus calls us; o'er the tumult	549,550			128,129			■
Lead us, heavenly Father, lead us	559						
My song is love unknown	458						
O Jesus, I have promised	655					■	
Thou didst leave thy throne				126			
What does it mean to follow Jesus?					89		
Will you come and follow me		757					

Same tune, but not text   [S] Seasonal   [C] Collect   [P] Psalm   [GR] Gospel-related   [SC] Semi-continuous

Proper 9 | Year C

Anthem	Solo	Handbells	Voicing	Title	Collection	Composer
				Collect		
■				A New Commandment	OXASH	Richard Shephard
■						Thomas Tallis
			SSATBB	Huc me sydereo	ANTH	Josquin Desprez
				I Give You a New Commandment	OXNEA	Peter Aston
			SSA or SSAA	If Ye Love Me		Harvey B Gaul
			SSA			Daniel Pinkham
						Thomas Tallis
			SSA			Healey Willan
				2 Kings 5:1-14 SC Track See Epiphany 6B		
■				I've Just Come from the Fountain		arr Robert Hobby
				Psalm 30 SC Track See Proper 5C		
				Isaiah 66:10-14 GR Track		
				Dixit Dominus		Multiple
	s			Ihr habt nun Traurigkeit, *A German Requiem*		Johannes Brahms
■				O Comfort Now My People	SEW	Thomas Pavlechko
	t			Comfort Ye, *Messiah*		G F Handel
	s			Rejoice Greatly, *Messiah*		G F Handel
				Psalm 66:1-8 GR Track See Easter 6A and Ps 100, Thanksgiving		
			2 pt	Come All That Love the Lord		Robert J Powell
				Make a Joyful Noise unto God		Heinz Werner Zimmerman
			SATB or TTBB	Praise God Ye Lands		H Schütz
			U	Psalm 66		Jane Marshall
						Walter Pelz
				Say Unto God		Tchesnokoff
				Sing Forth		Carl F Mueller
				The First Song of Isaiah		Jack Noble White
				With a Voice of Singing	AUG	Kenneth Jennings
						Martin Shaw
■				Bring to the Lord God, *Five Sht Scrd Concer.*		Heinrich Schütz
				Sing Ye A Joyful Song		A Dvorák
				Galatians 6:(1-6), 7-16		
				Adoramus te		Multiple
				Christus factus est		Multiple
				Faithful Cross		Thomas Pavlechko
				Greater Love Hath No Man		John Ireland
						Carl F Mueller
			SATB, t	Grieve Not the Holy Spirit		T Tertius Noble
			SATB, s	Jesus Walked That Lonesome Valley		arr John Ferguson, *et al*
				When I Survey the Wondrous Cross		arr Gilbert Martin
				Ye Servants of God	OXEA	arr Henry Coleman
■				Spirit of Gentleness		James K Manley
				Luke 10:1-11, 16-20		
				All Who Believe and Are Baptized	BFAS	J S Bach
				Bring Low Our Ancient Adam	BFAS	J S Bach
				Dona nobis pacem, *Mass in B Minor*, BWV 232	BFAS	J S Bach
				Lord, Thee I Love with All My Heart	BFAS	J S Bach
				Peace Be unto You		Knut Nystedt
				Peace, Perfect Peace		Libby Larsen
				Transcendent, Holy God	BFAS	J S Bach
				What God Ordains is Good Indeed	BFAS	J S Bach
■				Peace Be unto You	LIFT	Franz Schubert
				Add'l Music, Cantatas, Major Works		
				Father in Heaven	TCS	G F Handel
	s			I Follow with Gladness, *St. John Passion*		J S Bach
				Lord to Whom Our Prayers	RNMS	F Schubert
				The Song of the Pilgrims		R Vaughan Williams
			satb	44: Sie werden euch in den Bann tun		J S Bach

Year C | Proper 9

	H82	WLP	LEVAS II	VF	MHSO	CG descant	Inst descant
Love divine, all loves excelling [C]	657						
2 Kings 5:1-14 SC Track							
Crashing waters at creation				67	95		
Wade in the water		740	143				
Isaiah 66:10-14 GR Track							
All you who love Jerusalem				157			
Bring many names				106			
Glorious things of thee are spoken	522,523						
Make a joyful noise unto the Lord [P 66]	710						
Mothering God, you gave me birth				71,72	142		
O Zion, tune thy voice	543						
Surely it is God who saves me	678,679						
Galatians 6:(1-6,)7-16							
Beneath the cross of Jesus	498						
In the cross of Christ I glory	441,442						
Jesus, keep me near the cross			29				
Lord Christ, when first thou cam'st to earth	598						
My God, accept my heart this day	697						
Nature with open volume stands	434						
On a hill far away stood an old rugged cross			38				
Praise the Lord, rise up rejoicing	334						
The head that once was crowned with thorns	483						
We know that Christ is raised and dies no more	296					o	
We sing the praise of him who died	471						
When I survey the wondrous cross	474						
Luke 10:1-11,16-20							
As we gather at your table		763				o	
Awake, thou Spirit of the watchmen	540						
Come, labor on	541						
For the fruit of all creation	424						
"Go preach my gospel," saith the Lord			161				
Jesus shall reign, where'er the sun	544						
Let us talents and tongues employ				79	50		
Lord, you give the great commission	528	780					
My God, thy table now is spread	321						
O Spirit of the living God	531						
O Zion, haste, thy mission high fulfilling	539						
Out in the highways and byways of life			158				
Ye servants of God, your Master proclaim	535						

o Same tune, but not text   [S] Seasonal   [C] Collect   [P] Psalm   [GR] Gospel-related   [SC] Semi-continuous

Proper 10 | Year C

Anthem/Solo/Handbells	Voicing	Title	Collection	Composer
		Collect		
A		Hear My Prayer (O God)		Multiple
A		Let Thy Merciful Ears, O Lord		Thomas Mudd
		Amos 7:7-17 SC Track		
		Psalm 82 SC Track		
		Judge Eternal		Gerre Hancock
		Let Justice and Judgment, *Coron Anthem, No. 2*		G F Handel
		Deuteronomy 30:9-14 GR Track		
		Lead Me, Lord		Samuel Wesley
		Lord, Make Me to Know Thy Ways		William Byrd, arr Lovelace
		Praise to the Lord		Hugo Distler
	SATB, t	Seek Ye the Lord		J V Roberts
		Show Me Thy Ways	AUG	Walter Pelz
		Teach Me O Lord		T Attwood; W Byrd; D Hurd
		Psalm 25:1-9 GR Track		
		Ad te, Domine, levavi		Andreas Hakenberger
		Call to Remembrance, O Lord	TUD, OXNCAB	Richard Farrant
	SSAATTBB			John Hilton
		Leite mich in deiner Wahrheit, *Cantata 150*		J S Bach
		Lord, I Trust Thee		G F Handel
		Lord, Make Me to Know Thy Ways		William Byrd, arr Lovelace
		Nach dir, Herr, verlanget mich, *Cantata 150*		J S Bach
		O Lord, My God, To Thee	OXCAB, OXNC	Jacques Arcadelt
		Psalm 25		Harold Friedell
	U or 2 pt	Psalm for Advent		John Karl Hirten
	SAB	Show Me Your Ways		F J Haydn
		Teach Me O Lord		T Attwood; W Byrd; D Hurd
	TB	To Thee, O Lord		Benedetto Marcello
			AFC 1	S Rachmaninoff
		To Thee, O Lord, Have I Lifted…		Gerald Near
		To You O Lord I Lift Up My Soul		Sam Batt Owens
		Universi, qui te exspectant		Michael Haydn
	SATB or 2 pt	Unto Thee I Lift Up My Soul		Franz Schubert
	s or t	Turn unto Me, *Biblical Songs*		A Dvořák
		Unto Thee I Lift Up My Soul	LIFT	Peter Cornelius
		Colossians 1:1-14		
	SA	Canticle	SOP TR	Arthur Wills
		He That Shall Endure, *Elijah*		F Mendelssohn
	U	We Give Thanks, *Prayer Intonation*		Jack C Goode
		Luke 10:25-37		
		A New Commandment	OXASH	Richard Shephard
				Thomas Tallis
		God Is Love *(Playing Gospel Piano)*		Carl MaultsBy
	SSATBB	Huc me sydereo	ANTH	Josquin Desprez
		I Give You a New Commandment	OXNEA	Peter Aston
		Greater Love Hath No Man		John Ireland; Carl F Mueller
	t	Grieve Not the Holy Spirit		T Tertius Noble
	children	The Good Samaritan, *Three Parables in Song*		Wilha Hutson
		Ubi caritas		Maurice Duruflé
		Love Is of God		Donald Busarow
		Love Ye the Lord		G F Handel
		The Greatest of These Is Love		Daniel Moe
	s or t	Ubi caritas et amor		Flor Peeters
	a or b	Wenn ich mit Menschen…, *Four Serious Songs*		J Brahms
		Add'l Music, Cantatas, Major Works		
	atb	33: Allein zu dir, Herr Jesu Christ		J S Bach
	satb	77: Du sollt Gott, deinen Herren, lieben		J S Bach
	satb	164: Ihr, die ihr euch von Christo nennet		J S Bach

Year C | Proper 10

	H82	WLP	LEVAS II	VF	MHSO	CG descant	Instr descant
Amos 7:7-17 SC Track							
Come, thou Holy Sprit bright	226,227						
O day of God, draw nigh	600,601						
Praise to the living God	372					o	
Deuteronomy 30:9-14 GR Track							
Lead us, O Father, in the ways of peace [P 25]	703						
Praise to the living God!	372					o	
Praise to the Lord, the Almighty, the King of creation	390						
The stars declare his glory	431						
Colossians 1:1-14							
Come, we that love the Lord	392						
From glory to glory advancing, we praise thee, O Lord	326						
Lord, dismiss us with thy blessing	344						
Love divine, all loves excelling	657						
O Master, let me walk with thee	659,660						
Luke 10:25-37							
"Come now, you blessed, eat at my table"					155		
I come with joy to meet my Lord	304						
In Christ there is no East or West	529		62				
Jesu, Jesu, fill us with your love	602		74				
Lord, whose love through humble service	610						
Out in the highways and byways of life			158				
When Christ was lifted from the earth	603,604						
Where charity and love prevail	581						
Where cross the crowded ways of life	609						

o Same tune, but not text   [S] Seasonal   [C] Collect   [P] Psalm   [GR] Gospel-related   [SC] Semi-continuous

Proper 11 | Year C

Anthem/Solo/Handbells/Voicing	Title	Collection	Composer
	Collect		
	Almighty God, the Fountain of All Wisdom	AFC 1	Ernest Farrar
			Thomas Weelkes
	Amos 8:1-12 SC Track		
	Kyrie		Multiple
	Let Justice and Judgment, *Coron. Anth. No. 2*		G F Handel
	Lord for Thy Tender Mercy's Sake		Richard Farrant
SSATB or ATB	Lord How Long Wilt Thou Be Angry?		Henry Purcell
SATB, s, a	O Remember Not Our Old Sins		Samuel Wesley
	Remember Not Our Offenses		Henry Purcell
	Psalm 52 SC Track		
	Ich danket dir Ewiglich		Johann Ludwig Freydt
	Genesis 18:1-10a GR Track		
SSA	God's Promise		Samuel Adler
	Laudate pueri		Multiple
	Magnificat		Multiple
	Offertory, *Requiem Mass*		Multiple
	Psalm 15 GR Track		
	Beatitudes		Russian Chant
	Blessed Be the Lord Who Schools Me		Dolores Hruby
	Lord, Who Shall Abide		Glenn W Darst
	Lord, Who Shall Abide in Thy Tabernacle?		Arthur Bliss
	Lord, Who Shall Abide, *Four Motets*		Alan Hovhaness
SAB, gtr, fl	Who Shall Abide		Walter Pelz
	Who May Lodge in Thy Tabernacle?		Daniel Pinkham
	Who Shall Abide in Thy Tabernacle?		G B Pergolesi
	Colossians 1:15-28		
instr	All Glory Be to God on High		Johann Crüger
SA	Canticle	RSCM TR	Arthur Wills
	Non nobis, Domine		Multiple
	Rockin' Jerusalem		John Work
	Salvation unto Us Has Come	BFAS	J S Bach
	Sing My Soul His Wondrous Love		Ned Rorem
	Verbum caro factum est		Multiple
	Luke 10:38-42		
	Be Thou My Vision		John Rutter; Bob Chilcott
	Blessed Jesus at Thy Word		harm J S Bach
	Dear Lord and Father of Mankind		Charles H H Parry
s	There Is a Balm in Gilead		arr William Dawson
a	O Rest in the Lord, *Elijah*		F Mendelssohn
	Add'l Music, Cantatas, Major Works		
	Prayer	RNMS	Beethoven
	So Art Thou to Me	RNMS	K Lee Scott
satb	3: Ach Gott, wie manches Herzeleid		J S Bach

Year C | Proper 11

	Entrance	Sequence	Offertory	Communion	Postcommunion		H82	WLP	LEVAS II	VF	MHSO	CG descant	Inst. descant
Amos 8:1-12 SC Track													
Judge eternal, throned in splendor							596						
O day of God, draw nigh							600,601						
The Lord will come and not be slow							462						
Genesis 18:1-10a GR Track													
God it was who said to Abraham (1-2,5)											85		
God moves in a mysterious way							677						
In the bulb there is a flower											86		
The God of Abraham praise							401						
Colossians 1:15-28													
All glory be to God on high							421						
Come now, O Prince of Peace								795			82		
Hail, thou once despised Jesus!							495						
Lord, enthroned in heavenly splendor							307						
Sing, my soul, his wondrous love							467						
Luke 10:38-42													
Be thou my vision, O Lord of my heart							488						
Blessed Jesus, at thy word							440						
Come with us, O blessed Jesus							336						
In boldness look to God for help										94			
In life's busy moments										22			
Jesus, all my gladness							701						
Lord, dismiss us with thy blessing							344						
O Mary, O Martha									17				
Seek ye first the kingdom of God							711						
This is the hour of banquet and of song							316,317						

Same tune, but not text [S] Seasonal [C] Collect [P] Psalm [GR] Gospel-related [SC] Semi-continuous

Proper 12 | Year C

Anthem/Solo/Handbells/Voicing	Title	Collection	Composer
	Collect		
Anthem	Jesu meine Freude, Chorales	BFAS	J S Bach
	Hosea 1:2-10 SC Track		
	Psalm 85 SC Track *See also Advent 2B*		
Solo	Benedixisti, Domine		Giovanni Gabrieli
SA sa duet	Drop Down Ye Heavens	OXEA	Heathcote Statham
	Order My Steps		Glenn Burleigh
	Not unto Us, O Lord	AFC 1	Thomas Walmisley
	Genesis 18:20-32 GR Track		
	Judge Eternal		Gerre Hancock
	Kyrie		Multiple
	Let Justice and Judgment, *Coron. Anth., No. 2*		G F Handel
	Lord for Thy Tender Mercy's Sake		Richard Farrant
SSATB or ATB	Lord How Long Wilt Thou Be Angry?		Henry Purcell
SATB, s, a	O Remember Not Our Old Sins		Samuel Wesley
	Psalm 138 GR Track		
U	A Joyous Psalm		Eugene Butler
	Attend to the Music Divine (Ps. 134)		Richard Webster
	Confitebor tibi, *Solemn Vespers*		W A Mozart
SATB/STTB	Confitebor tibi		Francesco Cavalli
	He Watching Over Israel, *Elijah*		F Mendelssohn
	I Was Glad (Ps 122) *See Advent 1A*		Multiple
U	I Will Worship		George Dyson
	Laetatus sum (Ps 122)		Marc-Antonio Charpentier
			Michael Haydn
			Claudio Monteverdi
	Let Thy Hand Be..., *Coron. Anth. No. 2*		G F Handel
	Locus iste		Anton Bruckner
SAB	O Give Thanks unto the Lord		John Wood
	Psalm 138		Thomas Hoekstra
			Knut Nystedt; J P Sweelinck
Anthem	Bring to Jehovah, *Five Sacred Songs*		Heinrich Schütz
Anthem	Bring to the Lord God, *5 Sht Sac Concertos*		Heinrich Schütz
Anthem	Give God the Glory		Heinrich Schütz
	Colossians 2:6-15 (16-19)		
	All Who Believe and Are Baptized	BFAS	J S Bach
	Christ Our Passover		R Dirksen; W C MacFarlane
	To See Your Glory		K Lee Scott
	Luke 11:1-13		
	Hear My Prayer		arr Moses Hogan
	Notre Père (The Lord's Prayer)		Maurice Duruflé
	Our Father *(Vater unser)*		Heinrich Schütz
	Our Father in Heaven		Eugene Hancock
	Our Prayer		Rickey Grundy
	Otche nash (The Lord's Prayer)		Anton Arensky
	Pater noster	OXESM	Jacob Handl
			Multiple
	Salvation unto Us Has Come	CHAN	Hugo Distler
	The Lord's Prayer	AFC 1	Robert Stone
	This Day, *African American Heritage Hymnal*		Edwin Hawkins
	Thou Wilt Keep Him in Perfect Peace	OXNCAB	Samuel Wesley
	Ubi caritas		Maurice Duruflé
s or t	Pater noster		Ernst Chausson
	The Lord's Prayer		Michael Head; Malotte
			Flor Peeters
ss duet	Vater unser in Himmelreich		Johann Hermann Schein
	Add'l Music, Cantatas, Major Works		
satb	86: Wahrlich, wahrlich, ich sage euch		J S Bach

Year C | Proper 12

	Entrance	Sequence	Offertory	Communion	Postcommunion		H82	WLP	LEVAS II	VF	MHSO	CG descant	Inst descant
				■		If thou but trust in God to guide thee [C]	635						
	■					O worship the King, all glorious above! [C]	488						■
						Hosea 1:2-10 SC Track							
	■					Creator of the earth and skies	148						
	■					The Lord will come and not be slow [P 85]	462						
						Genesis 18:20-32 GR Track							
	■					Judge eternal, throned in splendor	596						
			■			O day of God, draw nigh	600,601						
	■		■			Praise, my soul, the King of heaven	410						
						Colossians 2:6-15(,16-19)							
	■					All who believe and are baptized	298						
	■					Baptized in water	294	767	121				
	■					From God Christ's deity came forth	443						
	■					On this day, the first of days	47						
						Luke 11:1-13							
				■		Eternal Spirit of the living Christ	698						
				■		For the bread which you have broken	340,341						
			■			"Forgive our sins as we forgive"	674					■	
				■		Glory, love, and praise and honor	300						
				■	■	O God of Bethel, by whose hand	709					■	
						Our Father in heaven		833					
						Pater noster		834					
				■		Seek ye first the kingdom of God	711						■
				■		Thy kingdom come, O God!	613						
				■		"Thy kingdom come!" on bended knee	615						■
				■		Where charity and love prevail	581						
				■		Your kingdom come, O Lord				27			

○ Same tune, but not text   [S] Seasonal   [C] Collect   [P] Psalm   [GR] Gospel-related   [SC] Semi-continuous

Proper 13 | Year C

Anthem	Solo	Handbells	Voicing	Title	Collection	Composer
				Hosea 11:1-11 SC Track		
				Arise, O Jerusalem		Richard Webster
				Comfort, Comfort		John Ferguson
				I Rejoiced when I Heard Them Say		Richard Proulx
				I Was Glad *See Psalm 122, Advent 1A*		Multiple
				Jerusalem surge	CHES FLEM	Heinrich Isaac
				Laetatus sum *See Psalm 122, Advent 1A*		Marc-Antonio Charpentier
				Look Toward the East		Thomas Pavlechko
				O Pray for the Peace of... *See Psalm 122, Advent 1A*		
				Peace Be within Thy Walls		Jean Berger
				Pray for Peace		Alice Parker
				Pray that Jerusalem May Have Peace and Felicity		Charles V Stanford
■	■			Glorious Jerusalem		Horatio Parker
			t	Then Shall the Righteous Shine		F Mendelssohn
				Psalm 107:1-9, 43 SC Track *See also Proper 26A*		
			SSA	Cry unto the Lord		Ellen Keating
				The Eyes of All Wait upon Thee		Multiple
				The Eyes of All Wait upon You		William H Harris
				Ecclesiastes 1:2, 12-14; 2:18-23 GR Track		
				I Am All-Fair		Andrew Carter
				The Fear of the Lord		Herbert Howells
				Nobody Knows the Trouble I've Seen		Spiritual, Multiple
				Vanity of Vanities, *Three Songs from Ecclesiastes*		Daniel Pinkham
				Psalm 49:1-11 GR Track		
				Ah, Thou Poor World	AFC 1	J Brahms
				Jesu, meine Freude, Chorales	BFAS	J S Bach
				The Paper Reeds..., *The Peaceable Kingdom*		Randall Thompson
				Colossians 3:1-11		
				At the Name of Jesus		Ralph Vaughan Williams
				Christ Is the World's True Light	OXEA	W K Stanton
				Come Down O Love Divine		arr David Ashley White
				Is Any Afflicted		William Billings
				Lord, Make Me an Instrument		Roger Holland
				O Divine Redeemer		Charles Gounod
				Ubi caritas		Maurice Duruflé
			U	You Are the People of God		Gerhardt Becker
	■			Awake All Ye People, *Cantata 15*	LIFT	J S Bach
				O Divine Redeemer		Charles Gounod
				One Bread, One Body		John Foley
				Luke 12:13-21		
				Ah Thou Poor World	AFC 1	Johannes Brahms
				Come Sweetest Death		arr J S Bach
				Have No Fear Little Flock		Heinz Werner Zimmerman
				Jesu meine Freude		J S Bach
				O Mortal World		J S Bach
				In Peace and Joy I Now Depart		Multiple
				My Lord, What a Morning		Spiritual, Multiple
				On Jordan's Stormy Banks		Spiritual, Multiple
				Soon and Very Soon		Spiritual, Multiple
				Be Not Proud	SCY	C P E Bach
				Behold the Son of God	LIFT	W A Mozart
				Bist du bei mir		J S Bach
			a	Ich liebe den Höchsten, *Cantata 174*		J S Bach
			a	Man nehme sich in Acht, Cantata No. 166		J S Bach
				My Source of Joy	TCS	F J Haydn
				Recitative and Chorale, *Cantata No. 95*	LIFT	J S Bach
				Add'l Music, Cantatas, Major Works		
■			satb	94: Was frag ich nach der Welt		J S Bach

Year C | Proper 13

	Entrance	Sequence	Offertory	Communion	Postcommunion		H82	WLP	LEVAS II	VF	MHSO	CG descant	Inst descant
				■		Father, we thank thee who hast planted [C]	302,303						
						Hosea 11:1-11 SC Track							
	■					How wondrous and great thy works, God of praise	532,533					■	
	■					In your mercy, Lord, you called me	706						
						Sing praise to God who reigns above	408					o	
						Ecclesiastes 1:2,12-14; 2:18-23 GR Track							
	■					Come, Holy Spirit, heavenly Dove	510					■	
						Lead us, heavenly Father, lead us	559						
						Nobody knows the trouble I've seen			175				
						Colossians 3:1-11							
			■			At the Name of Jesus	435		135			■	
						Christ is the world's true Light	542						
						Come down, O Love divine	516					■	
			■			In Christ there is no East or West	529		62				
						Muchos resplandores/Many are the lightbeams		794					
						One bread, one body			151				
						Pan de Vida					93		
						Where charity and love prevail	581						
						Luke 12:13-21							
		■				All my hope on God is founded	665					■	
		■				Before thy throne, O God, we kneel	574,575						
		■				Creator of the earth and skies	148						
		■				God of grace and God of glory	594,595					■	
		■				Jesus, all my gladness	701						
						Some folk would rather have houses and land			68				

o Same tune, but not text   [S] Seasonal   [C] Collect   [P] Psalm   [GR] Gospel-related   [SC] Semi-continuous

Proper 14 | Year C

Anthem/Solo/Handbells/Voicing	Title	Collection	Composer
	Isaiah 1:1, 10-20 SC Track *See also Proper 26C*		
	Asperges me, Domine		Multiple
	Create in Me		Multiple
	Psalm 50:1-8, 23-24 SC Track *See Epiphany Last B*		
	Genesis 15:1-6 GR Track		
SSA	God's Promise		Samuel Adler
	Laudate pueri		Multiple
	Magnificat		Multiple
	Offertory, *Requiem Mass*		Multiple
a	O Rest in the Lord, *Elijah*		Felix Mendelssohn
	Psalm 33:12-22 GR Track *See also Pentecost Vigil*		
	A Choral Flourish		Ralph Vaughan Williams
	All Who Are Just		Couperin/Proulx
	Exultate just in Domino		Andreas Hakenberger
	Of the Kindness of the Lord		Richard Proulx
children	Rejoice!		Nancy Hill
	Rejoice in the Lord		Thomas Weelkes
	Hebrews 11:1-3, 8-16		
	Behold I Make All Things New		Robert J Powell
	Hold On!		J Hairston; Moses Hogan
	Ich ruf zu dir harm		J S Bach
	My Soul, There Is a Country	OXCAB	Charles H H Parry
	O Lord Increase My Faith		Henry Loosemore
	Luke 12:32-40		
	Ah Thou Poor World	AFC 1	J Brahms
	Arise, Arise, This Day Rejoice		Johann Walther
	Blessed Are Those Servants	NNOV	E J Moeran
	Don't Let Him Catch You with Your Work...		Ashford & Simpson
	Give Almes of Thy Goods		Christopher Tye
	Have No Fear Little Flock		Heinz Werner Zimmermann
	Jesu meine Freude		J S Bach
	Jesu meine Freude, Chorales	BFAS	J S Bach
	Keep Your Lamps		André Thomas
	Somebody's Knockin at My Door		Spiritual, Multiple
	Sleepers, Awake!		arr J S Bach
	Wachet auf		arr J S Bach
	In Peace and Joy I Now Depart		arr J S Bach
	My Lord, What a Morning		Spiritual, Multiple
	On Jordan's Stormy Banks		Spiritual, Multiple
	Rise Up! Rise Up!	CHAN	Johann Walter
	Sleepers, Wake, A Voice is Calling, *St. Paul*		F Mendelssohn
	Soon and Very Soon		Spiritual, Multiple
	Wachet auf		J S Bach
	Wake, Awake, for Night Is Flying	BFAS	J S Bach
	Wohlauf, wohlauf, mit hellem Ton	CHAN	Johann Walter
	You Better Mind How You Talk		J Hairston; Moses Hogan
	Zion Hears the Watchmen Singing	BFAS	J S Bach
	Awake All Ye People, *Cantata 15*	LIFT	J S Bach
	Behold the Son of God	LIFT	W A Mozart
	Dearest Lord Jesus, *Scrd Sngs-Schemellis Gesang.*		J S Bach
	Fear Not Little Flock		J S Bach
sb duet	I Seek Thee, My Life, *Cantata 140*		J S Bach
a	Prepare Thyself Zion, *Christmas Oratorio*		J S Bach
	Recitative and Chorale, *Cantata No. 95*	LIFT	J S Bach
	The Call	SSJ	K Lee Scott
t or b	The Call, *Five Mystical Songs*		R Vaughan Williams
	Add'l Music, Cantatas, Major Works		
satb	115: Mache dich, mein Geist, bereit		J S Bach

130

Year C | Proper 14

						Hymn	H82	WLP	LEVAS II	VF	MHSO	CG descant	Inst descant
				■		Lead us, O Father, in the paths of peace [C]	703						
						Isaiah 1:1,10-20 SC Track							
	■					Come, Holy Spirit, heavenly Dove	510					■	
■						How wondrous and great thy works, God of praise	532,533						■
■						Judge eternal, throned in splendor	596						
				■		Strengthen for service, Lord	312						
		■				What does the Lord require	605						
				■		What does the Lord require of you?					153		
						Genesis 15:1-6 GR Track							
■						It rained on the earth forty days, forty nights (2-4)					97		
				■		The God of Abraham praise	401					■	
				■		We are on our way to the promised land					96		
						Hebrews 11:1-3,8-16							
		■				Bless now, O God, the journey that all your people make				142			
■						How firm a foundation, ye saints of the Lord	636,637						
			■			I call on thee, Lord Jesus Christ	634						
			■			If thou but trust in God to guide thee	635						
			■			Lo! what a cloud of witnesses	545						
	■					O God of Bethel, by whose hand	709						
			■			O God of gentle strength		770,771				o	
			■			O what their joy and their glory must be	623						
	■					Only begotten, Word of God eternal	360,361						
■						Praise our great and gracious Lord	393						
						We've come this far by faith			208				
						When from bondage we are summoned		753,754					
						Luke 12:32-40							
			■			Better be ready			4				
			■			Give me oil in my lamp					61		
			■			Jesus, all my gladness	701						
	■					Rejoice! rejoice, believers	68						
■						"Sleepers, wake!" A voice astounds us	61,62						
						Stay awake, be ready					62		
			■			This is the hour of banquet and of song	316,317						

o Same tune, but not text   [S] Seasonal   [C] Collect   [P] Psalm   [GR] Gospel-related   [SC] Semi-continuous

Proper 15 | Year C

Anthem/Solo/Handbells	Voicing	Title	Collection	Composer
		Isaiah 5:1-7 SC Track		
		Judge Eternal		Gerre Hancock
H	SA	The Song of the Vineyard		Thomas Keesecker
		Vinea mea Electa		Multiple
		Woe unto Them, *The Peaceable Kingdom*		Randall Thompson
		Psalm 80:1-2, 8-18 SC Track		
		Advent Anthem		Richard Proulx
		Cibavit eos		William Byrd
		Exultate Deo		Palestrina
		From Thy Throne, O Lord		Richard Proulx
		Hear, O Thou Shepherd of Israel		William Mathias
		O Adonai, et Dux domus Israel	OXNOV	Roderick Williams
		Ring Out Your Joy		Harrison Oxley
		We Shall All Be Saved *(The Coming)*		Leon Roberts
		Who Shall Ascend into the Hill of the Lord		John Bertalot
		Jeremiah 23:23-29 GR Track		
		God Be in My Head		H Walford Davies
				John Rutter
S		Is Not His Word like a Fire? *Elijah*		F Mendelssohn
S	t	Seek Ye the Lord		Roberts
		Thou Knowest Lord the Secrets of My Heart		Henry Purcell
S	b	Is Not His Word like a Fire? *Elijah*		F Mendelssohn
S	t	Thou Shalt Break Them, *Messiah*		G F Handel
S	b	Why Do the Nations, *Messiah*		G F Handel
		Psalm 82 GR Track		
		Judge Eternal		Gerre Hancock
		Let Justice and Judgment, *Coron. Anth. No. 2*		G F Handel
		Hebrews 11:29—12:2		
	instr	All Glory Be to God on High		arr Johannes Crüger
		Fight the Good Fight		John Gardner
H	U, 2 pt, instr	I Sing A Song of the Saints of God		arr Wayne Wold
		Go Down Moses		Spiritual, Multiple
		Joshua Fit the Battle of Jericho		arr Moses Hogan
		Let Nothing Disturb Thee		David Diamond
		Refrain Thy Voice from Weeping		Arthur Sullivan
		Luke 12:49-56		
		Christ Is the World's True Light	OXEA	W K Stanton
		Judge Eternal		Gerre Hancock
		Let Nothing Disturb Thee		David Diamond
		Refrain Thy Voice from Weeping		Arthur Sullivan
S	ss duet	Vater unser in Himmelreich		Johann Hermann Schein
S	b	Why Do the Nations, *Messiah*		G F Handel
		Add'l Music, Cantatas, Major Works		
S	a or b	But Who May Abide/ For He Is Like…, *Messiah*		G F Handel
		Merciful God		G F Handel
	satb	146: Wir müssen durch viel Trübsal		J S Bach

Year C | Proper 15

	H82	WLP	LEVAS II	VF	MHSO	CG descant	Inst descant
Isaiah 5:1-7 SC Track							
God the sculptor of the mountains		746,747			130		
Judge eternal, throned in splendor	596						
Open your ears, O faithful people	536						
Jeremiah 23:23-29 GR Track							
God be in my head	694						
Lord, speak to me that I may speak				98			
Open your ears, O faithful people	536						
Seek the Lord while he wills to be found	S217-S222						
The Lord will come and not be slow [P 82]	462						
Hebrews 11:29-12:2							
All glory be to God on high	421						
Awake, my soul, stretch every nerve	546						
Fight the good fight with all thy might	552,553						
Give us the wings of faith to rise	253						
Guide my feet, Lord		819					
Hail, thou once despised Jesus!	495						
Holy God, we praise thy Name	366						
How firm a foundation, ye saints of the Lord	636,637						
I want to walk as a child of the light	490						
If thou but trust in God to guide thee	635						
Lo! what a cloud of witnesses	545						
When from bondage we are summoned		753,754					
Women of faith, loving and kind				26			
Luke 12:49-56							
Before thy throne, O God, we kneel	574,575						
Go forth for God; go to the world in peace	347						
Hope of the world, thou Christ of great compassion	472						
Judge eternal, throned in splendor	596						
They cast their nets in Galilee	661						

Same tune, but not text   [S] Seasonal   [C] Collect   [P] Psalm   [GR] Gospel-related   [SC] Semi-continuous

Proper 16 | Year C

Anthem/Solo/Handbells/Voicing	Title	Collection	Composer
	Jeremiah 1:4-10 SC Track		
	Be Not Afraid, *Elijah*		F Mendelssohn
t	Be Thou Faithful unto Death, *St. Paul*		F Mendelssohn
b, vio	Behold I Have Put My Words in Your Mouth		Stephen P Folkemer
	How Lovely Are the Messengers, *St. Paul*		F Mendelssohn
	Thou Knowest Lord the Secrets		Henry Purcell
	Psalm 71:1-6 SC Track		
	Descendit sicut pluvial	MCS	Orlando Lassus
	Go Not Far from Me O God		Nicola Zingarelli
SSATB	Herr, auf dich Traus ich		Heinrich Schütz
	I Go to the Rock		Briggs & Rambo arr Lloyd Larsson
	I Waited on the Lord, *Lobgesang*, vs 14		F Mendelssohn
	In te, Domine speravi		Josquin; Halsey Stevens
SATTB	In te speravi		Palestrina
	In Thee, O Lord		Jane Marshall
b			Thomas Weelkes
	My God Is a Rock		Shaw/Parker
	O How Amiable		Ralph Vaughan Williams
	O Lord in Thee Have I Trusted		G F Handel
2 pt	O Lord, My God (Bist Du bei mir)		J S Bach, arr Hopson
	They That Wait upon the Lord		Jean Berger
st duet	My Song Shall Be…, *Lobgesang*, vss 22-24		F Mendelssohn
	Isaiah 58:9b-14 GR Track		
U	A Lenten Carol		Glen Darst
	His Yoke Is Easy, *Messiah*		G F Handel
	The Glory of the Lord		Vernon deTar
st	This Is the Fasting I Ask		Michael Connolly
2 pt	True Fasting		George Brandon
	You Shall Go Out in Joy		Leland Sateren
sa	He Shall Feed …Come Unto Him, *Messiah*		G F Handel
a	O Rest in the Lord, *Elijah*		F Mendelssohn
	Psalm 103:1-8 GR Track		
	Benedic anima mea	CHES FR	Claudin de Sermisy
	Bless the Lord		Ippolitoff
	Bless the Lord O My Soul		Multiple
	Canticle of Praise		John Ness Beck
	In Ecclesiis		Giovanni Gabrieli
2 pt or 3 pt	Like as A Father		Luigi Cherubini
	Lord for Thy Tender Mercy's Sake	TUD	Richard Farrant
	Not unto Him/Bless Thou the Lord, *St. Paul*		F Mendelssohn
	O My Soul, Bless God the Father		Edward Kerr
	Praise the Lord, My Soul		Samuel Wesley
	Praise the Lord, O My Soul		Thomas Tomkins
	The Lord Has Established His Throne		Daniel Pinkham
	Hebrews 12:18-29		
	But Thanks Be to God, *Messiah*		G F Handel
	With Awe and Confidence		George Brandon
	Luke 13:10-17		
	He Touched Me		Milton Biggham
	Touch Me, Lord Jesus *(Playing Gospel Piano)*		Lucie E. Campbell
	Tu solus qui facis mirabilia	CHES FL	Josquin des Prez
	A Song of Trust	SSJ	F Schubert
	I Know De Lord's Laid His Hands on Me		arr Harry T Burleigh
	I Know the Lord Laid His Hands on Me	SOS	Edward Boatner
	Add'l Music, Cantatas, Major Works		
sb	192: Nun danket alle Gott		J S Bach

134

Year C | Proper 16

Liturgical Use	Hymn	H82	WLP	LEVAS II	VF	MHSO	CG descant	Inst descant
C	Come now, O Prince of Peace [C]		795			82		
C	I come with joy to meet my Lord [C]	304						
C	Our Father, by whose name [C]	587						
C	Praise the Lord, rise up rejoicing [C]	334						
C	Put forth, O God, thy Spirit's might [C]	521						
C	Thou, who at thy first Eucharist didst pray [C]	315						
C	Unidos/Together [C]		796					

Jeremiah 1:4-10   SC Track

	Hymn	H82	WLP	LEVAS II	VF	MHSO	CG descant	Inst descant
	Be not dismayed what e'er betide			183				
	From my birth, from my birth					126		
	God of the prophets, bless the prophets' heirs	359						
	Rock of ages, cleft for me [P 71]	685						

Isaiah 58:9b-14   GR Track

	Hymn	H82	WLP	LEVAS II	VF	MHSO	CG descant	Inst descant
	Bless the Lord, my soul [P 103]		825					
	Bless the Lord, O my soul [P 103]			65				
	Jesus, Lover of my soul	699		79				
	Morning has broken	8						
	O bless the Lord [P 103]					28		
	O bless the Lord, my soul! [P 103]	411						

Hebrews 12:18-29

	Hymn	H82	WLP	LEVAS II	VF	MHSO	CG descant	Inst descant
	Glorious things of thee are spoken	522,523						
	Holy Father, great Creator	368						
	Jerusalem the golden	624						
	O what their joy and their glory must be	623						

Luke 13:10-17

	Hymn	H82	WLP	LEVAS II	VF	MHSO	CG descant	Inst descant
	From miles around the sick ones came		774					
	From thee all skill and science flow	566						
	God, creator, source of healing				93			
	Heal me, hands of Jesus		773					
	Heal me, Lord				91			
	In boldness, look to God for help				94			
	O Christ, the healer, we have come		772					
	O for a thousand tongues to sing	493						
	Thine arm, O Lord, in days of old	567						
	Word of God, come down on earth	633						

Same tune, but not text   [S] Seasonal   [C] Collect   [P] Psalm   [GR] Gospel-related   [SC] Semi-continuous

Proper 17 | Year C

Anthem/Solo/Handbells/Voicing	Title	Collection	Composer
	Collect See Holy Name		
	Immortal, Invisible		Eric Thiman
	Jeremiah 2:4-13 SC Track		
	Kyrie		Multiple
	Let Justice and Judgment, *Coron. Anthem II, No. 2*		G F Handel
	Lord for Thy Tender Mercy's Sake		Richard Farrant
SSATB or ATB	Lord How Long Wilt Thou Be Angry?		Henry Purcell
SATB, s, a	O Remember Not Our Old Sins		Samuel Wesley
	Psalm 81:1, 10-16 SC Track		
SAATB	Exsultate Deo		Andreas Hakenberger
			Hans Leo Hassler
		OXESM	G P Palestrina
			Francis Poulenc
			Alessandro Scarlatti
	Nocturne		Randall Thompson
	O Sing Joyfully	16th	Adrian Batten
	Sing Aloud and Shout for Joy		Kent Newbury
SSAATB	Sing Joyfully		William Byrd
	Sing to God Our Great Protection		W A Mozart
2 pt	Sing We Merrily		Sydney Campbell
		AFC 2	Christopher Symons
2 pt	Sing We Merrily unto God		Donald E Clawson
			William Byrd
	Sirach 10:12-18 GR Track *See Gospel below*		
	Proverbs 25:6-7, alt *See Gospel below*		
	Psalm 112 GR Track		
	Beatus vir		G. Carissimi
			Orlando Lassus
		OXESM	Claudio Monteverdi
	Beatus vir, *Solemn Vespers*		W A Mozart
			A Vivaldi
			Multiple
	Blessed Are the Men Who Fear Him, *Elijah*	NNOV	F Mendelssohn
SATB/SSAB	O Happy Man		Henry Purcell
	Hebrews 13:1-8, 15-16		
b	For We Have on Earth…, *A German Requiem*		J Brahms
	He That Is Down Need Fear No Fall		Philip Moore
	He Won't Leave You		Richard Smallwood
	Now the God of Peace		Gerald Knight
	Ubi caritas		Maurice Duruflé
	Luke 14:1, 7-14		
	At the Name of Jesus		Ralph Vaughan Williams
	Christus factus est		Multiple
	He That Is Down Need Fear No Fall		Philip Moore
			Ralph Vaughan Williams
	Let This Mind Be in You		Lee Hoiby
	Magnificat		Multiple
	Non nobis, Domine		Multiple
t	Ev'ry Valley, *Messiah*		G F Handel
	He That Is Down Need Fear No Fall		R Vaughan Williams
s	I Will Look unto the Lord, *Cantata 93*		J S Bach
	Add'l Music, Cantatas, Major Works		
	Peccator videbit/ Beatus vir		A Vivaldi
sb	47: Wer sich selbst erhöhet		J S Bach
satb	114: Ach, lieben Christen, seid getrost		J S Bach
at	148: Bringet dem Herrn Ehre seines Namens		J S Bach

Year C | Proper 17

	Hymn	H82	WLP	LEVAS II	VF	MHSO	CG descant	Inst descant
C	Immortal, invisible, God only wise [C]	423						
C	Joyful, joyful, we adore thee [C]	376						
C	Lord, dismiss us with thy blessing [C]	344						

Jeremiah 2:4-13   SC Track

	Hymn	H82	WLP	LEVAS II	VF	MHSO	CG descant	Inst descant
	Come, thou fount of every blessing	686		111				
	I, the Lord of sea and sky [P 81]		812		77			
	Sing praise to God who reigns above	408					o	

Sirach 10:12-18   GR Track

	Hymn	H82	WLP	LEVAS II	VF	MHSO	CG descant	Inst descant
	Creator of the earth and skies	148						
	Father all loving, who rulest in majesty	568						
	Lord Christ, when first thou cam'st to earth	598						
	My heart sings out with joyful praise					60		
	My soul gives glory to my God				117			
	Tell out, my soul, the greatness of the Lord!	437,438						

Proverbs 25:6-7   GR Track

	Hymn	H82	WLP	LEVAS II	VF	MHSO	CG descant	Inst descant
	Lord, for ever at thy side	670						

Hebrews 13:1-8,15-16

	Hymn	H82	WLP	LEVAS II	VF	MHSO	CG descant	Inst descant
	All my hope on God is founded	665						
	Christ is the King! O friends upraise	614						
	Circle the table, hands now extend				85			
	Cuando el pobre nada tiene/ When the poor one who has nothing		802					
	For thy dear saints, O Lord	279						
	How firm a foundation, ye saints of the Lord	636,637						
	Lo! what a cloud of witnesses	545						
	Lord, whose love through humble service	610						

Luke 14:1,7-14

	Hymn	H82	WLP	LEVAS II	VF	MHSO	CG descant	Inst descant
	All praise to thee, for thou, O King divine	477					o	
	All who hunger, gather gladly		761		87	52		
	As we gather at your table		763				o	
	Brother, sister, let me serve you				124	94		
	I'm a-going to eat at the welcome table			148				
	My God, thy table now is spread	321						
	We gather at your table, Lord				89			

o Same tune, but not text   [S] Seasonal   [C] Collect   [P] Psalm   [GR] Gospel-related   [SC] Semi-continuous

Proper 18 | Year C

Anthem	Solo	Handbells	Voicing	Title	Collection	Composer
				Jeremiah 18:1-11 SC Track		
■				Turn Back O Man		Gustav Holst
	■			My Lord, What a Morning		Spiritual, Multiple
	■			Search Me, O God, *Biblical Songs*	LIFT	A Dvorák
				Psalm 139:1-5, 12-17 SC Track		
				Lord, You Have Searched Me		David Hurd
			SAATB	Mihi autem nimis		Thomas Tallis
				O for the Wings of a Dove		F Mendelssohn
				Psalm 139		Warren Benson
				Search Me, Lord		Thomas A. Dorsey
				The Lord Is My Light		Peter Hallock
				Thou Knowest, Lord, the Secrets of Our Hearts		Henry Purcell
				Thou Wilt Keep Him in Perfect Peace		Bruce Neswick
					NNOV	Robert Walker
					OXCAB	Samuel Wesley
				Whither Shall I Go?		Malcolm Williamson
				Deuteronomy 30:15-20 GR Track		
				Blessed Are the Undefiled		Healey Willan
				Create in Me a Clean Heart		Paul Bouman; J Brahms
				Gloria in Excelsis, *All Night Vigil*		Sergei Rachmaninoff
				If Ye Love Me		Thomas Tallis
						Philip Wilby
				Immortal, Invisible		Eric Thiman
				Lead Me Lord		Charles Wesley
				Miserere		Gregorio Allegri
				O for a Closer Walk with God	AFC 1	Charles Villiers Stanford
				Teach Me O Lord		David Hurd
				Teach Me, O Lord, the Way of Thy Statutes		Thomas Attwood
				Psalm 1 GR Track		
			SA	Beatus vir		Orlando Lassus
						W A Mozart
			ss duet, s, t			A Vivaldi
			SA	Blessed Is He Who Walks Not in the Path…		Heinrich Schütz
			SAB	Blessed Is the Man		Archangelo Corelli
						Sven Lekberg; Jane Marshall
				Blessed Is the Man, *All Night Vigil*		S Rachmaninoff
				Blest Is the Man		Hans Leo Hassler
			SSA			Orlando Lassus
			U, ob, fl	Happy Is the Man Who Fears the Lord		Richard Proulx
				O For a Closer Walk	AFC 1	C V Stanford
				Psalm 1		S Rachmaninoff; H Stevens
				Philemon 1-21		
				Christus factus est		Anton Bruckner
				Ubi Caritas		Maurice Duruflé
				Luke 14:25-33		
				Ain'-a That Good News!		arr William Dawson
				Crux fidelis		Multiple
				Day by Day		Martin How
				Dear Lord and Father of Mankind		Charles H H Parry
				Faithful Cross		Thomas Pavlechko
				The Summons		John Bell
				Witness		Spiritual, Multiple
				Come, Follow Me	WB	Siegfried Karg-Elert
				Courage, My Heart	RNMS	Georg Böhm
				I Follow Thee Also, *St. John Passion*		J S Bach
				Add'l Music, Cantatas, Major works		
				No Way Is Hard, *Three Odes of Solomon*		Alan Hovhaness
			satb	8: Liebster Gott, wann werd ich sterben?		J S Bach

Year C | Proper 18

Hymn	H82	WLP	LEVAS II	VF	MHSO	CG descant	Inst descant
If thou but trust in God to guide thee [C]	635						
Jeremiah 18:1-11 SC Track							
Everywhere I go, the Lord is near me [P 139]					143		
From my birth, from my birth [P 139]					126		
God the sculptor of the mountains		746,747			130		
Have thine own way, Lord! Have thine own way!			145				
Lord, thou hast searched me and dost know [P 139]	702						
Lord, You have searched my heart [P 139]				16			
Deuteronomy 30:15-20 GR Track							
Come, Gracious Spirit, heavenly Dove	512						
God of grace and God of glory	594,595						
Immortal, invisible, God only wise	423						
Lord, be thy word my rule	626						
Now that the daylight fills the skies	3,4						
Praise to the living God!	372					○	
Philemon 1-21							
Creating God, your fingers trace	394,395						
Go forth for God; go to the world in peace	347						
God is love, and where true love is	576,577						
Pan de Vida					93		
Ubi caritas et amor		831					
When Christ was lifted from the earth	603,604						
Where charity and love prevail	581						
Where true charity and love dwell	606						
Luke 14:25-33							
Day by day	654				33		
Hope of the world, thou Christ of great compassion	472						
I can hear my Savior calling			144				
I have decided to follow Jesus			136				
New every morning is the love	10						
Not here for high and holy things	9						
Praise the Lord through every nation	484,485						
Take up your cross, the Savior said	675						
What does it mean to follow Jesus?					89		
Will you come and follow me		757					
You laid aside your rightful reputation		734					

○ Same tune, but not text   [S] Seasonal   [C] Collect   [P] Psalm   [GR] Gospel-related   [SC] Semi-continuous

Proper 19 | Year C

Anthem/Solo/Handbells	Voicing	Title	Collection	Composer
		Jeremiah 4:11-12, 22-28 SC Track		
		Kyrie		Multiple
		Let Justice and Judgment, *Coronation Anthem, No. 2*		G F Handel
		Lord For Thy Tender Mercy's Sake	TUD	Richard Farrant
	SSATB or ATB	Lord How Long Wilt Thou Be Angry?		Henry Purcell
	SATB, s, a	O Remember Not Our Old Sins		Samuel Wesley
	SSAATTBB, a	Steal Away		arr Dale Adelmann
		Psalm 14 SC Track		
	SS(A)TB	O That Salvation for Israel Would Come		Johann Geisler
	SSAATTBB, a	Steal Away		arr Dale Adelmann
		The Fool Hath Said in His Heart		Alan Hovhaness
		There Is a God		Andrew Cooper
		When the Lord Turned Again	16th	Adrian Batten
		Exodus 32:7-14 GR Track		
		Confitemini Domino		Multiple
		Create in Me, O God: Cast Me Not…; Grant Unto…		Johannes Brahms
	2 pt	Create in Me		Paul Bouman; C F Mueller
		Create in Me A Clean Heart O God		Healey Willan
	SAATB	In ieiunio et fletu	ANTH	Thomas Tallis
		Lord For Thy Tender Mercy's Sake		Richard Farrant
		Make Thou in Me O God		J Brahms
		Miserere mei, Deus		Multiple
	SATTB	Ne irascaris	ANTH	William Byrd
		O For a Closer Walk with God	AFC 1	Charles Stanford
		Turn Thy Face from My Sins	OXCAB	Thomas Attwood
		Consume Them All, Lord Sabaoth, *St. Paul*		Felix Mendelssohn
		God Hath Led His People On	LIFT	Felix Mendelssohn
		Make Me A Clean Heart O God, *Anthem III*		G F Handel
		Psalm 51:1-11 GR Track *See also Proper 13B*		
		Cast Me Not Away from Thy Presence		Samuel Wesley
		Hide Not Thou Thy Face	TUD	Richard Farrant
		Kyrie		Multiple
		O God Have Mercy on Me, *St. Paul*		F Mendelssohn
		Schaffe in mir		Johannes Brahms, et al
		Wash Me Throughly	OXNEA	David Halls
	b	O God, Have Mercy, *St. Paul*		F Mendelssohn
		1 Timothy 1:12-17		
		Immortal, Invisible		Eric Thiman
		The First Song of Isaiah		Jack Noble White
		The Secret of Christ		Richard Shephard
		To God Be the Glory		arr. Roger Holland
		Wondrous Love		arr Alice Parker
		Luke 15:1-10		
		Amazing Grace		Multiple
	U or 2 pt	Rejoice! I Found the Lost		Rusty Edwards, arr Wold
		Savior Like a Shepherd Lead Us		David Ashley White
		See What Love, *St. Paul*		F Mendelssohn
		Sheep May Safely Graze		J S Bach
	SSAATTBB, a	Steal Away		arr Dale Adlemann
		The First Song of Isaiah		Jack Noble White
		Thou Knowest, Lord, the Secrets…		Henry Purcell
		When Some Kind Shepherd from His Fold		Alice Parker
		I'm So Glad Jesus Lifted Me		Spiritual, Multiple
		Our Loving Father, *Nine Sacred Songs*	LIFT	Peter Cornelius
		Add'l Music, Cantatas, Major Works		
	stb	21: Ich hatte viel Bekümmernis		J S Bach
	atb	135: Ach Herr, mich armen Sünder		J S Bach
	sat	184: Erwünschtes Freudenlicht		J S Bach

Year C | Proper 19

	Entrance	Sequence	Offertory	Communion	Postcommunion		H82	WLP	LEVAS II	VF	MHSO	CG descant	Inst descant
Jeremiah 4:11-12,22-28 SC Track													
Creator of the earth and skies							148						
How wondrous and great thy works, God of praise!							522,523						
O worship the King, all glorious above!							388						
Exodus 32:7-14 GR Track													
God the Omnipotent! King, who ordainest							569						
O for a closer walk with God							683,684						
Praise, my soul, the King of heaven							410						
Praise our great and gracious Lord							393						
Sing praise to God who reigns above							408					o	
The God of Abraham praise							401						
When all thy mercies, O my God							415						
Wisdom freed a holy people								905		155			
1 Timothy 1:12-17													
Immortal, invisible, God only wise							423						
In your mercy, Lord, you called me							706						
O love, how deep, how broad, how high							448,449						
Out in the highways and byways of life									158				
The great Creator of the worlds							489						
What wondrous love is this							439						
Luke 15:1-10													
A long lost lamb is in the fold										95			
I sought the Lord, and afterward I knew							689						
Now the silence							333						
Praise the Lord, rise up rejoicing							334						
Savior, like a shepherd lead us							708						
The King of love my shepherd is							645,646						
There's a wideness in God's mercy							469,470						

o Same tune, but not text   [S] Seasonal   [C] Collect   [P] Psalm   [GR] Gospel-related   [SC] Semi-continuous

Proper 20 | Year C

Anthem	Solo	Handbells	Voicing	Title	Collection	Composer
				Collect		
				Ah, Thou Poor World	AFC 1	J Brahms
				Jesus, Priceless Treasure		J S Bach
				Praise to the Lord		Hugo Distler
				The Law and the Prophets		Egil Hovland
				Jeremiah 8:18—9:1 SC Track		
				Dear Lord and Father		Charles H H Parry
	s			There Is A Balm in Gilead		arr William L. Dawson
			TTBB			Sam Batt Owens
				Your Love Divine		Richard Smallwood
				Psalm 79:1-9 SC Track		
				Dear Lord and Father		Charles H H Parry
			U	From Your Throne, O Lord		Gordon Binkerd
			SSATB	Lord, How Long Wilt Thou Be Angry?		Henry Purcell
			ATB	O Remember Not		Henry Purcell
				Remember Not Our Offenses		Henry Purcell
				Remember Not Our Old Sins		Samuel Wesley
				Amos 8:4-7 GR Track		
				Kyrie		Multiple
				Let Justice and Judgment, *Coron. Anthem, No. 2*		G F Handel
				Lord For Thy Tender Mercy's Sake		Richard Farrant
			SSATB or ATB	Lord How Long Wilt Thou Be Angry?		Henry Purcell
			SATB, s, a	O Remember Not Our Old Sins		Samuel Wesley
				Remember Not Our Offenses		Henry Purcell
				Psalm 113 GR Track		
				All From the Sun's Uprise	OXEA	Philip Tomblings
				From the Rising of the Sun	AFC 1	Frederick Ouseley
				Give Laud Unto the Lord	OXEA	arr Ernest Bullock
				Laudate Pueri		G F Handel; W A Mozart
				Laud Ye the Name of the Lord, *All Night Vigil*		S Rachmaninoff
				O Come, Ye Servants of the Lord	OXNEA	Christopher Tye
			U	Praise God, Ye Servants..., *Twelve Songs of Praise*		Samuel Adler
				Praise the Lord		Heinz Werner Zimmermann
				Praise the Lord, Ye Servants	ANTH, AFC 1	John Blow
				Praise the Name of the Lord, *Sev.Short Anthems*		Peter Hallock
			U or SATB	Praise to the Lord	SAS	Ron T. Klusmeier
			U/U	Praise Ye the Lord		Henry Pfohl
				Praise Ye the Lord, Ye Children		Richard Proulx
				Ye Servants of God	OXEA	arr Henry Coleman
				1 Timothy 2:1-7		
				Glory and Worship, *Coronation Anthem, No. 3*		G F Handel
				Hear My Prayer		Felix Mendelssohn; et al
				Let This Mind Be in You		Lee Hoiby
				O Sing Unto the Lord *excerpts*		Henry Purcell
				One Bread, One Body		John Foley
			SAB	There Is One God and One Mediator		Johann C. Geisler, arr Cogin
				Luke 16:1-13		
				Ah, Thou Poor World	AFC 1	Johannes Brahms
				Be Faithful		Richard Smallwood
			U	Be Thou My Vision		arr Marie Pooler
						John Rutter
				Jesu, meine Freude		J S Bach
				The Law and the Prophets		Egil Hovland
				Recitative and Chorale, O Mortal World		J S Bach
				Add'l Music, Cantatas, Major Works		
	satb			105: Herr, gehe nicht ins Gericht		J S Bach
	satb			Solo Cantata 168: Tue Rechnung! Donnerwort		J S Bach
				Motet: Jesu, meine Freude		J S Bach

Year C | Proper 20

	Entrance	Sequence	Offertory	Communion	Postcommunion		H82	WLP	LEVAS II	VF	MHSO	CG descant	Inst descant
						Commit thou all that grieves thee [C]	669						
						Praise to the Lord, the Almighty [C]	390						
						Sing praise to God who reigns above [C]	408					o	
						Jeremiah 8:18-9:1 SC Track							
						Give praise and glory unto God	375						
						Savior, again to thy dear Name we raise	345						
						Sing praise to God who reigns above	408					o	
						There is a balm in Gilead	676		203				
						Amos 8:4-7 GR Track							
						Father all loving, who rulest in majesty	568						
						God of freedom, God of justice				90			
						Judge eternal, throned in splendor	596						
						O holy city, seen of John	582,583						
						1 Timothy 2:1-7							
						God of mercy, God of grace	538						
						Holy Father, great Creator	368						
						O day of God, draw nigh	600,601						
						Luke 16:1-13							
						Be thou my vision, O Lord of my heart	488						
						God himself is with us	375						
						God of grace and God of glory	594,595						
						Jesus, all my gladness	701						
						Jesus calls us; o'er the tumult	549,550				128,129		

o Same tune, but not text   [S] Seasonal   [C] Collect   [P] Psalm   [GR] Gospel-related   [SC] Semi-continuous

Proper 21 | Year C

Anthem/Solo/Handbells	Voicing	Title	Collection	Composer
		Collect		
		Kyrie		Multiple
		Treasures in Heaven		Joseph W. Clokey
		Jeremiah 32:1-3a, 6-15 SC Track		
		Psalm 91:1-6, 14-16 SC Track		
		For He Has Commanded His Angels…, *Elijah*		F Mendelssohn
	SSAATTB	For He Shall Give His Angels…, *Elijah*		F Mendelssohn
		Lord, Thou Hast Been Our Refuge		Edward Bairstow
				John Joubert
				Ralph Vaughan Williams
		On Eagle's Wings		Michael Joncas
		Swing Low, Sweet Chariot		arr Dale Adelmann, et al
		I've Got Peace Like a River		Spiritual, Multiple
	a	Lobe den Herren, *Cantata 137*		J S Bach
	sb	Lobe den Herren, *Cantata 137*		J S Bach
		Amos 6:1a, 4-7 GR Track		
		Psalm 146 GR Track		
		Bless the Lord O My Soul	OXEA	C Armstrong Gibbs
		Exultate justi		Viadana
		Fight the Good Fight		John Gardner
		Lauda anima mea Dominum		Orlando DiLasso
		My Soul, Sing the Praise …, *Seven Short Anthems*		Peter Hallock
		Praise the Lord		Emma Lou Diemer
	SSAATTBB	Praise the Lord, O My Soul	ANTH	John Blow
				Thomas Tomkins
		Praise the Lord, O My Soul, *Psalmfest*		John Rutter
		Praise to the Lord		Hugo Distler
		Praise Ye		Emma Lou Diemer
		Praise Ye the Lord	ANTH	John Blow
		Psalm 146		Samuel Adler
				Jean Berger
				Peter Hallock
				Stanley Hoffman
				Robert J Powell
				John Rutter
		To Thee, O Lord	AFC 1	S Rachmaninoff
	s or a	Then Shall the Eyes of the Blind, *Messiah*		G F Handel
		1 Timothy 6:6-19		
		Ah, Thou Poor World	AFC 1	Johannes Brahms
		Eternal Life		Kirk Franklin
		Fight the Good Fight		John Gardner
				Leo Sowerby
		Jesu, meine Freude, Chorales	BFAS	J S Bach
		Christ the World's Redeemer		Stephen H Prussing
		Immortal, Invisible		Eric Thiman
		Jesu, meine Freude		J S Bach
		Jesus, Priceless Treasure		J S Bach
		Luke 16:19-31		
		Ain'-a That Good News!		arr William L. Dawson
	sstb, 2 vln	Father Abraham, Have Mercy on Me		H Schütz
		In Paradisum, *Requiem*		Multiple
		Poor Man Lazarus		Jester Hairston
	sstb, 2 vln	Vater Abraham, erbarme Dich mein		H Schütz
		Add'l Music, Cantatas, Major Works		
	atb	20: O Ewigkeit, du Donnerwort		J S Bach
	satb	75: Die Elenden sollen essen, Part I		J S Bach

Year C | Proper 21

	H82	WLP	LEVAS II	VF	MHSO	CG descant	Inst descant
Awake, my soul, stretch every nerve [C]	546						
Guide my feet, Lord, while I run this race [C]		819					
Lo! what a cloud of witnesses [C]	545						
Jeremiah 32:1-3a,6-15 SC Track							
As those of old their first fruits brought	705						
Give praise and glory unto God [P 91]	375						
O God of Bethel, by whose hand [P 91]	709						
Amos 6:1a,4-7 GR Track							
Before thy throne, O God, we kneel	574,575						
I'll praise my Maker while I've breath [P 146]	429						
1 Timothy 6:6-19							
All to Jesus I surrender			133				
Crown him with many crowns	494						
Fight the good fight with all thy might	552,553						
God of grace and God of glory	594,595						
Immortal, invisible, God only wise	423						
Jesus, all my gladness	701						
You have longed for sweet peace			135				
Luke 16:19-31							
Father all loving, who rulest in majesty	568						
I will trust in the Lord			193				
Into paradise may the angels lead you	354						
May choirs of angels lead you	356						
Open your ears, O faithful people	536						
Tell out, my soul, the greatness of the Lord	437,438						
Ye holy angels bright	625						

Same tune, but not text   [S] Seasonal   [C] Collect   [P] Psalm   [GR] Gospel-related   [SC] Semi-continuous

145

Proper 22 | Year C

Anthem/Solo/Handbells	Voicing	Title	Collection	Composer
		Lamentations 1:1-6 SC Track		
	SSAATB	Aspice Domine	CHES ENG6	William Byrd
	SSATB	Lord, Thou Know'st All My Desire	ANTH	John Blow
	2 pt	O God, I Cry in the Daytime	AFC 2	John Reynolds
		The Lamentation	OXASH	Edward C. Bairstow
	2 pt	The Sorrows of My Heart	AFC 2	William Boyce
	satb	Cast Thy Burden upon the Lord, *Elijah*	CAB	F Mendelssohn
		Canticle Lamentations 3:19-26 SC Track		
		A Song of Thanksgiving	AUG	John Ferguson
		I Waited on the Lord, *Hymn of Praise*		F Mendelssohn
	2 pt	The Sorrows of my Heart	AFC 2	William Boyce
	a/b	O Rest in the Lord, *Elijah*		F Mendelssohn
		Psalm 137, alt SC Track		
	SSAATB	Aspice Domine	CHES ENG6	William Byrd
		By the Babylonian Rivers	AUG	arr Richard Erickson
		By the Rivers of Babylon		T Tertius Noble
	U	By the Waters of Babylon, *Four Ps Settings*		Colin Mawby
		Super flúmina	CHES ITAL	G P da Palestrina
	2 pt	The Sorrows of my Heart	AFC 2	William Boyce
	s or t	By the Still Waters…, *Biblical Songs*		Antonin Dvorák
		Habakkuk 1:1-4; 2:1-4 GR Track		
	U	Be Thou My Vision		arr Marie Pooler
				John Rutter
	SAB	Climb to the Top of the Highest Mountain		Richard W Gieseke
		Good Tidings to the Meek, *Requiem*		Randall Thompson
	U tr	He Delivered the Poor, *Hear My Words*		Charles H H Parry
	U	I Will Greatly Rejoice in the Lord		Philip M Young
	U	O Thou Art of Purer Eyes		David Francis Urrows
	U or 2 pt	With the Help of the Spirit of the Lord		Jayne Southwick Cool
		Psalm 37:1-10 GR Track		
		Commit Your Life to the Lord		Liebhold
		Habe deine Lust an dem Herrn		Christopher Bernhard
	ss duet	I Waited for the Lord, *Lobgesang, Hymn of Praise*		F Mendelssohn
	div	Os justi	OXESM	Anton Bruckner
		Proclaim the Lord		Dan Locklair
		Psalm 37		John Leavitt
	U			Jane Marshall
		Novit Dominus	CHES FG6	Leonhard Lechner
		The Paper Reeds…, *The Peaceable Kingdom*		Randall Thompson
	b	Habe deine Lust…, *Cantata 4, Alles was ihr tut*		Dietrich Buxtehude
		2 Timothy 1:1-14		
		Ah, Thou Poor World	AFC 1	Johannes Brahms
		Amazing Grace		Multiple
		Draw Us in the Spirit's Tether		Harold Friedell
		Fight the Good Fight		John Gardner
		Grace Is Sufficient		James Cleveland
		Jesu, meine Freude, Chorales	BFAS	J S Bach
		Jesus, Priceless Treasure		J S Bach
		Kindle the Gift of God		Gerre Hancock
		We Rely on the Power of God		Richard Hillert
		Luke 17:5-10		
		An Anthem of Faith		Carl F Mueller
		He'll Be There (When You Need Him)		Walter Hawkins
		O Lord, Increase Our Faith		Henry Loosemoore
		Thee We Adore		T Frederick Candlyn
		Add'l Music, Cantatas, Major Works		
	satb	75: Die Elenden sollen essen, Part II		J S Bach
		Motet: Jesu, meine Freude		J S Bach

146

Year C | Proper 22

	H82	WLP	LEVAS II	VF	MHSO	CG descant	Instr descant
Eternal Spirit of the living Christ [C]	698						
Only-begotten, Word of God eternal [C]	360,361						
Lamentations 1:1-6 SC Track							
Great is thy faithfulness, O God my Father [Lam 3]			189				
In deepest night, in darkest days [P 137]				97			
Let us, with a gladsome mind [Lam 3]	389						
New every morning is the love [Lam 3]	10						
O what their joy and their glory must be [P 137]	623						
The steadfast love of the Lord never ceases [Lam 3]		755					
When all thy mercies, O my God [Lam 3]	415						
Habakkuk 1:1-4;2:1-4 GR Track							
Be thou my vision, O Lord of my heart	488						
Commit thou all that grieves thee [P 37]	669						
O God of every nation	607						
2 Timothy 1:1-14							
Amazing grace! how sweet the sound	671		181				
Hope of the world, thou Christ of great compassion	472						
O thou who camest from above	704						
We praise thee, O God			157				
Luke 17:5-10							
Awake, my soul, and with the sun	11						
Come, labor on	541						
I call on thee, Lord Jesus Christ	634						
Lord, whose love through humble service	610						
O Jesus, I have promised	655						
O Master, let me walk with thee	659,660						
Rise up, ye saints of God!	551						
Strengthen for service, Lord	312						
Ye servants of God, your Master proclaim	535						

Same tune, but not text   [S] Seasonal   [C] Collect   [P] Psalm   [GR] Gospel-related   [SC] Semi-continuous

Proper 23 | Year C

Anthem	Solo	Handbells	Voicing	Title	Collection	Composer
				Jeremiah 29:1, 4-7 SC Track		
■				Praise to the Lord		Hugo Distler
■				O Praise Our God		H Schütz
				Psalm 66:1-11 SC Track See Ps 100, Thanksgiving		
■			2 pt	Come All That Love the Lord		Robert J Powell
■				Jubilate, *Offertorium pro omni tempore*		W A Mozart
■			SATB, s	O Be Joyful in God		Healey Willan
■				O Come Hither		Maurice Greene
■				Make a Joyful Noise unto God		Heinz Werner Zimmerman
■			SATB or TTBB	Praise God Ye Lands		H Schütz
■			U	Psalm 66		Jane Marshall
■						Walter Pelz
■				Say unto God		Tchesnokoff
■				Sing Forth		Carl F Mueller
■				The First Song of Isaiah		Jack Noble White
■				We've Come to Praise Him		arr Don Hart
■				With a Voice of Singing	AUG	Kenneth Jennings
■						Martin Shaw
■				Bring to the Lord God, *Five Short Sacred Con.*		Heinrich Schütz
■				Sing Ye A Joyful Song		A Dvořák
				2 Kings 5:1-3, 7-15c GR Track		
■				Asperges me, Domine		Multiple
■				Create in Me, O God		J Brahms
■				Create in Me		Carl F Mueller
■				Wade in the Water		Spiritual, Multiple
■				Wash Me Throughly		G F Handel; Samuel Wesley
■				Wade in the Water		Spiritual, Multiple
				Psalm 111 GR Track		
■				Beatus vir		W A Mozart, et al
■				Confitebor tibi		W A Mozart, et al
■				Haec Dies *(Ps 118)*		Multiple
■				Haec es Dies *(Ps 118)*		Multiple
■				My Heart Is Full Today		Richard Proulx
■				This Is the Day *(Ps 118)*		Bortniansky; C Callahan
■						Richard Proulx; Eric Thiman
■				I Sing to the Lord, *Five Short Sacred Concertos*		Heinrich Schütz
				2 Timothy 2:8-15		
■				Christ Is the World's Redeemer		Stephen H Prussing
■				Fight the Good Fight		John Gardner; Leo Sowerby
■				He That Shall Endure, *Elijah*		F Mendelssohn
■				Since by Man Came Death, *Messiah*		G F Handel
■				Since by Man	SEW	Thomas Pavlechko
■				Jesu meine Freude, *Chorales*	BFAS	J S Bach
■				Jesus Priceless Treasure	BFAS	J S Bach
■				We Rely on the Power of God		Richard Hillert
				Luke 17:11-19		
■				Be Faithful		Richard Smallwood
■				Be Grateful		Walter Hawkins
■				Now Thank We All Our God	BFAS	J S Bach
■				Now Thank We All Our God (Chorale)	BFAS	J S Bach
■			SATB/SATB	Nun danket alle Gott		Johann Pachelbel
■				O Lord, Increase My Faith		Henry Loosemore
■				Thee We Adore		T Frederick Candlyn
				Add'l Music, Cantatas, Major Works		
			satb	17: Wer Dank opfert, der preiset mich		J S Bach
			stb	25: Es ist nicht Gesundes an meinem Leibe		J S Bach
			atb	67: Halt im Gedächtnis Jesum Christ		J S Bach

Year C | Proper 23

			Hymn	H82	WLP	LEVAS II	VF	MHSO	CG descant	Inst descant
			Jeremiah 29:1,4-7 SC Track							
			All who love and serve your city	570,571						
			Praise to the Lord, the Almighty, the King of creation	390						
			Sing to celebrate the city!				116			
			2 Kings 5:1-3,7-15c GR Track							
			Crashing waters at creation				67	95		
			Healing river of the Spirit				96			
			Wade in the water		740	143				
			2 Timothy 2:8-15							
			Help us, O Lord, to learn	628						
			No saint on earth lives life to self alone		776					
			O Jesus, I have promised	655						
			The head that once was crowned with thorns	483						
			Word of God, come down on earth	633						
			Luke 17:11-19							
			Give praise and glory unto God	375						
			God of mercy, God of grace	538						
			God of the sparrow					129		
			Heal me, Lord				91			
			I love the Lord, he heard my cry			67				
			O bless the Lord, my soul!	411						
			O Christ, the healer, we have come		772					
			O for a thousand tongues to sing	493						
			Praise, my soul, the King of heaven	410						
			Thine arm, O Lord, in days of old	567						
			When all thy mercies, O my God	415						

Same tune, but not text   [S] Seasonal   [C] Collect   [P] Psalm   [GR] Gospel-related   [SC] Semi-continuous

Proper 24 | Year C

Anthem/Solo/Handbells/Voicing	Title	Collection	Composer
	Jeremiah 31:27-34 SC Track		
	Kyrie		Multiple
	Teach Me, O Lord, the Way of…		Thomas Attwood
	This Is the Covenant		Jean Berger
	Thou Knowest, Lord, the Secrets…		Henry Purcell
	Psalm 119:97-104 SC Track		
	Everyday with Jesus		Myrna Summers
	Like as the Hart		Herbert Howells
2 pt	Lord, What Love Have I	AFC 2	William Croft
U	The Twin Commandments, *God Speaks*		Jane Marshall
U	True Goodness, *God Speaks*		Jane Marshall
U	Words of Faith, *God Speaks*		Jane Marshall
	Genesis 32:22-31 GR Track		
	Come O Thou Traveler Unknown		Erik Routley
	Wrestling Jacob		Malcolm Williamson
SATB/SATB	Motet: Ich lasse dich night		J S Bach
	Psalm 121 GR Track		
U	A Song of Trust		C V Stanford
	Ad te levavi	CHES ENG6	Robert White
	Auxilium meum	CHES FR	Passereau
2 pt	Coverdale's Psalm 121		John Bertalot
	He Watching over Israel, *Elijah*		Mendelssohn
U	I Lift Mine Eyes, *Twelve Songs of Praise*		Samuel Adler
	I Lift My Eyes to the Hills		Jean Berger
2 pt tr			Paul Bouman
			David Hurd
			John Rutter
			Leo Sowerby
	I to the Hills Lift Up Mine Eyes	AUG	Jean Berger
2 pt	I Will Lift Up Mine Eyes		Malcolm Williamson
			Leo Sowerby
	I Will Lift Up Mine Eyes, *Psalmfest*		John Rutter
SSA	Lift Thine Eyes, *Elijah*		F Mendelssohn
	Our Help Comes from the Lord		David Ashley White
	Processional Psalms		Sydney Nicholson
TTBB	Psalm 121		Samuel Adler
SSA			Charles Callahan
			Zoltan Kodaly
2 pt			Robert J Powell
	Psalm CXXI, *Cantata 71*		J S Bach
s or t	I Will Lift Up Mine Eyes, *Biblical Songs*		Antonin Dvorák
	I Will Lift Up Mine Eyes	LIFT	Peter Pindar Stearns
	Psalm 121		Harold Friedell
	2 Timothy 3:14—4:5		
	Thy Word Is a Lamp unto My Feet		Multiple
	Thy Word Is a Lantern		John Bertalot
	We Rely on the Power of God		Richard Hillert
	Luke 18:1-8		
U	Be Thou My Vision		arr Marie Pooler
			John Rutter
	Judge Eternal		Gerre Hancock
	Let Justice and Judgment, *Cor. Anthem, No. 2*		G F Handel
	Lord, You Have Searched Me		David Hurd
	O Lord, Increase Our Faith		Henry Loosemoore
	Search Me, Lord		Thomas A. Dorsey
	Add'l Music, Cantatas, Major Works		
satb	10: Was Gott tut, das ist wohlgetan		J S Bach

Year C | Proper 24

		H82	WLP	LEVAS II	VF	MHSO	CG descant	Inst descant
	Jeremiah 31:27-34 SC Track							
	Help us, O Lord, to learn	628						
	O God of Bethel, by whose hand	709						
	Praise to the living God!	372					o	
	Genesis 32:22-31 GR Track							
	Come, O thou Traveler unknown	638,639						
	I to the hills will lift mine eyes [P 121]	668						
	With awe approach the mysteries		759					
	2 Timothy 3:14-4:5							
	Book of books, our people's strength	631						
	Lamp of our feet, whereby we trace	627						
	Lord, be thy word my rule	626						
	Spread, O spread, thou mighty word	530						
	Thanks to God, whose Word was spoken	630						
	Ye servants of God, your Master proclaim	535						
	Luke 18:1-8							
	And now, O Father, mindful of the love	337						
	By gracious powers so wonderfully sheltered	695,696						
	Commit thou all that grieves thee	669						
	Eternal Spirit of the living Christ	698						
	It's me, O Lord, standin' in the need of prayer		797	177				
	Jesus describes a forceful woman				25			
	New every morning is the love	10						
	O God of Bethel, by whose hand	709						
	Seek ye first the kingdom of God	711						
	Sweet hour of prayer			178				

o Same tune, but not text   [S] Seasonal   [C] Collect   [P] Psalm   [GR] Gospel-related   [SC] Semi-continuous

Proper 25 | Year C

Voicing	Title	Collection	Composer
	Collect		
	O Lord, Increase Our Faith		Henry Loosemoore
	Thee We Adore		T Frederick Candlyn
	Ubi Caritas		Maurice Duruflé
	Joel 2:23-32 SC Track *See also Thanksgiving B*		
2 pt or SAB	And I Will Praise Thee O God		Mary Lynn Lightfoot
	Fear Not, O Land	OXNEA	William H Harris
2 pt or SATB	I Will Pour Out My Spirit on the Earth		Hal Hopson
	Lord, Pour Out Your Spirit		Hal Hopson
SATB, ss	Motet for Whitsunday		Bernard Naylor
	Open Our Eyes		Will C MacFarlane
	The First Song of Isaiah		Jack Noble White
	Psalm 65 SC Track *See also Thanksgiving A*		
	Thou, Oh God, Art Praised in Sion		Malcolm Boyle
2 pt			Joseph Corbe
		AFC 4	Ian Hare
	Sirach 35:12-17 GR Track		
	Give Almes of Thy Goods	AFC 1	Christopher Tye
	How Lovely Is Thy... *See Psalm 84, Proper 16B*		
	Judge Eternal		Gerre Hancock
	Jeremiah 14:7-10, 19-22, alt GR Track		
	All My Hope on God Is Founded		Herbert Howells, arr Rutter
	Psalm 84:1-6 GR Track *See also Proper 16B*		
	How Dear to Me		David Hurd
	I Was Glad (Ps 122) and Jubilate Deo (Ps 100)		Multiple
	Laetatus sum (Ps 122)		Marc-Antonio Charpentier
			M Haydn; C Monteverdi
SSA	Psalm 84		Jan Bender
			Richard Proulx
	Quam Dilecta!		Gerald Bales
	The Lord Is My Strength		Daniel Moe
st	O How Amiable Are Thy Dwellings, *Psalmfest*		John Rutter
	2 Timothy 4:6-8, 16-18		
	Ain'-a That Good News		arr William Dawson
	Fight the Good Fight		John Gardner
	Lo, Round the Throne, A Glorious Band		Henry Ley
	Not Only unto Him/Bless Thou the Lord, *St. Paul*		F Mendelssohn
	O Happy Souls		Alice Parker
	To God Be the Glory		arr Roger Holland
	We Rely on the Power of God		Richard Hillert
st	And They All.../Be Thou Faithful..., *St. Paul*		F Mendelssohn
s	And Though He Be Offered, *St. Paul*		F Mendelssohn
	Luke 18:9-14		
U, 2 pt	Be Merciful, O Lord		John Karl Hirten
	Blessed Are the Pure in Heart		H Walford Davies
	Create in Me: Cast Me Not..., Grant Unto Me...		J Brahms
	He That is Down Need Fear No Fall		Philip Moore
	Kyrie, Lord Have Mercy		Multiple
	Miserere mei, Deus, Ps 51		Multiple
	O Sinner Man		arr Howard Roberts
	Thee We Adore		T Frederick Candlyn
	The Pharisee and the Publican		H Schütz
SA	Tilge, Höchster, meine Sünden, *Motet*		J S Bach
	Lass mich Freud und Wonne spüren, *Motet*		J S Bach
	Add'l Music, Cantatas, Major Works		
satb	113: Herr Jesu Christ, du höchstes Gut		J S Bach
stb	179: Siehe zu, dass deine Gottesfurcht		J S Bach
s	Solo Cantata 199: Mein Herze schwimmt im Blut		J S Bach

Year C | Proper 25

		H82	WLP	LEVAS II	VF	MHSO	CG descant	Inst descant
Joel 2:23-32 SC Track								
	For the fruit of all creation	424						
	I sing the almighty power of God	398					o	
	Let all creation bless the Lord		885					
	Let us, with a gladsome mind	389						
	O all ye works of God, now come	428	884					
	O day of God, draw nigh	600,601						
	Praise the Spirit in creation	506,507						
	Surely it is God who saves me	678,679						
	"Thy kingdom come!" on bended knee	615						
Sirach 35:12-17 GR Track								
	All who love and serve your city	570,571						
	How lovely is thy dwelling-place [P 84]	517						
	Judge eternal, throned in splendor	596						
	Put forth, O God, thy Spirit's might	521						
	The Lord will come and not be slow	462						
Jeremiah 14:7-10,19-22 GR Track								
	All my hope on God is founded	665						
	Come, thou fount of every blessing	686		111				
	Creator of the earth and skies	148						
	Eternal light, shine in my heart	465,466						
	How lovely is thy dwelling-place [P 84]	517						
	O God, our help in ages past	680						
2 Timothy 4:6-8,16-18								
	Awake, my soul, stretch every nerve	546						
	Fight the good fight with all thy might	552,553						
	Guide my feet, Lord, while I run this race			819				
	How firm a foundation, ye saints of the Lord	636,637						
Luke 18:9-14								
	Blest are the pure in heart	656						
	Humbly I adore thee, Verity unseen	314						
	Let all creation bless the Lord		885					
	Lord, for ever at thy side	670						
	Lord Jesus, think on me	641	798					
	O all ye works of God, now come	428	884					
	O, I couldn't hear nobody pray			171				
	Take, O take me as I am					46		

[S] Seasonal   [C] Collect   [P] Psalm   [GR] Gospel-related   [SC] Semi-continuous

Proper 26 | Year C

Anthem/Solo/Handbells/Voicing	Title	Collection	Composer
	Collect		
	Fight the Good Fight		John Gardner; Leo Sowerby
	Habakkuk 1:1-4; 2:1-4 SC Track *See Proper 22C*		
U	Be Thou My Vision		arr Marie Pooler
			John Rutter
	Good Tidings to the Meek, *Requiem*		Randall Thompson
U tr	He Delivered the Poor, *Hear My Words*		Charles H H Parry
U	I Will Greatly Rejoice in the Lord		Philip M Young
	I'll Stand Until		Kirk Franklin
	Stand		Donnie McClurkin
satb	Cast Thy Burden upon the Lord, *Elijah*	CAB	F Mendelssohn
	Psalm 119:137-144 SC Track		
	I Call with My Whole Heart		Michael Sullivan
	I Will with My Whole Heart		Leo Sowerby
SAB or SATB, s	Righteous, O Lord, Art Thou		A Vivaldi, arr W Ehret
	Isaiah 1:10-18 GR Track		
	Asperges me, Domine		Multiple
U, 2 pt	Be Merciful, O Lord		John Karl Hirten
	Create a Pure Heart in Me		Daniel Pinkham
	Create in Me: Cast Me Not…, Grant unto Me…		J Brahms
2 pt	Create in Me		Paul Bouman; Haydn Morgan
			C Mueller; C Schalk; H Willam
ATB	Have Mercy upon Me, O Lord	NOV ENG 3	Thomas Tomkins
	Hide Not Thou Thy Face		Richard Farrant
	Judge Eternal		Gerre Hancock
	Kyrie		Multiple
	Lord, for Thy Tender Mercy's Sake		Richard Farrant
	Miserere mei, Deus		Multiple
SA	Tilge, Höchster, meine Sünden, *Motet*		J S Bach
	Lass mich Freud und Wonne spüren, *Motet*		J S Bach
	Turn Thy Face from My Sins	OXCAB	Thomas Attwood
		CON	Arthur Sullivan
	Wash Me Throughly		G F Handel; Samuel Wesley
	Make Me a Clean Heart, O God	LIFT	G F Handel
	Psalm 32:1-7 GR Track		
	A Choral Flourish		Ralph Vaughan Williams
SAB	Be Glad You Righteous		Robert J. Powell
	Beati quorum via (Ps. 119)		C V Stanford
ATB	Blessed Is He Whose Unrighteousness…		Thomas Tomkins
	Exultate Deo		Multiple
	Exultate justi		Multiple
SST or SAB	Psalm 32		Paul Weber
	Thou Knowest, Lord, the Secrets of Our Hearts		Henry Purcell
TTBB	Whom the Lord Hath Forgiven		Alan MacMillan
	2 Thessalonians 1:1-4, 11-12		
	O Lord, Increase Our Faith		Henry Loosemoore
	Thee We Adore		T Frederick Candlyn
	Ubi caritas		Maurice Duruflé
	Luke 19:1-10		
	Amazing Grace		arr John Rutter
	Come on Down, Zacchaeus		Robert Leaf
	Give Almes of Thy Goods		Christopher Tye
	Go Climb a Sycamore Tree		Roman Lavore
	Salvation is Free		Shelton Becton
	Salvation unto Us Has Come	BFAS	J S Bach, J Brahms
	Today Is Salvation Come		Raymond Hahn
	Add'l Music, Cantatas, Major Works		
t	55: Ich armer Mensch, ich Sündenknecht		J S Bach

154

Year C | Proper 26

	H82	WLP	LEVAS II	VF	MHSO	CG descant	Inst descant
Awake, my soul, stretch every nerve [C]	546						
Fight the good fight with all thy might [C]	552,553						
Guide my feet, Lord, while I run this race [C]		819					
Lo! what a cloud of witnesses [C]	545						
Habakkuk 1:1-4;2:1-4 SC Track							
Be thou my vision, O Lord of my heart	488						
O God of every nation	607						
Isaiah 1:10-18 GR Track							
Come, Holy Spirit, heavenly Dove	510						
How wondrous and great thy works, God of praise	532,533						
Judge eternal, throned in splendor	596						
Strengthen for service, Lord	312						
What does the Lord require	605						
What does the Lord require of you?					153		
2 Thessalonians 1:1-4,11-12							
Gracious Spirit, give your servants		782					
I call on thee, Lord Jesus Christ	634						
Lord, speak to me that I may speak				98			
O thou who camest from above	704						
Luke 19:1-10							
A long lost lamb is in the fold					95		
And now, O Father, mindful of the love	337						
Before thy throne, O God, we kneel	574,575						
Bread of the world, in mercy broken	301						
From God Christ's deity came forth	443						
God it was who said to Abraham (1,4-5)					85		
Here, O my Lord, I see thee face to face	318						
If I have wounded any soul today			176				
In love you summon, in love I follow					125		
In your mercy, Lord, you called me	706						
King of glory, King of peace	382						
Let thy Blood in mercy poured	313						
Lord Jesus, think on me	641	798					
My God, how wonderful thou art	643						
O bless the Lord, my soul!	411						
O love, how deep, how broad, how high	448,449						
Praise, my soul, the King of heaven	410						
The great Creator of the worlds	489						
There's a wideness in God's mercy	469,470						

Same tune, but not text [S] Seasonal [C] Collect [P] Psalm [GR] Gospel-related [SC] Semi-continuous

155

Proper 27 | Year C

Anthem/Solo/Handbells/Voicing	Title	Collection	Composer
	Collect		
	Lo! He Comes with Clouds Descending		David H Williams
	Haggai 1:15b—2:9 SC Track		
	Ain'a That Good News		arr William Dawson
	And He Shall Purify, *Messiah*		G F Handel
	Immortal, Invisible		Eric Thiman
a or b	Thus Saith the Lord; But Who May Abide, *Messiah*		G F Handel
	Psalm 145:1-5, 18-22 SC Track *See also Proper 20A*		
	Every Eye Waiteth upon Thee		H Schütz
	I Will Extol Thee		Richard Webster
	I Will Extol You		Peter Hallock
	Oculi Omnium		Charles Wood
	Prope est Dominus	CHES CHR	Jacob Regnart
	The Eyes of All Wait upon Thee		Jean Berger; O Gibbons
			William Harris; R E Smith
U			Richard Proulx
		SEW	Richard Shephard
	The Lord Is Good to All		Jean Berger
s or t	Lord, a New Song I Would Fashion, *Biblical Songs*		Antonin Dvořák
	Psalm 98, alt SC Track *See Easter 6B*		
	Cantate Domino		Jonathan Pitkin
			Giuseppe Pitoni; H Purcell
	Jesu dulcis memoria Domino	OXNOV	Francis Pott
	O Sing unto the Lord a New Song		Healey Willan
	O Ye That Love the Lord		Frederick Ouseley
	Sing to the Lord	CHAN	Heinrich Schütz
	Sing to the Lord a New Song		Johann Pachelbel, et al
	Job 19:23-27a GR Track		
SATTB	Domine, secundum multitudinem	ANTH	William Byrd
	Give Me Jesus	AUG	arr Larry L Fleming
	I Know That My Redeemer Lives	OXCAB	J M Bach; H Schütz
s	I Know That My Redeemer Liveth *(Born to Die)*		Glenn Burleigh
	Ich weiss, dass mein Erlöser lebt		H Schütz
	Jesus Christ, My Sure Defense—Alleluia	CHAN	F Mendelssohn
	Scio enim	CHES FLEM	Orlandus Lassus
	Psalm 17:1-9 GR Track *See also Proper 13A*		
U	Evening Air Psalm		Malcolm Williamson
	Exaudi Domine	CHES IS6	Giovanni Gabrieli
U	Hold Thou Me Up		Benedetto Marcello/Weinhorst
	O Lord Our Governor		Healey Willan
	Thou Knowest, Lord, the Secrets of Our Hearts		A Hammerschmidt, et al
	We Call on You O Lord		Hal Hopson
	Why Are Thou So Heavy O My Soul?		Orlando Gibbons
	2 Thessalonians 2:1-5, 13-17		
	A Parting Blessing		Michael Cox
	Come Ye Faithful Raise the Strain	OXEA	R S Thatcher
	Ein feste Burg	BFAS	J S Bach
	God Be with You Till We Meet Again		Barry Rose
	I Want Jesus		Jester Hairston
	The Lord Bless You and Keep You		H Hopson; P Lutkin; J Rutter
	Luke 20:27-38		
	Christ Our Passover		R Dirksen; W C MacFarlane
	Come Ye Faithful Raise the Strain	OXEA	R S Thatcher
	Immortal, Invisible		Eric Thiman
	In Dat Great Gittin' Up Mornin'		Jester Hairston
	Since By Man	SEW	G F Handel, T Pavlechko
	Add'l Music, Cantatas, Major Works		
	Motet: O Jesu Christ, mein Lebens Licht		J S Bach

Year C | Proper 27

	H82	WLP	LEVAS II	VF	MHSO	CG descant	Inst descant
Before thy throne, O God, we kneel [C]	574,575						
O heavenly Word, eternal Light [C]	63,64						
Haggai 1:15b-2:9 SC Track							
God, my King, thy might confessing [P 145]	414						
New songs of celebration render [P 98]	413						
We will extol you, ever-blessed Lord [P 145]	404						
Job 19:23-27a GR Track							
Jesus lives! thy terrors now	194,195						
Love's redeeming work is done	188,189						
2 Thessalonians 2:1-5,13-17							
God be with you			234				
God be with you till we meet again		801					
Nada te turbe				88			
Nothing distress you				146			
Sing praise to our Creator	295						
Luke 20:27-38							
For the bread which you have broken	340,341						
Hosanna to the living Lord!	486						
Let saints in earth in concert sing	526						
Praise to the living God!	372					o	
The God of Abraham praise	401						
Ye holy angels bright	625						

[o] Same tune, but not text   [S] Seasonal   [C] Collect   [P] Psalm   [GR] Gospel-related   [SC] Semi-continuous

Proper 28 | Year C

Anthem	Solo	Handbells	Voicing	Title	Collection	Composer
				Isaiah 65:17-25 SC Track		
				And I Saw a New Heaven		Edgar L Bainton
				Blessed City, Heavenly Salem		Edward Bairstow
				How I Got Over		Clara Ward
				I Heard a Voice from Heaven	OXCAB	John Goss
				I Saw a New Heaven and a New Earth	AUG	Carl Schalk
				Lo, God Is Here	AFC 1	Francis Jackson
				Locus iste		Anton Bruckner
				Peace in the Valley		Thomas A. Dorsey
				Soon Ah Will Be Done		William Dawson
				Surge illuminare		Richard Webster, et al
				The First Song of Isaiah		Jack Noble White
				City Called Heaven	SOS	Spiritual, arr Boatner
				Canticle 9, Isaiah 12:2-6 SC Track		
				Behold, God Is My Salvation		Jean Berger
			SA			Robert J Powell
			SA			Leo Sowerby
			TTBB	Cry Out and Shout		Knut Nystedt
				Ecce Deus		Ned Rorem
			TTBB	God Is My Salvation		Samuel Adler
						Theron Kirk
				O Lord I Will Praise Thee	OXEA	Gordon Jacob
			U			Gerhard Krapf
			2 pt	Song of Isaiah		Richard Proulx
			2 pt, fl	Surely It Is God Who Saves Me		David Ashley White
						Alec Wyton
				The First Song of Isaiah		Jack Noble White
				The Wells of Salvation		Alice Parker
				Malachi 4:1-2a GR Track		
				Ain't Got Time to Die		Hall Johnson
				Christ Whose Glory Fills the Skies		T Frederick Candlyn
				Hark the Herald Angels Sing		Carol, Multiple
				Judge Eternal		Gerre Hancock
				Psalm 98 GR Track		*See Proper 27C SC Track*
				2 Thessalonians 3:6-13		
				Ain't Got Time to Die		Hall Johnson
				My Master		Frances McPhail
				Luke 21:5-19		
			U	And There Will Be Signs		Jan Bender
				But Thanks Be to God, *Messiah*		G F Handel
				My Lord, What a Morning		Spiritual, Multiple
				Once He Came in Blessing		John R Addenour
						Mark Sedio
						Charles Wood
			2 pt	See the Fig Tree		H Schütz, arr Bowman
				Steal Away		arr Dale Adelmann, et al
				There Shall Be Signs in the Sun		F W Wadley
			a or b	But Who Shall Abide, *Messiah*		G F Handel
				My Lord, What a Morning		Spiritual, Multiple
			at	O Death Where Is Thy Sting? *Messiah*		G F Handel
			b	Why Do the Nations, *Messiah*		G F Handel
				Add'l Music, Cantatas, Major Works		
			satb	183: Sie werden euch in den Bann tun		J S Bach

Year C | Proper 28

	Entrance	Sequence	Offertory	Communion	Postcommunion		H82	WLP	LEVAS II	VF	MHSO	CG descant	Inst descant
		■				Help us, O Lord, to learn [C]	628						
						Lord, be thy word my rule [C]	626						
				■		O Christ, the Word Incarnate [C]	632						
			■			Word of God, come down on earth [C]	633						
						Isaiah 65: 17-25 SC Track							
						All who love and serve your city	570,571						
						All you who love Jerusalem				157			
	■		■			Come, we that love the Lord	392		12				
						Goin' to lay down my sword and shield			210				
				■		Jerusalem, my happy home	620					■	
						Jerusalem the golden	624						
						O day of peace that dimly shines	597						
	■					O God of every nation	607					■	
						Surely it is God who saves me [Cant 9]	678,679						
				■		This is the hour of banquet and of song	316,317						
						Malachi 4:1-2a GR Track							
■						Christ, whose glory fills the skies	6,7						
						I want to walk as a child of the light	490						■
						Judge eternal, throned in splendor	596						
		■				New songs of celebration render [P 98]	413						
						O very God of very God	672						
						Sometimes a light surprises	667						
						The Lord will come and not be slow	462						
■						Thou, whose almighty word	371					■	
						2 Thessalonians 3:6-13							
■						Awake, my soul, and with the sun	11						
						Lord of all hopefulness, Lord of all joy	482			131			
						Not here for high and holy things	9						
		■				Teach me, my God and King	592					o	
						Luke 21:5-19							
		■				All my hope on God is founded	665					■	
						If thou but trust in God to guide thee	635						
						Lord Christ, when first thou cam'st to earth	598					■	
						My Lord, what a morning			13				
						O day of God, draw nigh	600,601						
						Once he came in blessing	53						
			■			Steal away		804	103				
						"Thy kingdom come!" on bended knee	615						■

o Same tune, but not text   [S] Seasonal   [C] Collect   [P] Psalm   [GR] Gospel-related   [SC] Semi-continuous

159

Proper 29 | Year C

Anthem/Solo/Handbells/Voicing	Title	Collection	Composer
	Jeremiah 23:1-6 SC Track *See also Proper 11B*		
	Lauda Sion		Multiple
	Let Justice and Judgment, *Coron. Anth. No. 2*		G F Handel
	Savior, Like a Shepherd Lead Us		William Bradley Roberts
	Surrexit a mortuis		Charles-Marie Widor
	Surrexit pastor bonus		Multiple
SAB	The Prophecy		Robert J Powell
	Canticle 4 or 16, Luke 1:68-79 SC Track		
	Benedictus		Multiple
	Blessed Be the God of Israel		John Carter
	Jeremiah 23:1-6 GR Track *See Proper 11B*		
	Psalm 46 GR Track *See Proper 4A*		
	A Mighty Fortress Is Our God	CHAN	Hans Leo Hassler
	Dominus regnavit		Josquin des Prez
	Esto mihi in Deum protectorum		Michael Haydn
tr div	God Is Our Hope		John Bertalot
	I Build on God's Strong Word	CHAN	Johann Walther
	O Salutaris Hostia		Multiple
	Psalm 46		D Cherwien; R Dirksen
			John Ferguson; H Schütz
	The Secret of Life	OXNCAB	Richard Shephard
	The Song of the Tree of Life	AFC 2	Ralph Vaughan Williams
	Colossians 1:11-20		
instr	All Glory Be to God on High		Johannes Crüger
SA	Canticle	RSCM TR	Arthur Wills
	Christ Is Made the Sure Foundation		Dale Wood
	Christus factus est		Multiple
	Immortal, Invisible		Eric Thiman
	I've Got Peace Like a River		Spiritual, Multiple
	King of Glory, King of Peace		Howard Helvey
	Non nobis, Domine		Multiple
	Salvation unto Us Has Come	BFAS	J S Bach
			J Brahms
	Sing My Soul His Wondrous Love		Ned Rorem
	Verbum caro factum est		Multiple
	Luke 23:33-43		
	A Lamb Goes Uncomplaining Forth	CHAN	Hugo Distler
	Ain'-a That Good News!		arr William L Dawson
	Christus factus est		Multiple
	Crucifixus, *Mass in B Minor*		J S Bach
	Crucifixus		Multiple
	I Wonder as I Wander		Multiple
	In Paradisum, *Requiem*		Multiple
SSA	In Praise of God	AFC 3	Francois Couperin
	In the Resurrection Glorious	CHAN	Johann C F Bach
	King of Glory, King of Peace	OXCAB	J S Bach/arr W H Harris
	Lord Jesus Christ, God's Only Son	BFAS	J S Bach
SAA	O Domine Jesu Christe	AFC 3	Claudio Monteverdi
	Ride on, King Jesus		Shaw/Parker
	The King Shall Rejoice, *Coron. Anthem No. 3*		G F Handel
	Tristis est anima mea		Multiple
b	Heute, wirst du mi mir..., *Cantata 106*		J S Bach
s or t	How Hast Thou Offended		Heinrich Schütz
a	Mit Fried und Freud ich..., *Cantata 106*		J S Bach
	Add'l Music, Cantatas, Major Works		
2 trp	Crown Him with Many Crowns		arr Robert J Powell
atb	182: Himmelskönig, sei willkommen		J S Bach
satb	*Coronation Mass*, K. 317		W A Mozart

160

Year C | Proper 29

	Entrance	Sequence	Offertory	Communion	Postcommunion		H82	WLP	LEVAS II	VF	MHSO	CG descant	Inst descant
						All praise to thee, for thou, O King divine [S]	477					o	
						Alleluia! sing to Jesus! (1,3-5) [S]	460,461						
						At the Name of Jesus [S]	435			135			
						Christ is the King! O friends upraise [S]	614						
						Crown him with many crowns [S]	494						
						He is King of kings, he is Lord of lords [S]			96				
						Jesus came, adored by angels [S]	454						
						Jesus shall reign where'er the sun [S]	544						
						King of glory, King of peace [S]	382						
						Let all mortal flesh keep silence [S]	324						
						Lo! he comes with clouds descending [S]	57,58						
						Rejoice, the Lord is King! [S]	481						
						Ye servants of God, your Master proclaim [S]	535						
						Jeremiah 23:1-6 SC/GR Track							
						A mighty fortress is our God [P 46]	687,688						
						Blessed be the God of Israel [Cant 4/16]		889					
						Blessed be the God of Israel [Cant 4/16]	444						
						Give praise and glory unto God	375						
						Hail to the Lord's Anointed	616						
						How bright appears the Morning Star	496,497						
						Jesus, our mighty Lord	478						
						Savior, like a shepherd lead us	708						
						To God with gladness sing	399						
						Colossians 1:11-20							
						All glory be to God on high	421						
						Christ is made the sure foundation	518						
						Come now, O Prince of peace		795			82		
						From glory to glory advancing, we praise thee, O Lord	326						
						From the dawning of creation		748					
						Lord, enthroned in heavenly splendor	307						
						Sing, my soul, his wondrous love	467						
						Luke 23:33-43							
						Draw nigh and take the Body of the Lord	327,328						
						Hail, thou once despised Jesus!	495						
						King of my life I crown thee now			31				
						Lord Christ, when first thou cam'st to earth	598						
						Lord Jesus, think on me	641	798					
						My song is love unknown	458						
						Ride on, King Jesus			97				
						The head that once was crown with thorns	483						
						To mock your reign, O dearest Lord	170						

Same tune, but not text   [S] Seasonal   [C] Collect   [P] Psalm   [GR] Gospel-related   [SC] Semi-continuous

The Presentation (Feb 2) | Year C

Anthem	Solo	Handbells	Voicing	Title	Collection	Composer
				Collect		
			SA	Create in Me		Paul Bowman
						J Brahms; Carl F Mueller
				Malachi 3:1-4		
				And He Shall Purify, *Messiah*		G F Handel
	b			Thus Saith the Lord, *Messiah*		G F Handel
	b or a			But Who May Abide, *Messiah*		G F Handel
				Psalm 84		*see Proper 16B*
				I Was Glad (Ps 122)		Multiple
				Jubilate Deo (Ps 100)		Multiple
				Laetatus sum (Ps 122)		M A Charpentier; M Haydn
						Claudio Monteverdi
				O How Amiable		Multiple
				Quam Dilecta!		Gerald Bales
				The Lord Is My Strength		Daniel Moe
	st			O How Amiable Are Thy Dwellings, *Psalmfest*		John Rutter
				Psalm 24:7-10, alt		
				Lift Up Your Heads	16th	John Amner
			SATB/SATB, 3 tr			Jean Berger
						J Blow; J Carter; Wm Croft
			Unison			Earle Cooper
			SSAATB			Orlando Gibbons
			SSATBB			Andreas Hammerschmidt
				Lift Up Your Heads, *Messiah*		G F Handel
				Lift Up Your Heads		Wm Mathias; H Schütz
			SSA or SATB			Healey Willan
			SATB & Unison	The King of Glory		Austin Lovelace
			Unison	Who Is This King of Glory		Malcolm Williamson
				Hebrews 2:14-18		
				Adoramus te, Christe		Multiple
				Ave verum Corpus		Multiple
				Christus factus est		Multiple
				O admirabile commercium		Multiple
				O bone Jesu		Multiple
				Since by Man Came Death, *Messiah*		G F Handel
				Since by Man	SEW	Thomas Pavlechko
				Luke 2:22-40		
				Behold This Child Is Set for the Fall		Heinrich Schütz
				Blessed Are the Pure in Heart		H Walford Davies
				Canticle of Simeon		John Karl Hirten
				Christ, Whose Glory Fills the Skies	OXCAB	Thomas Armstrong
				Christ, Whose Glory Fills the Skies		T Frederick Candlyn
				Dies sanctificatus		Multiple
				Depart in Peace		John Rutter
				Holy Is the True Light		William Harris
				Joys Seven		arr. Stephen Cleobury
				Let All Mortal Flesh Keep Silence		Edward Bairstow; G Holst
				Nunc dimittis		Multiple
			SATTB	O nata lux		William Byrd; T Tallis
				O nata lux		William Mathias
				Song of Simeon		A Gretchaninoff; J Marshall
						Alice Parker; R Schulz-Widm
				When to the Temple Mary Went	OXCAB	Johann Eccard
				Add'l Music, Cantatas, Major Works		
	b			Solo Cantata 82: Ich habe genung		J S Bach
	atb			83: Erfreute Zeit im neuen Bunde		J S Bach
	atb			125: Mit Fried und Freud ich fahr dahin		J S Bach
	a			Solo Cantata 200: Bekennen will...Namen		J S Bach

Year C | The Presentation (Feb 2)

						H82	WLP	LEVAS II	VF	MHSO	CG descant	Inst descant
			■		How lovely is thy dwelling-place [P]	517						
					When candles are lighted on Candlemas Day [S]				31			
					Malachi 3:1-4							
■					Angels, from the realms of glory	93						
			■		Love divine, all loves excelling	657						
					Hebrews 2:14-18							
		■			How bright appears the Morning Star	496,497						
			■		Sing of Mary, pure and lowly	277						
		■			The great Creator of the worlds (1-4)	489						
					Luke 2:22-40							
			■		Blest are the pure in heart	656						
■					Christ, whose glory fills the skies	6,7						
■					Hail to the Lord who comes	259						
		■			Let all mortal flesh keep silence	324						
				■	Lord God, you now have set your servant free	499						
					Lord I have seen thy salvation			153				
					Lord, you have fulfilled your word		891					
				■	Sing we of the blessed Mother	278						
				■	Virgin-born, we bow before thee	258						

[o] Same tune, but not text   [S] Seasonal   [C] Collect   [P] Psalm   [GR] Gospel-related   [SC] Semi-continuous

The Annunciation (Mar 25) | Year C

Anthem	Solo	Handbells	Voicing	Title	Collection	Composer
				Isaiah 7:10-14		
				Ecce concipies	CHES	Jacob Handl
				Ecce virgo concípiet	CHES	Heinrich Isaac
			SSATB			J P Sweelinck
				Lo, How a Rose E'er Blooming		Hugo Distler
			stb	Wie shön leuchtet..., *Cantata 1*		J S Bach
			a	Behold, A Virgin Shall Conceive, *Messiah*		G F Handel
				What You Goin' to Name the Baby?	SOS	Spiritual, arr Boatner
			stb	Cantata 1: Wie shön leuchtet der Morgenstern		J S Bach
				Psalm 45		
				Affrentur regi virgines		Anton Bruckner
			SSATB	Constitues eos principes		Samuel Wesley
				King's Daughters, *Coronation Anthem No 4*		G F Handel
				Kings Shall Be Thy...*Coron. Anthem No 4*		G F Handel
			ssaattbb	My Heart is Inditing, *Coron. Anthem No 4*		G F Handel
				O God My King	AFC 1	John Amner
				Upon Thy Right Hand, *Coron. Anthem No 4*		G F Handel
				Psalm 40:5-11, alt		
				Expectans expectavi		Orlando Di Lasso
				Great and Glorious		F J Haydn
			2 pt	I Waited Patiently for the Lord		Ronald Arnatt
				Psalm 40		Samuel Adler
				Thy Law Is Within My Heart		Robert Powell
				Canticle 3 or 15, alt		
				Canticle of Mary; Song of Mary; Magnificat		Multiple
				My Soul Doth Magnify the Lord		Multiple
				My Soul Magnifies the Lord		Multiple
				Hebrews 10:4-10		
				O Morning Star, How Fair and Bright	BFAS	J S Bach
				Salvation unto Us Has Come	BFAS	J S Bach, J Brahms
				Luke 1:26-38		
				Ave Maris Stella		Multiple
				Ave Gratia plena		Multiple
				Dixit Maria	CHES CHR	Hans Leo Hassler
				Ecce virgo concípiet	CHES CHR	Heinrich Isaac
			SSATB			J P Sweelinck
			2 pt	I Sing of a Maiden		Bruce Neswick
				Jesu, dulcis memoria		Multiple
				Mary Had A Baby		arr William Dawson
			Unison or 4 pt	Mary Said Yes		Russell Schulz-Widmar
				Ne timeas Maria		Tomas Luis de Victoria
				Nova, Nova		Multiple
			SAATBB	O virgo prudentissima	ANTH	Josquin Desprez
				The Angel Gabriel		Basque Carol, Multiple
				The Hunter		J Brahms
				The Linden Tree Carol		Multiple
				Ave Maria		Multiple
		a		Behold, A Virgin Shall & O Thou..., *Messiah*		G F Handel
			duet	I Sing of a Maiden		Bruce Neswick
				I Sing of a Maiden		Multiple
				What You Goin' to Name the Baby?	SOS	Spiritual, arr Boatner
				Add'l Music, Cantatas, Major Works		
			SATTB	Illibata dei virgo	ANTH	Josquin Desprez
			SATTBB	Praeter rerum seriem	ANTH	Josquin Desprez
			satb	147: Herz und Mund und Tat und Leben		J S Bach

Year C | The Annunciation (Mar 25)

	H82	WLP	LEVAS II	VF	MHSO	CG descant	Inst descant
From east to west, from shore to shore (1-3) [S]	77						
God himself is with us [S]	475						
Mary, when the angel's voice [S]				64			
Sing of Mary, pure and lowly [S]	277						
Virgin-born, we bow before thee [S]	258						
Isaiah 7:10-14							
Lo, how a Rose e'er blooming	81						
My heart sings out with joyful praise [Cant.]					60		
My soul gives glory to my God [Cant.]				117			
Tell out, my soul, the greatness of the Lord [Cant.]	437,438						
Hebrews 10:4-10							
How bright appears the Morning Star	496,497						
The great Creator of the worlds (1-4)	489						
Luke 1:26-38							
Gabriel's message does away	270						
Nova, nova	266						
Praise we the Lord this day	267						
Salamu Maria / Hail Mary, O Mother			51	11			
Sing we of the blessed Mother	278						
The angel Gabriel from heaven came	265						
The Word whom earth and sea and sky	263,264						
Ye who claim the faith of Jesus	268,269						

Same tune, but not text [S] Seasonal [C] Collect [P] Psalm [GR] Gospel-related [SC] Semi-continuous

The Visitation (May 31) | Year C

Anthem	Solo	Handbells	Voicing	Title	Collection	Composer
				1 Samuel 2:1-10		
			SA/opt SATB	A New Magnificat	AUG	Carolyn Jennings
				Behold O God Our Defender		John Blow
				Magnificat		Multiple
				My God Is a Rock		Robert Shaw
			2 pt tr, narr	My Heart Rejoices in the Lord		John Horman
				My Soul Doth Magnify the Lord		Multiple
				My Soul Magnifies the Lord		Multiple
				Psalm 113		
				All from the Sun's Uprise	OXEA	Philip Tomblings
				Give Laud unto the Lord	OXEA	arr Ernest Bullock
				Laudate Pueri		Multiple
				Laud Ye the Name of the Lord, *All Night Vigil*		S Rachmaninoff
				O Come, Ye Servants of the Lord	OXNEA	Christopher Tye
				Praise the Lord, Ye Servants		John Blow
			Unison or SATB	Praise to the Lord	SAS	Ron T. Klusmeier
			Unison/Unison	Praise Ye the Lord		Henry Pfohl
				Ye Servants of God	OXEA	arr Henry Coleman
				Romans 12:9-16b		
				Ubi Caritas		Maurice Duruflé
				Luke 1:39-57		
			SA/opt SATB	A New Magnificat	AUG	Carolyn Jennings
				Canticle of Mary		Multiple
				Magnificat		Multiple
				Mary's Magnificat	OXNCAB	Andrew Carter
				My Soul Doth Magnify the Lord		Multiple
				My Soul Magnifies the Lord		Multiple
				Song of Mary		Multiple
				Add'l Music, Cantatas, Major Works		
			SATTB	Illibata dei virgo	ANTH	Josquin Desprez
			SAATBB	O virgo prudentissima	ANTH	Josquin Desprez
			SATTBB	Praeter rerum seriem	ANTH	Josquin Desprez
			satb	10: Meine Seel erhebt den Herren		J S Bach
			satb	147: Herz und Mund und Tat und Leben		J S Bach

Year C | The Visitation (May 31)

	H82	WLP	LEVAS II	VF	MHSO	CG descant	Inst. descant
Mary, when the angel's voice [S]				64			
Sing of Mary, pure and lowly [S]	277						
Sing we of the blessed Mother [S]	278						
Virgin-born, we bow before thee [S]	258						
Ye watchers and ye holy ones [S]	618						
1 Samuel 2:1-10							
If thou but trust in God to guide thee	635						
Media sida					103		
To God with gladness sing	399						
Romans 12:9-16b							
Lord, make us servants of your peace	593						
Rejoice, ye pure in heart	556,557						
Luke 1:39-57							
Jerusalem, my happy home	620						
My heart sings out with joyful praise					60		
My soul gives glory to my God				117			
Tell out, my soul, the greatness of the Lord	437,438						
The first one ever, oh, ever to know	673						
Ye who claim the faith of Jesus	268,269						

Same tune, but not text   [S] Seasonal   [C] Collect   [P] Psalm   [GR] Gospel-related   [SC] Semi-continuous

The Transfiguration (Aug 6) | Year C

Voicing	Title	Collection	Composer
	Exodus 34:29-35		
	The Lord Bless You and Keep You		Peter Lutkin
			John Rutter
	Psalm 99		
SATB/SATB	Derr Herr ist König		Johann Pachelbel
	Dominus Regnavit		Peter Hallock
	Let All Mortal Flesh Keep Silence		Edward Bairstow
			Gustav Holst
	Sanctus		Multiple
	The Lord is King		David Ashley White
	2 Peter 1:13-21		
	Christ Is the World's True Light	OXEA	W K Stanton
	Christ, Whose Glory Fills the Skies	OXCAB	Thomas Armstrong
			T Frederick Candlyn
	O Paschal Lamp of Radiant Light	AUG	Sam Batt Owens
a	O Thou That Tellest, *Messiah*		G F Handel
	The Only Son from Heaven	BFAS	J S Bach
	This Is My Beloved Son		Knut Nystedt
	Worthy Is the Lamb, *Messiah*		G F Handel
	Luke 9:28-36		
	And Then Shall Your Light Break Forth, *Elijah*		F Mendelssohn
	Beautiful Savior		F Melius Christiansen
	Christ upon the Mountain Peak		John Bertalot
			Paul Bouman
	Christ, Whose Glory Fills the Skies	OXCAB	Thomas Armstrong
			T Frederick Candlyn
		AUGXMAS	Walter L Pelz
SAB	Fairest Lord Jesus		Russell Schulz-Widmar
U	Jesus on the Mountain Peak	AUGXMAS	Mark Sedio
	O Christ Who Art the Light and Day (evening)	OXCAB	William Byrd
	O Gladsome Light, O Grace (evening)	OXCAB	Bourgeois/Goudimel
	O nata lux		William Byrd
			William Mathias
			Thomas Tallis
a	O Thou That Tellest, *Messiah*		G F Handel
	The Spirit of the Lord Is..., *The Apostles*		Edward Elgar
	This Is My Beloved Son		Knut Nystedt
	Of the Father's Heart Begotten	100 CFC, AFC	arr David Willcocks
	Of the Father's Love Begotten	AUG	arr William Miller
	The Only Son from Heaven	AUGXMAS, BF	J S Bach
	The Spirit of The Lord Is upon Me		Edward Elgar
	The Transfiguration		Sven-Erik Bäck
	The Transfiguration of Christ		Hampson A Sisler
	The Transfiguration of our Lord		Nancy Maeker
	This Is My Beloved Son		Knut Nystedt
			Dan Uhl
	Transfiguration		Alan Hovhaness
	Add'l Music, Cantatas, Major Works		
	O Morning Star How Fair and Bright	BFAS	J S Bach
U & SATB			arr Donald Bursarow
	Te Deum		Multiple
	The Heavens Are Telling		Beethoven
			F J Haydn
	130: Herr Gott, dich loben alle wir		J S Bach

Year C | The Transfiguration (Aug 6)

						H82	WLP	LEVAS II	VF	MHSO	CG descant	Inst descant
					Exodus 34:29-35							
	■				O Zion, tune thy voice	543						
					2 Peter 1:13-21							
				■	Christ is the world's true Light	542						■
■		■			Christ, whose glory fills the skies	6,7						
	■				From God Christ's deity came forth	443						
			■		Jesu, joy of our desiring			75				
■					When morning gilds the skies	427					■	
			■		Yo soy la luz del mundo/I am the world's true light					75		
					Luke 9:28-36							
	■				Christ upon the mountain peak	129,130						
	■				O Light of Light, Love given birth	133,134						
	■				O wondrous type, O vision fair	136,137					■	

○ Same tune, but not text   [S] Seasonal   [C] Collect   [P] Psalm   [GR] Gospel-related   [SC] Semi-continuous

169

Holy Cross Day (Sept 14) | Year C

Anthem/Solo/Handbells/Voicing	Title	Collection	Composer
	Collect		
	Adoramus te, Christe		Multiple
	Christus factus est		Multiple
SATB div	Faithful Cross		Thomas Pavlechko
	Isaiah 45:21-25		
	Above All Praise and All Majesty	OXEA	F Mendelssohn
	At the Name of Jesus		Ralph Vaughan Williams
	Great and Glorious		F J Haydn
	Psalm 98:1-4, (5-10)		
	Cantate Domino		Multiple
	Let All the Rivers Clap Their Hands		Mark Schweizer
Unison, fl	Make a Joyful Noise		Maureen I Sindlinger
	Psalm 98		Multiple
SSAATB	Recordatus est	CHES FG6	Philippe Rogier
	Ring Out Your Joy		Harrison Oxley
	Shout for Joy! (Ps 100)		John Carter
	Singet dem Herrn		J S Bach
	Singet dem Herrn ein neues Lied		Heinrich Schütz
	Sing to the Lord a New Song		Multiple
	Sing unto the Lord a New Song		Healey Willan, et al
	Sing a New Song, *Biblical Songs*		A Dvořák
	Philippians 2:5-11		
	Adoramus te, Christe		Multiple
	At the Name of Jesus		Ralph Vaughan Williams
	Christus factus est		Multiple
	Jesu, dulcis memoria		Multiple
SAB	Jesus, Name of Wondrous Love		Everett Titcomb
	Let This Mind Be in You		Lee Hoiby
	Let Thy Hand Be..., *Coronation Anthem No 2*		G F Handel
	Non nobis, Domine		Multiple
	Praise to You Lord Jesus	CHAN	Heinrich Schütz
	Wondrous Love		Multiple
	Galatians 6:14-18, alt		
	Adoramus te, Christe		Multiple
	Christus factus est		Multiple
div	Faithful Cross		Thomas Pavlechko
	Thee We Adore		T Frederick H Candlyn
	John 12:31-36a		
	As Moses Lifted Up the Serpent		Edward Bairstow
	Jesus, So Lowly		Harold Friedell
	Lift Up Your Heads	16th	John Amner
	Lift Up Your Heads, *Messiah*		G F Handel
	Sicut Moses serpentem		Heinrich Schütz
	The Way to Jerusalem		Harold Friedell
va	Who Is This?		John Ferguson
SSATB	Yet a Little While		Knut Nystedt
b	The People That Walked in Darkness, *Messiah*		G F Handel
	Add'l Music, Cantatas, Major Works		
	Behold the Lamb of God, *Messiah*		G F Handel
	But Thanks Be to God, *Messiah*		G F Handel
	Crux fidelis		Multiple
	God So Loved the World *See Lent 2A, Trinity B*		
	O Saviour of the World	OXNEA	John Goss
SAATB	Salvator mundi		Thomas Tallis
	Since by Man Came Death, *Messiah*		G F Handel
	Since by Man	SEW	Thomas Pavlechko
SSAATTBB	The Veneration of the Cross, *All Night Vigil*		S Rachmaninoff
at duet	O Death Where Is Thy Sting? *Messiah*		G F Handel

Year C | Holy Cross Day (Sept 14)

	Entrance	Sequence	Offertory	Communion	Postcommunion		H82	WLP	LEVAS II	VF	MHSO	CG descant	Inst descant
						Alas! And did my Savior bleed [S]			30				
						Beneath the cross of Jesus [S]	498						
						Cantad al Señor [P]		786					
						Faithful cross, above all other [S]		737					
						Jesus, keep me near the cross [S]			29				
						New songs of celebration render [P]	413						
						On a hill far away stood an old rugged cross [S]			38				
						Sing, my tongue the glorious battle [S]	165,166						
						The flaming banners of our King [S]	161						
						The royal banners forward go [S]	162						
						Isaiah 45:21-25							
						Holy God, we praise thy name	366						
						How wondrous and great, thy works God of praise!	532,533						
						Philippians 2:5-11							
						All hail the power of Jesus' Name!	450,451						
						All praise to thee, for thou, O King divine	477					o	
						At the name of Jesus	435			135			
						Cross of Jesus, cross of sorrow	160						
						Gracious Spirit, give your servants		782				o	
						Jesus! Name of wondrous love!	252						
						Morning glory, starlit sky	585						
						O Spirit of the living God	531						
						Sing, ye faithful, sing with gladness	492						
						The head that once was crowned with thorns	483						
						What wondrous love is this	439						
						Galatians 6:14-18							
						In the cross of Christ I glory	441,442						
						Nature with open volume stands	434						
						We sing the praise of him who died	471						
						When I survey the wondrous cross	474						
						John 12:31-36a							
						Lift high the cross	473						
						Lift him up			159				
						When Christ was lifted from the earth	603,604					o	

[o] Same tune, but not text   [S] Seasonal   [C] Collect   [P] Psalm   [GR] Gospel-related   [SC] Semi-continuous

All Saints' Day (Nov 1) | Year C

Anthem/Solo/Handbells/Voicing	Title	Collection	Composer
	Daniel 7:1-3, 15-18		
	Blessing and Honor, *Messiah*		G F Handel
	Glory and Worship, *Coron. Anthem, No. 3*		G F Handel
	Glory and Worship	OXEA	F Mendelssohn
	Let All Mortal Flesh		Edward Bairstow
	Lo, Round the Throne a Glorious Band	OXCAB	Henry Ley
	Psalm 149 *See also Proper 18A*		
	Cantate Domino Canticum Novum		Richard Wayne Dirksen
	Psalm 149		H Schütz
	Ephesians 1:11-23 *See Ascension or Proper 29A*		
	Luke 6:20-31		
	Beatitudes		Russian Chant
	Beatitudes II and Chorale		Micki Grant
	Blessed Are the Pure in Heart	OXCAB	H Walford Davies
	Blessed Are They		David Haas
	Blessed Are Those Who Mourn, *Requiem*		Johannes Brahms
SSAATTBB	Blessed Is the Man, *All Night Vigil*		Serge Rachmaninoff
	Exceeding Glad, *Coronation Anthem, No. 2*		G F Handel
	Glory and Worship, *Coron. Anthem , No. 3*		G F Handel
	How Blest Are They	CON	P I Tchaikovsky
	I Heard a Voice	TUDOR	Thomas Tomkins
	I Heard a Voice from Heaven	OXCAB	John Goss
	Let Nothing Ever Grieve Thee		Johannes Brahms
	Let All the People Sing Praise		Lena McLin
	O Give Thanks unto the Lord	NNOV	Arthur Bliss
	Soon-Ah Will Be Done		arr William Dawson
	Swing Low, Sweet Chariot		arr Dale Adelmann, *et al*
	There Is a Balm in Gilead		arr William Dawson
	Way Over in Beulah Lan'		H Johnson; Stacey V Gibbs
	Add'l Music, Cantatas, Major Works *See also All Saints A & B*		
	Agnus Dei, *Requiem*		John Rutter
	Audivi, Media Nocte	16th	Thomas Tallis
	Give Us the Wings of Faith	AFC 4	Ernest Bullock
	Happy and Blest Are They, *St. Paul*		F Mendelssohn
	Herr, lehre doch mich, No. III, *A German Requiem*		J Brahms
SSA	In Praise of God	AFC 3	Francois Couperin
	In the Resurrection Glorious	CHAN	Johann C F Bach
SSATB	Justorum animae		William Byrd
		CHES FG5	Orlandus Lassus
2 pt	Let Saints on Earth in concert Sing	AFC 2	Alan Ridout
b	Lord, Teach Me That I Must Have an End, *Requiem*		J Brahms
	O quam gloriosum	CHES FL	Jacob Vaet
			T L de Victoria
	Purge Me, O Lord	ANTH	Thomas Tallis
	Sing Alleluia Forth in Duteous Praise		Jane Marshall
			Gerald Near
SSAT/SSAATTBB	The Souls of the Righteous		David Cherwien
	Their Bodies Are Buried in Peace	OXCAB	G F Handel
	They That Shall Endure to the End	CHAN	F Mendelssohn
	Thou Judge of Quick and Dead	OXCAB	Samuel Wesley
	We Are Not Our Own		Russell Schulz-Widmar
	There Is a Spirit in Man	LIFT	Peter Cornelius
	106: Gottes Zeit ist die Allerbeste Zeit		J S Bach
tb	157: Ich lasse dich nicht, du segnest...		J S Bach
	198: Trauerode		J S Bach
	Dies Gratiae, *Requiem Reflections*		Craig Phillips
	Requiem		Multiple

Year C | All Saints' Day (Nov 1)

						Hymn	H82	WLP	LEVAS II	VF	MHSO	CG descant	Inst descant
						By all your saints still striving (All Saints' Day) [S]	231,232						
						Christ, the Victorious, give to your servants [S]	358						
						For all the saints, who from their labors rest [S]	287						
						For the bread which you have broken [S]	340,341						
						For thy dear saints, O Lord [S]	279						
						From glory to glory advancing, we praise thee, O Lord [S]	326						
						Give rest, O Christ [S]	355						
						Give thanks for life [S]		775				o	
						Give us the wings of faith to rise [S]	253						
						Hark! the sound of holy voices [S]	275						
						I sing a song of the saints of God [S]	293						
						Let saints on earth in concert sing [S]	526						
						Lift up your heads, ye mighty gates [P]	436						
						No saint on earth lives life to self alone [S]		776					
						We sing of the saints (2: All Saints) [S]					118		
						Who are these like stars appearing [S]	286						
						Ye watchers and ye holy ones [S]	618						
						Daniel 7:1-3,15-18							
						Lead us, heavenly Father, lead us	559						
						Singing songs of expectation [P 149]	527						
						Ephesians 1:11-23							
						Be thou my vision, O Lord of my heart	488						
						Christ is made the sure foundation	518						
						Eternal light, shine in my heart	465,466						
						Loving Spirit, loving Spirit		742		51	111		
						My God, accept my heart this day	697						
						Luke 6:20-31							
						Beati		828					
						Blessed are the poor in spirit					74		
						Blessed Jesus, at thy word	440						
						Blest are the pure in heart	656						
						Gracious Spirit, give your servants		782					
						Lord, make us servants of your peace	593						
						Rejoice, ye pure in heart	556,557						
						Remember your servants, Lord	560						
						'Tis the gift to be simple	554						
						You shall cross the barren desert		811					
						At Baptism:							
						All who believe and are baptized	298						
						Baptized in water	294	767	121				
						Come away to the skies	213						
						I believe in God Almighty		768,769					
						You have put on Christ					122		
						You're called by name, forever loved		766					

o Same tune, but not text [S] Seasonal [C] Collect [P] Psalm [GR] Gospel-related [SC] Semi-continuous

Thanksgiving Day | Year C

Anthem/Solo/Handbells	Voicing	Title	Collection	Composer
		Deuteronomy 26:1-11		
A		Come See the Wonders		William Billings
S	sa	Go Down Moses		Robert Harris
A		Give Almes of Thy Goods	AFC 1	Christopher Tye
		Psalm 100		
A		A Song of Thanksgiving	AUG	John Ferguson
A	SAB	All From the Sun's Uprise	OXEA	Philip Tomblins
A		All People That on Earth Do Dwell	AFC	Thomas Tallis
A	SATB/SATB	Jauchzet dem Herren, alle Welt		J S Bach
A	SATB/SATB	Jauchzet dem Herren	OXESM	Heinrich Schütz
A	SA	Make a Joyful Noise		Carl F Mueller; Robin Orr
A			AFC 4	William Mathias
A		O Be Joyful in the Lord	AFC 4	Benjamin Britten
A		O Be Joyful in the Lord …, *Utrecht Jubilate*		G F Handel
A		O Be Joyful in the Lord, *Psalmfest*		John Rutter
A		O Go Your Way into…,		G F Handel
A		Old Hundredth Psalm Tune		Ralph Vaughan Williams
A		Psalm 100 or Jubilate Deo		Richard Dirksen, et al
A		Serve the Lord With Gladness, *Utrecht Jubilate*		G F Handel
A	SAB	To God Be Joyful		W A Mozart
A		Urah, hanevel! *Chichester Psalms*		Leonard Bernstein
		Philippians 4:4-9		
A		All Good Gifts, *Godspell*		Stephen Schwartz
A		Be Peace on Earth	OXEA	William Crotch, arr Ley
A		Rejoice in the Lord Always(s)	16th	Anon
S	atb			Andrew Carter; H Purcell
A			OXCAB	Henry G Ley
S	s	Rejoice Greatly, *Messiah*		G F Handel
		John 6:25-35		
A		Bread of Heaven		Roy Hopp
A		Ego sum panis vitae		Sven-Erik Bäck
A		Ego sum panis vivus	CHES IT	Palestrina
A		Gift of Finest Wheat		Robert Kreutz
A		Panis Angelicus		C Franck; Pierre Villette, et al
A		O Bread of Life from Heaven	BFAS	J S Bach
A		Verily, Verily I Say unto You	AFC 1	Thomas Tallis
A		Bread of Life, *Lauda Sion*	LIFT	F Mendelssohn
A		Thine O Father, Thine Is…, *Fall of Jerusalem*	LIFT	Martin Blumner
		Add'l Music, Cantatas, Major works		
A	SAB	All From the Sun's Uprise	OXEA	Philip Tomblings
A		All People That on Earth Do Dwell	AFC 1	Thomas Tallis
A		All Things Bright and Beautiful		John Rutter
A/H	SAB	Autumn Carol		Russell Schulz-Widmar
A		E'en So Lord Jesus Quickly Come		Paul Manz
A		For the Beauty of the Earth		John Rutter
A	2 pt	I Will Always Give Thanks	AFC 2	Charles King
A		Laud Ye the Name of the Lord, *All Night Vigil*		S Rachmaninoff
A		Now Thank We All Our God	BFAS	J S Bach
A	SATB/SATB	Nun danket alle Gott		J Pachelbel
A		O Taste and See		Ralph Vaughan Williams
A		Rorate caeli	CHES CHR AD	Francisco Guerrero
A		The Eyes of All Wait upon Thee		Jean Berger, et al
A		Every Day Will I Give Thanks	LIFT	G F Handel
A		Trust in the Lord, *Light of the World*	LIFT	Arthur Sullivan
A	satb	29: Wir danken dir, Gott, wir danken dir		J S Bach
A	b	(Solo)82: Ich habe genung		J S Bach
	s/a	82: Ich habe genung (Alt. version)		J S Bach
	sb	192: Nun danket alle Gott		J S Bach

Year C | Thanksgiving Day

	H82	WLP	LEVAS II	VF	MHSO	CG descant	Inst descant
All people that on earth do dwell [P]	377,378						
Before the Lord's eternal throne [P]	391						
Come, ye thankful people, come [S]	290						
For the beauty of the earth [S]	416						
For the fruit of all creation [S]	424						
From all that dwell below the skies [S]	380						
Give thanks to the Lord for he is good [S]			93				
Glory, love, and praise, and honor [S]	300						
God is so good [S]			214				
Grateful praise and hymns of adoration [S]				114			
Let all things now living [S]				107			
Make a joyful noise unto the Lord [P]	710						
Now thank we all our God [S]	396,397						
Praise to God, immortal praise [S]	288						
We gather together to ask the Lord's blessing [S]	433						
We plow the fields and scatter [S]	291						
We thank God for giving us life [S]					137		
When all thy mercies, O my God [S]	415						

Deuteronomy 26:1-11

	H82	WLP	LEVAS II	VF	MHSO	CG descant	Inst descant
As those of old their first fruits brought	705						
Wisdom freed a holy people		905		155			

Philippians 4:4-9

	H82	WLP	LEVAS II	VF	MHSO	CG descant	Inst descant
Rejoice in the Lord always				162			
Rejoice, the Lord is King!	481						

John 6:25-35

	H82	WLP	LEVAS II	VF	MHSO	CG descant	Inst descant
All who hunger, gather gladly		761		87	52		
Bread of life, hope of the world					48		
Bread of the world, in mercy broken	301						
Break thou the bread of life			146	73			
Completed, Lord, the Holy Mysteries	346						
Deck thyself, my soul with gladness	339						
Draw nigh and take the Body of the Lord	327,328						
Father, we thank thee who hast planted	302,303						
For the bread which you have broken	340,341						
I am the bread of life	335						
I am the bread of life		762					
I am the bread that came down from heaven			150				
Lord, enthroned in heavenly splendor	307						
My God, thy table now is spread	321						
O Food to pilgrims given	308,309						
O wheat whose crushing was for bread		760		74			
We the Lord's people, heart and voice uniting	51						

Same tune, but not text [S] Seasonal [C] Collect [P] Psalm [GR] Gospel-related [SC] Semi-continuous